W9-DDX-132

Contents

A God-Given Instrument

God's greatest desire is for us to live victorious lives and continually enjoy His blessings bequeathed to us in Christ Jesus. But one reason many are still struggling to live that glorious life is their inability to appropriate to themselves what God has already made available to them. God in His loving-kindness has, however, equipped you with a special instrument to help you appropriate and come into full possession of these manifold blessings. That instrument is your mind!

God has given us several amazing gifts, and they all have their specialised functions. He gave us mouths with which to chart the course of our lives, to confess ourselves into salvation, and beyond that, to where we enjoy the full benefits thereof (Romans 10:9-10). In **Romans 12:2**, Paul tells us about one of the wonderful gifts God gave us and its function; he said,

> *"And be not conformed to this world:*
> *but BE YE TRANSFORMED BY THE*
> *RENEWING OF YOUR MIND, that*
> *ye may prove what is that good, and*
> *acceptable, and perfect, will of God."*

This is an important revelation. Paul, by the Spirit, lets us know that God has given us our minds for our transformation. The English word "transformed" is from the Greek word "metamorphoo," which means "to be transfigured or changed from one form, state, or level to another."

Imagine that the Scripture stopped at *"...be ye transformed"*; we would have been at a loss as to how to be transformed. Thank God He told us how! He said we'll be transformed by the renewing of our minds, not by the renewing of our phones, cars, wardrobes, homes, or bank accounts. You can renew these things all you want, you still won't be transformed until your mind is renewed. That's because God has fashioned your mind as the instrument for your transformation. And this transformation we're talking about is from one level of glory to another, from one standard of living to a higher and better one, glory to God!

Your mind is unlimited in its potential to create whatever you desire. When you put your mind-power to work, the possibilities are endless. There're no limits to what you can achieve, and absolutely no restrictions to how high you can propel yourself in life.

Your prosperity is not essentially determined by your geographical location or the economy of the nation in which you live. What you become in life is largely determined by the content and quality of your mind, because with your mind you can change anything about you: with it, you can establish a perfect structure and administration for your life, and enjoy to the utmost the special life God has given you.

However, for all of these to happen, you must know how to use your mind. In other words, the content and character of your mind must be rich and positive enough to pull toward you what you want. Failure to use your mind rightly will only result in stagnation and retrogression, but if you want a transfiguration and transportation to the next level of glory and a higher and better quality of life, then you've got to learn to use your mind right.

This is what the Spirit of God is guiding me through this book to help you discover and understand, so you can effectively harness the power of your mind and channel its contents in a way that'll help you create a winning, successful, and vibrant life.

RENEWING YOUR MIND: THE CONCEPT OF MIND MANAGEMENT

After you come to Christ, God gives you new ways of thinking about Him, Heaven, yourself, your circumstances, the world around you, and life in general; He gives you new information and shows you how to relate with other people.

That's why Scripture tells us in Romans 12:2, "... *be ye transformed by the renewing of your mind....*" In other words, "Don't act like the rest of the world, but be transformed (transfigured, metamorphosed) by renewing your mind, changing your way of thinking, accepting God's thoughts and opinions, exchanging your ideas for His, and learning to think and talk like Him.

But you can't think like God except you have the

right material to think on, which is His Word. God's words are His thoughts clothed in vocabulary.

> THE WAY TO TRANSFORM, IMPROVE, AND UPGRADE YOUR LIFE IS BY RENEWING YOUR MIND.

God has shown us that we can influence our thinking in order to become more productive, successful, and prosperous. You can manage your mind and bring forth excellence, greatness, success, and prosperity. This is your responsibility, and God expects you to do it.

The Bible makes us understand how important it is to manage our minds; it not only determines the character of your personality, but the results you get and the quality of your life.

Romans 12:1-2:

> *"I beseech you therefore, brethren, by the mercies of God, that ye present your bodies a living sacrifice, holy, acceptable*

unto God, which is your reasonable service. And be not conformed to this world: but be ye transformed by the renewing of your mind, that ye may prove what is that good, and acceptable, and perfect, will of God."

Question: Do you want to transform your life? Do you want to have a better quality of life? Well, Paul says to you here by the Spirit that the way to transform, improve, and upgrade your life is by renewing your mind.

I've termed this spiritual principle **"MIND MANAGEMENT"**; it refers to the concept of reorganizing or reprogramming your mind (its contents and processes) with God's Word and aligning your thinking, perceptions and mindset about God, other people, the world, and yourself, with His Word.

If God is telling you to be transformed by the renewing of your mind, it means He's letting you know

you're the one to make it happen. He's instructing you
to do it because He's put the ability within you.

You're The Expression of Your Mind

Who you are today is a function of your mind.
Your personality is the expression of the contents and
working of your mind. The Bible says as a man thinks
in his heart, so is he (Proverbs 23:7). Your life and the
totality of your personality (how you live, what you do,
the character of your words, etc.) are the expression of
your mind.

Now, God has shown you that you can manage
your mind. That means you can work on your mind
and change its contents, and that change will show up
in your character and the results you have in life.

Increase Your Value

Managing your mind is the primary principle
for increasing your value, multiplying your success,

upgrading your state, and thus, enlarging your estate. Sometimes, you may have tried so hard and done all you thought you knew to do about something, without much success. What more can you do? Well, why don't you begin with mind management? Can you manage your mind differently regarding that situation? Can you access your mental hard drive to see what files you need to delete and the new ones you need to download and install?

Yes you can, and you should. You can make your life happier and much more fulfilling by making the right changes in the structure of your thinking.

We've established an important point here: you can transform your life by changing your way of thinking, i.e. by renewing—or managing—your mind.

But before we delve deeper into the contents of the mind and how to renew it, let us establish an understanding of the mind itself.

UNDERSTANDING THE MIND

Much as the human mind has been explored and discussed, it is yet to be discovered in the laboratory or revealed through scientific experimentation. Indeed, understanding of the mind is not something that even the world's best scientists, doctors, historians, or philosophers can give, for their finest explanations of the mind are speculatory at best.

That's because the mind is an intangible, spiritual entity, and only God's Word can shed the best light on it.

Hebrews 4:12 tells us:

> *"...the word of God is quick, and powerful, and sharper than any twoedged sword, piercing even to the dividing asunder of soul and spirit,*

> ***and of the joints and marrow, and is a***
> ***discerner of the thoughts and intents of***
> ***the heart."***

This is something the ordinary mind can't do or give you. It takes the revelation of the Word of God through the power of the Holy Spirit to make such distinctions between the soul and spirit known.

So we will begin with a simple definition of the mind:

> *The mind is the faculty of man's reasoning*
> *and thoughts. It holds the power of the*
> *imagination, recognition, and appreciation,*
> *and is responsible for processing feelings*
> *and emotions, resulting in attitudes and*
> *actions.*

There are some key words in this definition, the first of them being "thoughts."

> *Thought(s) is the creation, recalling,*

reviewing, and processing of images,
for meaning, reason, language, and
expression.

This means you can create, recall, review, and process images for meaning. In other words, you can give meaning to the images you get. You can also process those images for reason, language, and expression. All of these take place in the mind.

When your eyes focus on an image, it's your mind that interprets that image, and that's when you really see. If your mind can't interpret it, it doesn't matter what the image is, it'll make no sense to you. For instance, if you're given an Arabic book to read, and your mind hasn't been trained to understand Arabic letters, they'll be unrecognizable to you. Your first surprise would be that the words are written from right to left!

In studying this subject—whether in the Old or New Testaments—you'll discover that several words are used interchangeably to refer to the mind or its activities. Examples are "thoughts," "reason(ing)", "imagination," "thinking," and "inclination."

Sometimes, you'll read a scripture in one Bible version where the word "thought" is used, but another version expresses the same word as "reasoning."

You'll also find the words "mind," "soul," and "heart" being substituted for each other. But the mind is not the heart, and the heart is not the soul.

THE MIND IS AN INTANGIBLE, SPIRITUAL ENTITY, AND ONLY GOD'S WORD CAN GIVE THE BEST LIGHT ON IT.

Sometimes, "soul," "heart," "the hidden man of the heart," and "spirit," are used to describe the inward man (who comprises the human spirit and his soul).

But these are all just generic expressions of the inward man you'll find being used synonymously throughout the scriptures. And they're just a fraction of the vast number of synonyms that are used in expressing the phenomenon of the mind and its activities. Therefore, to better understand the mind, you need to have a clear understanding of the scriptural definition and description of the human person.

The Outward Man And The Inward Man

Man, primarily, has a twofold nature: the outward man and the inward man. In 2 Corinthians 4:16, Paul clearly distinguishes between these two when he said, *"For which cause we faint not; but though our OUTWARD MAN perish, yet the INWARD MAN is renewed day by day."*

He lets us know there's an outward man and there's an inward man.

The outward man is the physical body and its five senses (sight, hearing, smell, touch, taste). These senses are his medium for relating with his environment. That's why the human body can only receive information from this world through its five senses.

The inward man, however, is the human spirit and his soul (the seat of his mind, will, emotions, reasoning, and intellect). He's the one the Bible calls "the hidden man of the heart." He's not seen with the natural eyes, because he is the "man within the man."

Now, every one of us is a spirit being, and our inward man is the real person living in the physical body. That's the one who receives Christ's salvation. When you believed and confessed the Lordship of Jesus, it wasn't your body (your outward man) who was reborn; it was your inward man—your human spirit— that was born again.

Your human spirit has spiritual senses, and they function through your soul and its mind. This shows why your mind is so powerful and important, because it is the connector of your spirit to your body.

A Clearer Picture Of The Mind And Soul

Sometimes, spiritual things can be difficult to communicate, but the Bible shows that we can understand them by looking at the physical. That's because the spiritual gave birth to the physical. Hebrews 11:3 tells us, *"...the worlds were framed by the word of God, so that things which are seen were not made of things which do appear."*

To give you a better understanding of what I said about the inward man being the human spirit and his soul, and the outward man being the human body and its senses, I'll compare the nervous system and the soul:

What the nervous system is to the body, the soul is to the spirit.

Just as the nervous system is an integral part of the human body, the soul is inseparable from the human spirit; it belongs to and functions for the human spirit.

You'll get an even clearer picture of the soul with this comparison between it and its physical counterpart:

What the nervous system is to the body, the soul is to the spirit, and what the brain is to the nervous system, the mind is to the soul.

This therefore means that the mind is in the soul, just as the brain is part of the central nervous system. That's why you can see (imagine), hear, or feel with your mind. All the things the central nervous system and physical senses of the body can do are actually a reflection of the attributes of the inward man.

Thus, your mind has the ability to see, hear, perceive and interpret, even though you can't physically locate it in your body. It resides in your soul, and is a spiritual entity that only God can see.

The Human Brain

The American Heritage Stedman's Medical Dictionary gives the definition of the brain as *"the primary center for the regulation and control of bodily activities, receiving and interpreting sensory impulses and transmitting information to the muscles and body organs. It is also the seat of consciousness, thought, memory, and emotion."*

This is a great definition of the brain, but there's a part of it that isn't exactly right. The seat of consciousness, thought, memory, and emotions doesn't reside in the brain. In medical science and other fields, they know that the brain can be fully functional even when an individual isn't conscious. Consciousness, therefore, doesn't reside in the brain. Even memory can't be said to reside in the brain, because true memory goes beyond recording information to processing it. And such processing of information—usually for interpretation, meaning, language, and expression—is not in the power of the brain but the mind.

THE BRAIN IS NEITHER THE MIND NOR THE SOUL; IT'S A PHYSICAL ORGAN OF THE BODY, WHILE THE SOUL AND MIND ARE INTANGIBLE.

So the proper definition of the brain would be that it is the center for the regulation and control of bodily activities, receiving and interpreting sensory impulses and transmitting information to the muscles and organs of the body.

Even though *The American Heritage Stedman's Medical Dictionary* goes beyond the scope of the brain in its definition, there's some truth in it; it shows us there's a seat of consciousness, thought, memory, and emotion. That's because Science recognises there's a connection between the mind and the brain—i.e. between the inward man and the outward man—but it doesn't know how to make that connection.

The brain is neither the mind nor the soul; it's a physical organ of the body, while the soul and mind are intangible. However, the body's central nervous system (the brain and spinal cord) works in conjunction with the mind for optimum consciousness, cognition, and expression. These two—the central nervous system and the mind—are ultimately responsible for the character of a man. This is the connection between the mind and the brain and how they work together.

Educating The Inward Man

The mind is capable of receiving and processing information from the outward man and its senses, as well as from the inward man and his spiritual senses. It is the connector of the physical or outward man and the spiritual or inward man, thus giving the man his real character. The mind is ultimately responsible for the man's attitude and actions.

The best education in the world is an attempt to inform, refine, and develop the mind through the senses of the outward man. This is the most and farthest even the best schools and universities can go: the education of the mind through the senses. But man has a far better and more sublime potential than this. It is the education of the inward man, the human spirit, which ultimately leads to the education of the mind. This is only achievable through receiving and meditating on the Word of God.

Only through God's Word can the inward man be discovered and educated. You'll see this in **Hebrews 4:12**,

> *"For the word of God is quick, and powerful, and sharper than any twoedged sword, piercing even to the dividing asunder of soul and spirit, and of the joints and marrow, and is a discerner of the thoughts and intents of the heart."*

Notice it says the Word pierces "even to the dividing asunder of soul and spirit." This means it goes into the very core of our nature to distinguish and separate between the soul and the spirit. Only God's

Word can do that. It helps us discover our inward man. No school in the world that educates the mind through the senses can do this. The farthest they can go is train the mind to become educated in the sense-realm, but the real man—the spirit man—requires a different kind of education.

I'm not in any way belittling formal education, because the better educated a person is, the more advantages he can have in this world. When you know more about your environment, the world in which you live, and the people in it, you have an advantage over the one who doesn't.

Now think what better advantages you'll have with the education of your spirit and your spiritual senses. That's the advantage you get by reading spiritual material such as this that can help you discover the real you and improve the quality of your life from within. This critical education of your inward man is achieved through what I've termed MIND MANAGEMENT, and it's what Paul refers to in **Romans 12:1-2** where he tells us:

> *"I beseech you therefore, brethren, by the mercies of God, that ye present your bodies a living sacrifice, holy, acceptable unto God, which is your reasonable service. And be not conformed to this world: but be ye transformed by the renewing of your mind, that ye may prove what is that good, and acceptable, and perfect, will of God."*

Notice he says in the first verse, *"...ye present your bodies"*; this means you (the inward man) own your body. He lets you know that your human spirit has power over your outward man. Therefore, don't let your body control you; instead, take control of it and present it to God as a living sacrifice.

He then goes further in the second verse to talk about your spiritual education: *"be ye transformed by*

THE RENEWING OF YOUR MIND."

Just as a man is transformed through education of his natural senses, your inward man can also be transformed through the education of your spiritual senses.

Therefore, don't be conformed to this world. Don't live like them, or think like them, or see from their perspective. Instead, be transformed, transfigured, and translated by the renewing of your mind.

Don't say, "Oh God, take me to the next level!" It's your responsibility to transport yourself from one level of glory to another in your life. You can live a better and more glorious life by your choice, and He's shown you here exactly how to do it—by renewing (effectively managing) your mind.

A Better Understanding Of The Working Of The Heart, Soul, Mind, And Thoughts

I'll show you a few portions of Scripture that you'll find helpful in understanding the points we've made so far about the heart, soul, mind, and thoughts.

Matthew 15:1-11:

"Then came to Jesus scribes and Pharisees, which were of Jerusalem, saying, Why do thy disciples transgress the tradition of the elders? for they wash not their hands when they eat bread... And he called the multitude, and said unto them, Hear, and understand: Not that which goeth into the mouth defileth a man; but that which cometh out of the mouth, this defileth a man."

The scribes and Pharisees had charged Jesus' disciples with the offense of eating with unwashed hands. Understand that they weren't so concerned about hygiene here, but a ceremonial purification. So Jesus replied them, "It's not what goes through the mouth into the human body that defiles a man, but what comes out of his mouth." His disciples went to Him later, requesting further explanation of this parable, because they didn't understand it.

> *"And Jesus said, Are ye also yet without understanding? Do not ye yet understand, that whatsoever entereth in at the mouth goeth into the belly, and is cast out into the draught? But those things which proceed out of the mouth come forth from THE HEART; and they defile the man. For out of THE HEART proceed evil thoughts, murders, adulteries, fornications, thefts, false witness, blasphemies: These are the things which defile a man: but to eat with unwashen hands defileth not a*

man" (Matthew 15:16-20).

Watch Jesus' words here. The "heart" He's talking about isn't the physical organ beating beneath your chest and pumping blood through your body; rather, it's the human spirit and his soul (or more specifically, his mind), from where, He says, evil thoughts proceed. He's letting us know that evil thoughts don't come from the physical body (the brain), but from the mind.

> YOU'RE A REFLECTION OF YOUR THOUGHTS. YOUR LIFE IS THE OUTWARD MANIFESTATION OF THE INNER WORKINGS OF YOUR MIND.

This is remarkable! The Lord helps us see the difference between the human spirit and the physical body, and how a man is defiled (corrupted, made unclean) by evil thoughts that come, not from his brain, but from his inward man (his heart and mind).

There are different kinds of thoughts—good and evil—that come from the heart, and Jesus categorised these as evil, because they had been negatively processed in the mind.

Now, let's read another portion of the Bible from **Luke 24:36-37:**

> *"And as they thus spake, Jesus himself stood in the midst of them, and saith unto them, Peace be unto you. But they were terrified and affrighted, and supposed that they had seen a spirit"*

This was after the crucifixion and resurrection of Jesus. The disciples were all huddled together in a small room, discussing the harrowing events of the past few days, and wondering whether it was really true that Jesus had resurrected as some had reported.

While they were talking, Jesus suddenly appeared in their midst, with the doors being securely shut. They thought they'd seen a ghost, and, boy, were they terrified! Then Jesus said to them,

> *"Why are ye troubled? and why do*
> *THOUGHTS arise in your HEARTS?"*
> *(Luke 24:38).*

Again, I want you to observe the word "heart" closely. Remember, I told you the words "heart," "soul," and "mind" are used interchangeably in Scripture. Let's read from the NIV translation and see how this verse is rendered,

> *"Why are you troubled, and why do*
> *DOUBTS rise in your MINDS?" (Luke*
> *24:38 NIV).*

This time, the translators correctly used the word "mind" in place of "heart."

Jesus had told His disciples He was going to rise again from the dead; then they heard eyewitness reports from those who had seen Him alive after His crucifixion, but were still in doubt. Then the Man Himself showed up right in their midst, but they looked at Him and still doubted, thinking, "It must be His ghost."

Jesus' response to them was so beautiful. It helps us understand something about doubts and the mind. He asked them, "Why do these thoughts (doubts) arise in your minds," letting us know that doubt is a kind of thought that forms in the mind.

Observe something here about how the mind works. When Jesus appeared to His disciples, they thought they'd seen a ghost, and they were scared out of their wits. These men had obviously heard some terrifying stories about ghosts. They must have heard that ghosts are spirits of the dead that haven't gone to their place of rest and are wandering about the earth, even though they've passed over into the spirit realm.

Just because you've never seen a ghost doesn't mean they don't exist. They're real, and sometimes our eyes and ears can be opened in the spirit realm to see and hear them before they're taken away.

The disciples must have learnt about the reality of ghosts, but you know, people are often afraid of what they don't understand, or things beyond their control. In this case, the disciples were afraid of ghosts, even though they'd never seen one before. They didn't know what ghosts were, aside what they'd heard about them. Now, they thought they'd seen one and almost passed out from fear.

However, it wasn't a ghost they saw, but the Lord Jesus—the One they'd known and interacted closely with the last three years. But now He had a hard time convincing them He wasn't a ghost. He said, *"Look at my hands and my feet and see who I am! Touch me and find out for yourselves. Ghosts don't have flesh and bones as you see I have"* (Luke 24:39 CEV).

And to further prove His point to those who were still doubtful, He *"asked them, "Do you have something to eat?"* and in response, *"They gave him a piece of baked fish. He took it and ate it as they watched"* (Luke

24:41-43 CEV).

When they saw Him eat normally this way, it dawned on them that it was indeed the Master who had risen from the dead.

Where Did The Fear Come From?

Why were Jesus' disciples so afraid in the first place? Their fear came from the previous wrong and negative information they'd received regarding ghosts. That information had communicated fear to their hearts. Fear was already resident within them, and when Jesus showed up, their "fear files" were opened, and they manifested fright.

Understand this: what we hear (the information we receive) can produce faith or fear in us; it can generate weakness or strength. Fear doesn't exist by itself; it comes as a result of information.

In the next chapter, we'll go further to see the benchmarks against which the character and quality of your thinking are measured. Paul gave us that beautiful list in Philippians 4:8, and it's our responsibility to study it and conform our thinking to God's standard.

3

"THINK ON THESE THINGS..."

Protect Your Mind; It's Not An Open Field

There are people whose minds are like an open field that anyone (or animal, for that matter) can go through and drop unwanted seed. When you leave your mind open this way, any worthless seed can be thrown in it and it'll grow. It's your spirit that the Bible describes as a field, not your mind. And because your spirit is only accessible through your mind—which is the door to your spirit—nothing can get in there that you don't first allow in your mind.

That's why the Lord instructs us: *"Keep thy heart with all diligence; for out of it are the issues of life"* (Proverbs 4:23).

The word, "keep," used in this scripture is the

same used in Genesis 2:15: *"And the Lord God took the man and put him into the garden of Eden to dress it and to keep it."* It doesn't suggest putting or separating the garden away to somewhere safe. It actually implies taking care of it in a protective way and ensuring its security against any external aggressor.

The *Good News Bible* translation puts it clearer. It says, *"...the LORD God placed the man in the Garden of Eden to cultivate it and guard it."* The word "guard" has a military connotation, which suggests protecting from attack or maintaining in safety from danger.

You'd agree that if there's no enemy or adversary, there wouldn't be any need to guard something that belongs to you against an attacker. Truth is, there's an adversary, and that's why the Lord instructs you to keep—or guard—your heart with all diligence.

I love *James Moffat's* delivery of Proverbs 4:23-24. He says in his translation, *"Guard above all things, guard your inner self so you can live and prosper. Bar out all thoughts of evil and banish wayward words."*

Have you ever heard someone say, "I was barred from joining the team"? It means he was prevented, kept out, blocked, or disallowed from joining the team. That's how the Bible tells you to guard your heart, by barring (disallowing, keeping out) all thoughts that are not consistent with God's Word.

Now, this doesn't sound like the evil thoughts are originating from you, does it? What it simply shows is that there's a devil out there trying to send the wrong thoughts into your heart (through your mind). So you're admonished to bar his evil thoughts and banish his wayward words.

If someone says something to you that challenges God's Word, bar it from your mind! Don't try to accommodate it or reason it out. The Bible says to guard your heart with all diligence, so you must recognise that God is not going to guard your heart for you. The responsibility is yours. But the good news is that you're not helpless as to what to do. You've been equipped with "the whole armour of God" (Ephesians 6:11), and what you need to do is put it on and never take it off! With your armour in place, you'll be able to bar every evil thought or idea against God's Word that tries to assault your mind *(We'll be looking at this in greater detail in chapter seven).*

God's Yardstick For Measuring Good Thoughts

God didn't just instruct us to mount guard at the door of our hearts and disallow anything from passing through that shouldn't; He also shows us exactly how to place that guard over our minds— by choosing the thoughts we allow passage. In other words, He didn't just tell us to renew our minds without showing us

> IF SOMEONE SAYS SOMETHING TO YOU THAT CHALLENGES GOD'S WORD, BAR IT FROM YOUR MIND! DON'T TRY TO ACCOMMODATE IT OR REASON IT OUT.

how. He told us the files to delete from our minds and the new ones to download and replace them with.

> *"Finally, brethren, whatsoever things are TRUE, whatsoever things are HONEST, whatsoever things are JUST, whatsoever things are PURE, whatsoever things are LOVELY, whatsoever things are of GOOD REPORT; if there be any VIRTUE, and if there be any PRAISE, think on these things" (Philippians 4:8).*

How remarkable this is! It immediately shows us God's yardstick for measuring good thoughts. It says whatever things are consistent with truth [God's Word], excellent, lovely, of good report, and praiseworthy, focus your mind on these. In other words, let these thoughts occupy your mind and control your thinking-process.

What Are You Thinking About?

Imagine the kind of life you'll live if this verse of Scripture controlled your mind. How many times have you heard something that wasn't true, or honest, or pure, or of good report, but you kept it in your mind and thought about it?

Maybe you heard, saw, or experienced something that made you unhappy, and it kept you up all night, musing and tossing in your bed. Every time you closed your eyes, you saw those negative images and relived the nasty experience again, which only served to upset you even more. Why do you let yourself worry so? Free your mind of such self-inflicted, internal conflicts.

Why have you been thinking of something that's not true, honest, pure, or just? Why dwell on it if it's not lovely, virtuous, or praiseworthy? Why hold on to something that's a connection to unhappiness? Did you know that negative thoughts could reconstruct your face and cause you to look older than you actually are? This is the reason some folks look ten years older than their age!

You walk into the office and you see some colleagues huddled together, trading tales about another colleague, and you pull up a chair and join in the discussion. Then you wonder why you're unhappy, turning around in cycles, or going one step forward and two steps back. Well, it's because you've been dwelling on things that are not of good report!

> FACT AND TRUTH ARE TWO DIFFERENT THINGS. SOMETHING MAY BE A FACT, BUT IF IT DOESN'T ALIGN WITH THE WORD OF GOD, IT ISN'T TRUTH.

God's Word has shown you what to dwell on as His child. It says it must be HONEST, JUST, PURE, LOVELY, OF GOOD REPORT, VIRTUOUS, and PRAISEWORTHY. Now, you may hear something that sounds honest or true but isn't lovely or of a good report; don't dwell on it, because it falls short of the measure of God's standard of thoughts to allow.

Some folks like to set their minds on news or information that's not praiseworthy. Worse, they get others to join in with them, and together they form the "grumpy group." Refuse to be a dumping ground for their trash.

I believe you want to live a successful and brilliant life, filled with outstanding results and remarkable accomplishments. For that to happen, you cannot afford to be small in your mind. When you have big things to do, and you have a world to take, you can't afford to focus on frivolities and mundanities.

What God Expects You To Think Of Yourself

Perhaps, you're experiencing some challenges with your health, or the doctor has diagnosed you with a deadly sickness or disease. Now you're troubled and wondering what to do about your condition. I want you to realise that in the eyes of God, such a report isn't true, because it's not in line with His provisions for you revealed in His Word. That condition doesn't fall in line with God's definition of truth. So refuse to dwell on it. Reject it in Jesus' Name. Don't think on it, and don't voice it.

The doctor, by virtue of his training, may tell you the facts, but the Word of God is the truth (John 17:17). Fact and truth are two different things. Something may have been proven or verified as a fact, but if it doesn't align with the Word of God, it isn't truth.

The Bible already says, *"If any man be in Christ, he is a new creature: old things are passed away; behold, all things are become new"* (2 Corinthians 5:17). That means even if you were born with a sickness, now that you're in Christ, you don't have it anymore; it's passed away. You now live in divine health. So sickness or disease no longer have a place in you, praise God!

This is the consciousness that God wants you to have. This is how He wants you to think about yourself.

You Can Do It!

Now you may be reading this and thinking, "But this isn't realistic." Well, it's realistic and normal in God's Kingdom where I live! Remember, God's Word is "truth," meaning "verity" or "reality." So in our Kingdom, these are the realities by which we live. We don't participate in any kind of negative communication. The Lord said to me several years ago, "Son, look from the mountaintop." That's where I live, and it sure is no dumping ground for trash talk or thought!

"...Whatsoever things are JUST, whatsoever things are PURE, whatsoever things are LOVELY, whatsoever things are of GOOD REPORT; if there be any VIRTUE, and if there be any PRAISE, think on these things" (Philippians 4:8). God isn't telling us to do something He knows we can't. We're His children, and this is the life He's called us to. If He said these are the things we should think on, it means we can and we must, if we're to enjoy the full benefits of the life He's given us.

What you do with your mind is so important. Remember, you're the expression of your mind, and the quality of life you'll live here on earth isn't a function of the quality of your spirit but of the character of your mind. Your mind can make you poor or rich. It can place you on the pedestal of glory and greatness or dump you in the dust of suffering and shame. Choose glory. Choose life. Choose to use your mind right.

USE YOUR MIND RIGHT

I t's critical that you understand how to use your mind right, because that's your ticket to the next and higher level you desire. One of the first things you must learn to do with your mind is to focus it on the right thing. Isaiah 26:3 says,

> *"Thou wilt keep him in perfect peace,*
> *<u>whose mind is stayed on thee</u>: because*
> *he trusteth in thee."*

The Hebrew rendering of the phrase "perfect peace" is "shalom shalom," which in essence means "peace of prosperity." The Lord keeps him in the peace of prosperity whose mind is stayed (fixed, focused) on Him. Isn't this wonderful; not only is his life peaceful, but it's peaceful in prosperity, praise God!

*"Thou wilt **keep** him in perfect peace"* means

that when you enter into this realm of peace and prosperity, you remain in it and your life is maintained there, because God keeps you there.

"Thou wilt keep him in perfect peace, whose mind is stayed on thee..."

Now, notice the scripture doesn't say, "...whose hands and legs are stayed on thee," but "whose mind is stayed on thee." This is very instructive. He's telling us again about this instrument called the mind. If you've ever asked or wondered what you're supposed to do for the power of God to work in your behalf

ONE OF THE FIRST THINGS YOU MUST LEARN TO DO WITH YOUR MIND IS TO FOCUS IT ON THE RIGHT THING.

and keep you in peace and prosperity, you've got your answer right there—stay your mind on the Lord!

With All Your Mind

You may be thinking, "How do I stay my mind on the Lord and remain in the peace of prosperity?" Deuteronomy 6:5 tells us something very instructive in this regard; it says:

> *"And thou shalt love the LORD thy God with all thine heart, and with all thy soul, and with all thy might."*

Moses delivered this commandment from the Lord to the children of Israel, instructing them on how to love the Lord their God. Some other translations use the word "strength" in the place of "might." For example, the NIV reads:

> *"Love the Lord your God with all your heart and with all your soul and with all your strength" (Deuteronomy 6:5).*

Have you ever pondered this scripture and wondered how one could love the Lord with all his might or strength, since love as an emotion isn't necessarily expressed through physical energy?

Thankfully, the Lord Jesus gives us the answer. In one of His teachings, He picks up the same scripture from the Old Testament and decodes it ever so simply in response to a question that was thrown at Him:

> *"Then one of them, which was a lawyer, asked him a question, tempting him, and saying, Master, which is the great commandment in the law? Jesus said unto him, Thou shalt love the Lord thy God with all thy heart, and with all thy soul, and with all thy MIND" (Matthew 22:35-37).*

Here, the Lord Jesus introduces the word "mind" in place of "might," letting us know that loving the Lord with all your might (or strength) is the same as loving Him with all your mind. This implies focusing or channeling your mind in a certain direction. This is what you use your mind for. When you focus your mind, it helps to direct your energies and bring them to bear on a particular thing or activity.

> **WHEN YOU FOCUS YOUR MIND, IT HELPS TO DIRECT YOUR ENERGIES AND BRING THEM TO BEAR ON A PARTICULAR THING.**

So Jesus shows us how to love the Lord with all our might or strength by focusing our minds on Him.

Let's look at a few other scriptures that throw more light on this.

1 Chronicles 22:19:

> *"Now set your heart and your soul to seek the LORD your God; arise therefore, and build ye the sanctuary of the LORD God, to bring the ark of the covenant of the LORD, and the holy vessels of God, into the house that is to be built to the name of the LORD."*

David, the king of Israel, had become an old man,

and seeing that his days on earth were numbered, he installed his son Solomon as king, and gave him this important instruction for his life: "Set your heart and soul to seek the Lord your God."

This is how you bear that commandment in Deuteronomy 6:5—it's by setting your heart and soul to seek the Lord.

Remember, with your mind you create, recall, review, and process images for meaning, reasoning, language, and expression. So David was spot on when he said to his son, "Set your heart and soul to seek the Lord your God."

See how he puts the same point to Solomon in another verse:

> *"And thou, Solomon my son, know thou the God of thy father, and <u>serve him with a perfect heart and with a willing mind:</u> for the LORD searcheth*

all hearts, and understandeth all the imaginations of the thoughts: if thou seek him, he will be found of thee; but if thou forsake him, he will cast thee off for ever" (1 Chronicles 28:9)

How do you seek the Lord? By setting your mind on Him. You seek Him, not because He's missing and you're trying to find Him, but because you want to focus your heart, your mind, and your affections on Him.

Romans 8:5 also says the same thing:

"For they that are after the flesh do mind the things of the flesh; but they that are after the Spirit the things of the Spirit."

Those who are after the flesh set their minds on things of the flesh (carnal, worldly things), but if you're after God, you'll set your mind on Him and godly things.

You're In Control of Your Mind!

Setting your mind on something or someone presupposes that you're in control of your mind. Now that's one of the most profound truths you'll ever read or hear about your mind. Your mind is under your control, and you've got to acknowledge this truth, accept it, endorse it, and act like it!

> YOUR SPIRIT HAS THE CAPACITY TO CONTROL YOUR MIND

Let's look at Romans 8:5-6 again, this time from the New King James Version. It says,

> *"For those who live according to the flesh set their minds on the things of the flesh, but those who live according to the Spirit, the things of the Spirit. For to be carnally minded is death, but to be spiritually minded is life and peace."*

This means setting your mind on the ordinary plane of life—on fleshy, worldly things—produces death. But if it's peace you want, then be spiritually-minded. In other words, when you focus your mind on spiritual things, you'll have life and peace.

Your spirit has the capacity to control your mind. Paul lets us understand that we can control our minds from our spirits. You can decide that you want to set your mind on the things of God, and control your spiritual senses to conform to that decision. That decision is made by your spirit with his instrument of the soul (the seat of your mind, will and emotions); he decides what he wants to think about and sets his mind on it and starts thinking about it.

Set Your Mind on the Word

Now you ask, "How do I set my mind on the Lord and on spiritual things?" You do that by setting your mind on the Word of God! The Word shows you what spiritual things are and delivers them to you. That's because God's Word is Light (John 1:1; John 1:5), and light defines and reveals (Ephesians 5:13).

If you turned off all the lights in the room you're in right now, you won't be able to see anything with your natural eyes, because they require light to see. Your spiritual eyes also need God's light—His Word— to show you what spiritual things from Him are.

When I talk about setting your mind on "spiritual things," I'm not referring to every spiritual thing, because satan and his demons are spirits, and they also have their spiritual things. There are people who are spiritually-minded in that negative direction, but that's not what God wants you to do. The context here is "spiritual things toward God." So, Paul is not just telling you to be spiritually-minded, but to be spiritually-minded toward God.

THE CARNAL MIND VS. THE SPIRITUAL MIND

We just read in Romans 8:5 that those who are after the Spirit set their minds on spiritual things. That's what you're doing by reading this book. Your attention is on spiritual things concerning God, His Son Jesus Christ, the Holy Spirit, and the Kingdom of God. That's why you're giving time, attention, and effort to study such an important material as this.

Now, there are Christians who wouldn't be interested in this or any other kind of spiritual pursuit. They'd rather set their minds and attention on worldly things that are more appealing to the flesh. But Paul sounds a strong note of warning to such folks; he says in **Romans 8:6**,

> *"For to be carnally minded is death;"*

The carnal mind is the mind that has been trained to only recognise, appreciate, and desire worldly (sensual) things that have no spiritual benefits. It's concerned only with things of this earth, the gratification of the senses, and indulgence of the appetites, being devoted to this world and its pursuits rather than to spiritual affairs.

Paul, by the Spirit, warns that those who set their minds (by attention and affection) on carnal things programme themselves for spiritual death, and he tells us why: ***"Because the carnal mind is enmity against God: for it is not subject to the law of God, neither indeed can be"*** **(Romans 8:7).**

All that the carnal mind thinks about is worldly things and how to please itself; it doesn't think about the spiritual things of God in Christ, or things that please God. The Word declares that such a mind is in enmity against God, because it's not and cannot be subject to the law of God. And the reason for that is simple: it isn't controlled by the Spirit, but by the flesh or senses.

Paul goes on to deliver a thought-provoking point in **Romans 8:8:**

> *"So then they that are in the flesh cannot
> please God."*

How do you live your life? Do you live according to your senses and the things that appeal to your outward man? If you live that way, you can't please God. Paul, however, doesn't end his argument there; he follows up that grave submission with a vital and reassuring conclusion:

> *"But ye are not in the flesh, but in the
> Spirit, if so be that the Spirit of God
> dwell in you. Now if any man have not
> the Spirit of Christ, he is none of his"*
> *(Romans 8:9).*

If you're born again, your spirit is alive to God. You're not in the flesh but in the spirit, because God's Spirit dwells in you. So you're not going to live in the flesh, but you'll remain alive in Christ with the life He's given you, praise God!

You Have A Sound Mind

In learning to use your mind right, you've got to be conscious of the truth that you have a sound mind. In **2 Timothy 1:7**, Paul said:

> *"For God hath not given us the spirit of fear; but of power, and of love, and of a sound mind."*

Imagine if all your years growing up, your parents always told you that you had a sound mind, instead of telling you that you were a pig-headed, good-for-nothing. Imagine that whenever you did something wrong or messed up, they corrected you in love, and told you not to act that way, because you have a sound mind. Just imagine what that would have done for your confidence and self-image growing up.

Well, it's not too late. You can start today and

begin to tell yourself you have a sound mind. Just keep declaring, "My mind is sharp, and I'm sound. I'm super-intelligent and excellent." When you talk like this, people would say you're proud and braggadocious, but don't let that stop you. God has not given you the spirit of fear, but of power, and of love, and of a sound mind. This means you're powerful, loving, and mentally sound. When you put those three qualities— power, love, and a sound mind—together, the result is excellence. You're excellent!

Some people are powerful but not loving; some are loving but not sound. But that's not you; you've got all three; you're complete! You've got a sound mind, and you've got to use it to transform your life and your world.

6

THE POWER OF THOUGHTS

You must have observed that we've been talking a lot about thoughts. That's because there can't be any meaningful discourse on the mind without constant reference to the material with which it functions—thoughts.

In the second chapter, I defined thought as the creation, recalling, reviewing, and processing of images, for meaning, reason, language, and expression.

Now as we delve further into the subject, you'll see that thoughts are *pictures of the mind with constructive or destructive possibilities, functioning with or within human emotions.* In other words, they have the ability to influence your emotions. Sometimes they are imaginations, but they're more than that. Thoughts are conscious, mental constructions of your mind based on imaginations, information, or stimuli.

Thoughts, therefore, are a stream of images that

THOUGHTS ARE PICTURES OF THE MIND THAT HAVE CONSTRUCTIVE OR DESTRUCTIVE POSSIBILITIES, ENERGETIC FORCES THAT HAVE POWER WITH HUMAN EMOTIONS.

create meaning. You can't think without meaning; if you do, it just means you're not thinking. Real thinking is creating or setting one's mind on a stream of images that create or have a meaning, and thus give a message.

A man's thoughts, if wrongly employed, can keep him in bondage and clog the wheels of his success and progress. On the other hand, he can experience glorious liberty as a result of his thoughts. That's why the Bible in Philippians 4:8 counsels us to choose and think the right thoughts only.

Many times we underestimate the power and possibilities of our thoughts. Until you change your thinking, you can't change your life; you can't change your state, and therefore, can't change your estate. Your life will always go in the direction of your thoughts. Your life will never be different from the character of your thoughts.

You're a reflection of your thoughts. Your life is the outward manifestation of the inner workings of your mind. That's why understanding the importance of your thoughts and how to use them rightly is very vital.

Where Do Your Thoughts Come From?

By now, I trust that you must have understood the latent power of your mind and the importance of cultivating your thinking processes and creating the right pictures about everything that concerns you. I'm certain that you also now know how to effectively channel your thoughts in the way that God wants you to.

However, you mustn't be ignorant of the fact that there's an adversary (the devil) out there who's

> YOU'RE A REFLECTION OF YOUR THOUGHTS. YOUR LIFE IS THE OUTWARD MANIFESTATION OF THE INNER WORKINGS OF YOUR MIND.

constantly devising tricks to rob you of God's blessings. The Bible describes him as mimicking a roaring lion that prowls around, seeking whom he may devour (1 Peter 5:8). And one of the ways he'll try to sway you is by planting all kinds of wrong thoughts and pictures in your mind. He will try to mislead you into believing damaging thoughts that can put you in bondage. That's why, before you accept and dwell on any information that comes to you, you must first discern its source so you don't allow the wrong stuff get into your spirit.

You need to know how to distinguish the thoughts that come to you, because if you're not mindful of where the thoughts you process emanate from and examine them with God's Word, they could lead you astray.

Understanding The Different Sources Of Your Thoughts

1. Your Own Reasoning:

These are thoughts that emanate from you based on the information you've acquired. Such information, a lot of times, is conditioned by the happenings in your environment: what you've studied in school, read in the newspapers, listened to on radio, seen on TV, browsed on the Internet, or heard from someone else.

2. From God:

Thoughts can also come to you from God. God, sometimes, communicates His thoughts to you through your mind, which is the doorway to your spirit.

3. From Satan:

Evil or negative information, opinions and suggestions, if allowed, can be thrown to your mind by the devil. And all the thoughts he brings are to pollute your mind, blind you from God's truth, and rob you of the glorious life you ought to be enjoying. This is mostly done through imagination, pictures, and inaudible voices (2 Corinthians 4:4).

> EVERY THOUGHT THAT MAKES YOU RESENT OR DESPISE PEOPLE, OR MAKES YOU WORK AGAINST THE PURPOSES OF GOD IS FROM THE DEVIL, NOT FROM YOU.

You may wonder, "How then can I distinguish the thoughts that come to me?" How can I know the thoughts I should or shouldn't accept? It's simple.

If you're born again, the Bible says you have the mind of Christ: "*For who hath known the mind of the Lord, that he may instruct him? But we have the mind of Christ*" (1 Corinthians 2:16). Though you had a certain way of thinking before, now that you're God's child, your mind has been enabled and empowered to think like Him.

Before the new creation came, God said, *"For my thoughts are not your thoughts, neither are your ways my ways, saith the Lord"* (Isaiah 55:8). But now that you're born again, you have His life now; you're now a partaker of His divine nature. (2 Peter 1:4), glory to God! There's only one way of thinking and you're in that way now—in Christ.

Jesus said, *"I am the way, the truth, and the life"* (John 14:6). So every thought that is good for God and good for people is from heaven, and God's heaven is operational in your heart. Every thought that makes you resent or despise someone else, or makes you work against the purposes of God, is from the devil, not from you. When you find yourself thinking thoughts that frustrate or contradict God's plans for you, or for the Church, which is His Body, understand that they're not from you or God, but the devil. When such thoughts come to you, immediately discern and reject them.

Your thoughts are basically from the Lord's standpoint. He has declared you good, and so evil, unhealthy, or negative thoughts can't emanate from you.

You're Responsible For Your Thoughts

Scripture records in **Genesis 6:5** that God looked at man's life, the way he lived, and how he related with his fellow man, and

> *"...GOD saw that the wickedness of man was great in the earth, and that every IMAGINATION of the THOUGHTS of his HEART was only evil continually" (Genesis 6:5)*

"Imagination" is the word I want you to notice here. Some versions render it as "inclination." In other words, "every inclination of the thoughts of man's heart was only evil continually." This means man was constantly inclined to thinking and imagining evil. Wickedness was in his heart continually. So the Lord said, *"...I will destroy man whom I have created from the face of the earth; both man, and beast, and the creeping thing, and the fowls of the air; for it repenteth me that I have made them"* (Genesis 6:7).

God held man responsible for his thoughts. Otherwise, He wouldn't have pronounced this judgment upon him.

Some folks say, "Well, you know, these negative thoughts just come to my mind; I don't know how they come." Well, God holds you responsible for processing such thoughts.

Remember we defined "thought" as the creation, recalling, reviewing, and processing of images for meaning. Creating, recalling, reviewing, and processing are all up to you. It's up to you to process or not to process the images that you get. If you don't process them to have a meaning, they can't give you a meaning by themselves. You've got to give them a meaning, just as those disciples in Luke 24:37 gave ghosts a meaning (recall the narrative in Chapter 2).

They'd never seen anyone attacked or destroyed by a ghost, but they'd heard stories, and the fear of ghosts had become registered in their minds. So when they saw Jesus—the Healer of the broken hearted, the Kindness of God, the Expression of the love of God— they were afraid of Him, because they thought He was a ghost.

Just imagine that Jesus hadn't said anything to them to allay their fears? Think what would have happened if He had frowned at them. Maybe they would have passed out or even died from fear. Then the news would have gone around that a ghost killed them, when, in reality, they died of fear.

So with our minds we give meaning, interpretation, and reason to the images we receive and process. You can give reason to whatever you create in your mind, and also give it a language for expression.

Change Your Way of Thinking

I just told you that God holds you responsible for your thoughts. **Jeremiah 17:9** says,

"The heart is deceitful above all things,

and desperately wicked: who can know it?"

Until a man is born again, this is the description of the state of his inward man. No wonder Jesus said you must be born again, because the natural man's heart is desperately wicked.

Isaiah 55:7 also says,

"Let the wicked forsake his way, and the unrighteous man his thoughts: and let him return unto the LORD, and he will have mercy upon him; and to our God, for he will abundantly pardon."

These all show that God holds every man, even the unrighteous and unsaved, responsible for his thoughts. What then should the unrighteous do about his state, since, according to Jeremiah 17:9 and Genesis 6:5-6, his heart is desperately wicked and his thoughts are only evil continually? Jesus gives us the answer in John

3:3. He says he must be re-created; he must be born again and receive a new nature and a new heart.

But the question of his negative, evil thoughts still remains, even after he instantly receives a new heart by the miracle of salvation. And God still holds him responsible for his thoughts, in spite of his new nature. That's why Isaiah 55:7 says, *"Let the wicked forsake his way, and the unrighteous man his thoughts: and let him return unto the LORD, and he will have mercy upon him; and to our God, for he will abundantly pardon."* In other words, change your way of thinking. The Lord holds you responsible for your thoughts, and He expects you to change your way of thinking to conform with His Word.

Your Thoughts Affect Things Around You

Did you know that your thoughts can also affect things around you? That's because thoughts release signals, and those signals can be received by things around you and people connected to you.

You've probably had this experience where you were thinking about someone and that person suddenly showed up, or called you, or sent you a message. Or maybe you were thinking about a particular thing and even though you hadn't said anything about it to anyone, someone near you started thinking the same thing and actually voiced that thought. Science calls it telepathy: *a transference of thought from one mind to another by extrasensory means.* But if you understand the spirituality behind the science, you'll become ever more careful about the thoughts you allow.

I don't allow just any thought in my mind. If I don't want to create certain thoughts in someone near me, I won't think them, because I know I can transmit those thoughts.

We all transmit thoughts, and sometimes we inadvertently transmit negative thoughts into our environment that cause it to turn on us and attack us. Did you know, for instance, that your room has thoughts from you? The walls, furniture, clothing, etc., in your room are made from materials that have memory and can receive and retain information from you, and whatever they've gotten from you can remain in them. That's why you've got to be careful the kinds of thoughts you let run through your mind, so you don't make something happen that you don't want.

"Fear Not"

Why do you think the Lord so often tells us, "Fear not"? It's because if you allow thoughts of fear, they'll affect your mind and stop the power of God from flowing in your direction.

You're going to have to discipline your mind so you can use it correctly. Start learning to think happy thoughts. Practise it until you become good at it, such that whenever negative thoughts of discomfort, frustration, anger, annoyance, bitterness, etc., come to you, you can easily say no to them and change your mind.

Change your thinking; start by saying the right things, uttering words of gratitude, and singing songs of praise to God.

This is how you can use your mind to cause good things to flow in your direction and stop the wrong, negative, or evil things from happening around you.

PULLING DOWN STRONGHOLDS

We're At War!

One of the critical points we've established from our discourse so far is that our words and actions are guided by our predominant thoughts. Now, if you don't arrest and control your thoughts, you'll find yourself saying and doing terrible things you never dreamed you could say or do. That's because there's a constant assault of the devil against your mind. He's always seeking to attack and pollute your mind, so he can render you helpless and ineffective in the things of the spirit.

Scripture shows us that we're engaged in an on-going spiritual warfare:

"for though we walk in the flesh, we

do not war after the flesh..."

(2 Corinthians 10:3).

"For we wrestle not against flesh and blood, but against principalities, against powers, against the rulers of the darkness of this world, against spiritual wickedness in high places"
(Ephesians 6:12).

But it also lets us know we've been equipped with divine weaponry that assures our victory:

"(For the weapons of our warfare are not carnal, but mighty through God to the pulling down of strong holds;) Casting down imaginations, and every high thing that exalteth itself against the knowledge of God, and bringing into captivity every thought to the obedience of Christ;"

(2 Corinthians 10:4-5).

You'll observe that Paul, here, was speaking about things that go on (or reside) in the mind—strongholds, imaginations, thoughts, and "every high thing," indicating that our minds are the battlefield of that spiritual warfare.

Strongholds, Imaginations, Thoughts, and "Every High Thing"

"Strongholds," in the context in which it's used in 2 Corinthians 10:4, isn't talking about a fortified physical structure or some external force the devil stirs up against you. It's referring to ideas, theories, imaginations, reasonings, beliefs, etc., contrary to God's Word that attack and capture people's minds, causing them to think, act, and respond in a certain way and, consequently, holding them back

> STRONGHOLDS ARE MENTAL WALLS OF CONTAINMENT THAT PREVENT PEOPLE FROM ADVANCING IN THE THINGS OF GOD

from enjoying their inheritance in Christ.

Strongholds can also be thoughts that have been established in your mind as a result of your background and the way you were brought up to think. They're formed as the results of the things you've seen, heard, and experienced, and the habits and character you formed before or even after you were born again. They could also be cultural and traditional beliefs that may even be recognised and accepted as societal norms. But all they do is prevent new thoughts from God from entering your mind.

In essence, **strongholds are mental walls of containment that prevent people from advancing in the things of God.**

For example, someone thinks, "I'm never going to succeed," because his grandfather and his father before him were failures. Another one says, "Every time something good is about to happen to me, all hell breaks loose and I miss my opportunity," because that used to be his experience. These are strongholds!

Paul also talked about "every high thing":

> *Casting down imaginations, and* *<u>every high thing</u> that exalteth itself against the knowledge of God..." (2 Corinthians 10:5).*

This refers to falsely exalted systems of ethics, religion, philosophy, etc., set forth by men to oppose and defy the knowledge of God. These are vain, unfounded opinions, dogmas, mind-sets, biases, superstitions, and beliefs that have become mental barriers erected in people's minds against the knowledge of God.

But thanks be unto God who has fortified us with an impregnable armour and made us invulnerable to these satanic onslaughts against the mind. The Word shows us we've been equipped with weapons that are mighty through God to pull down every thought and cast down every imagination presented to us by the devil, to bring down every high thing that exalts itself above the knowledge of God, and to take captive every thought to obey Christ (the Word). We're able, with our weapons, to set men free who are held in bondage through these satanic manipulations, Hallelujah!

The Armour Of God

We've established that we're engaged in a conflict with satanic forces (whether or not we like it or are aware of it). And since it's a spiritual warfare, we can only engage the enemy, using spiritual weaponry (2 Corinthians 10:4).

In **Ephesians 6:13-17**, Paul itemises the different parts of our formidable and impregnable armour.

> *"Wherefore take unto you the whole armour of God, that ye may be able to withstand in the evil day, and having done all, to stand. Stand therefore, having your loins girt about with*

truth, and having on the breastplate of righteousness; And your feet shod with the preparation of the gospel of peace; Above all, taking the shield of faith, wherewith ye shall be able to quench all the fiery darts of the wicked. And take the helmet of salvation, and the sword of the Spirit, which is the word of God:"

So here's what our armour consists of:

1.The belt of truth

2.The breastplate of righteousness

3.The boots of preparedness of the gospel

4.The shield of faith

5.The helmet of salvation, and

6.The sword of the Spirit

Looking closely at each of these weapons, you'll observe that only one—the sword of the Spirit—is an offensive weapon; all the others are for defense against attacks.

Now, the rendering of the 16th verse in the KJV may be a little misleading. It says, *"Above all, taking the shield of faith, wherewith ye shall be able to quench all the fiery darts of the wicked,"* and it seems to suggest that the shield of faith is the final and most important item of the Christian's armour. An enlightening commentary by W. J. Conybeare argues that had this been the case, the shield of faith would have been listed last, but Paul went on to mention two more items of the armour after the shield of faith.

So instead of "above all," Conybeare says, *"...**take up** to cover you the shield of faith, wherewith you shall be able to quench all the fiery darts of the Evil One"* (Ephesians 6:16).

The Amplified Bible renders it thus: *"Lift up over all the [covering] shield of saving faith, upon which you can quench all the flaming missiles of the wicked [one]."*

In this teaching about the Christian's armour, Paul draws an interesting parallel with the Roman soldier's armour. The Greek word translated "shield" here is "thureos," and it is used specifically of the shield wielded by the heavily-armed Roman infantry. It was a large, four by two-and-a-half feet, oblong shield, and not the comparatively small, round one. One of the most dangerous weapons in ancient warfare was the fiery dart—an arrow tipped with tow dipped in pitch. The pitch-soaked tow was set alight and the flaming arrow launched at the enemy. To combat this, the Roman soldier, fully covered under or behind his shield, presented it to the arrow, which was quenched upon sinking into the shield.

Paul here was saying that your shield of faith should be big and strong enough to protect and defend every part of you, such that the fiery darts of the evil one wouldn't get through to any other part of your armour in the first place!

So take up your shield of faith to cover you completely, and quench all the fiery darts of the wicked one. These fiery darts are thoughts the devil fires at people's minds, and they've destroyed lives and families, ruined businesses, caused wars, and ravaged nations. But with your shield of faith, you can and should quench every single dart the enemy fires at you.

Overthrowing The Reasonings Of The Disputer

2 Corinthians 10:3 says,

> *"For the weapons which I wield are not of fleshly weakness, but mighty in the strength of God to overthrow the strongholds of the adversaries. Thereby can I overthrow the reasonings of the disputer, and pull down all lofty bulwarks that raise*

themselves against the knowledge of God, and bring every rebellious thought into captivity and subjection to Christ" (Conybeare).

What do you use to overthrow the strongholds of the adversary? The sword of the Spirit—the Word of God! Remember, this is the only offensive weapon in our arsenal. As you meditate on, mutter, and speak God's Word, those mental barriers based on the wrong things you've heard and believed all your life come crashing down like the walls of Jericho, glory to God!

This is why I love to teach and preach the Word, because as I do, the wrong ideas and theories in the minds of men that they've lived with for so long, and the ungodly cultures and traditions that they've built their lives and societies upon come tumbling down; those things can't stand the power of God's Word!

How about the reasonings of the disputer? You

overthrow those as well with the sword of the Spirit. Satan is the disputer of God's Word. When God instructed Adam not to eat of the tree of the knowledge of good and evil, satan (in the form of a serpent) went to Eve in the garden and questioned God's Word, and she was deceived (Genesis 3:1-6). He still operates the same way today.

For example, the Word declares that by Jesus' stripes, you were healed (1 Peter 2:24), but the devil will tell you, "Come on, do you think you were really healed? If you were, then why do you still feel the pain?"

You see, he'll challenge what God has said and try to cheat you out of your blessings through his negative reasonings and suggestions. But you can overthrow them all with the sword of the Spirit, and as Conybeare's translation of Ephesians 6:13 says, *"... having overthrown them all...stand unshaken."* So hold your ground and stand firm against the devil as you declare God's Word and lay claim to your inheritance in Christ.

With your armour in place, nothing the devil throws at you can penetrate. And with the sword of the Spirit, you can go on the offensive against him and tear down his strongholds. Glory to God!

DEALING WITH NEGATIVE THOUGHTS AND EMOTIONS

In our definition of the mind, we said it is responsible for processing feelings and emotions. This refers more particularly to different degrees of affection, disaffection, and passion. You can be more or less affectionate toward someone or something. So there can be affection or disaffection. You can also be passionate for or against. These are all products of the mind.

Don't Manufacture Worry and Pain

Nehemiah 8:10:

> *"Then he said unto them, Go your way, eat the fat, and drink the sweet, and send portions unto them for whom nothing is prepared: for this day is holy unto our*

> *Lord: neither be ye sorry; for the joy of*
> *the LORD is your strength."*

The part of this I want you to observe is where he says, *"Neither be ye sorry; for the joy of the LORD is your strength."* The expression, "Neither be ye sorry," isn't properly rendered in the KJV. In the Hebrew text, the word translated "sorry" is "awtsab," and it means "to carve, fabricate, or fashion worry, pain, anger, displeasure, grief, hurt." So Nehemiah was telling Israel, in essence, "Don't process, fabricate or manufacture these negative feelings and emotions of worry, pain, anger, displeasure, grief, or hurt, because the joy of the Lord is your strength."

Nehemiah had a focus here; he was looking at them being strong and not weak, successful and not failing, prosperous and not lacking. So he told them not to manufacture worry or pain, because those things would bring them down and destroy them.

The joy of the Lord is your strength, and God wants

you to be strong in the strength He's made available to you. Otherwise, He can't use you. Remember what He said to Joshua, "Be strong and very courageous" (Joshua 1:7), and now Nehemiah tells us that strength is in the joy of the Lord.

> IF SATAN WANTS YOU TO DISPLEASE GOD, HE'LL GO AFTER YOUR JOY.

This is why if satan wants you to displease God, he'll go after your joy; he'll try to stop you from being joyful and cause you to blame everybody around you for your bad feelings and emotions. If he succeeds, you'll find that you're constantly angry and upset, because someone somewhere is always offending you, hurting you, or annoying you. Then you develop an "attitude." But what's really happening is that you're becoming weaker spiritually, because you've allowed satan steal the joy of the Lord that should have been your strength.

If the Lord says, don't create, fabricate, process, or

> YOU'RE A MANIFESTOR OF GOD'S RIGHTEOUSNESS, A REVEALER OF HIS LIGHT, A DISPENSER OF HIS GOODNESS... DON'T LET SATAN'S CHARACTER SHOW ITSELF THROUGH YOU.

manufacture pain, displeasure, grief, and worry, He's letting you know that unless you reproduce or process them in your mind, they have no influence or power over you.

God said to Joshua, *"I am with you, wherever you go. I will not fail nor forsake you. As I was with Moses, so I'll be with you, and no man shall be able to stand against you all the days of your life. But this one thing I require of you—be strong and very courageous"* (Joshua 1:5-7).

Like Joshua, the Lord is asking you to be strong and very courageous. But how are you going to be strong? This strength comes from the joy of the Lord, and that joy is expressed in singing, laughter, dancing, words of praise, and the loving harmony you have with your brothers and sisters in the Lord, as you speak positive, uplifting, and encouraging words to them. Refuse to dwell on pain, displeasure, worry, and all such negative feelings and emotions.

Don't Set Your Mind On Failure

Don't set your mind on failure or on those who are trying to make trouble with you. Don't set your mind on their negative, hurtful, or hateful words. You're born of God, and you have His nature. You've been created in His image, so think and act like Him.

You're a child of God, a manifestor of His righteousness (2 Corinthians 5:20), a revealer of His light, and a dispenser of His goodness. So don't give vent to any negative thing; don't let satan's character show itself through you.

There may be someone you've declared persona non grata and decided to never talk to again because of something wrong they did to you. But such an attitude is contrary to God's nature. In our Kingdom, we don't make enemies; they may declare us their enemies, but we only make friends.

The Bible says, *"God commendeth His love towards us, in that, while we were yet sinners, Christ died for us"* (Romans 5:8). Be Christ-like in your attitude. Don't wait for the offender to apologise before you forgive and talk to him again. Act like God instead, Who extends His love to sinners even when they don't recognise Him. Extend your love (attention and care) to others, even if they despise and disrespect you. Give vent to the righteousness of God in your spirit, and you'll always be happy.

Respond Spiritually, Not Emotionally

People around you may be responding negatively emotionally, but you've got to learn to respond from your spirit. God wants His Word in your spirit, and to control your mind as well. That's why Paul tells us by the Spirit, *"Be renewed in the spirit (or character) of your mind"* (Ephesians 4:23).

We've learnt from Romans 12:2 how to transform our lives with our minds: *"And be not conformed to this world: but be ye transformed by the renewing of your mind, that ye may prove what is that good, and acceptable, and perfect, will of God."*

As a young Christian, this was one of the first verses I was taught and I memorised growing up in church. It says it's your responsibility to renew your mind. Also notice that it doesn't just stop at telling you to be transformed by the renewing of your mind. It goes further to let you know that in renewing your mind, you will prove what is that good, and acceptable, and perfect will of God.

Read this scripture slowly to yourself and meditate on it. It's God's Word, and it's designed to produce results in your life.

Let Only The Best In You Come Forth

If you ever surprise yourself by expressing any negative emotion or attitude, repent and correct yourself quickly. Say, "Father, I didn't know I could get impatient like this. From today, I reject impatience in Jesus' Name." If, instead of responding in love, you find yourself respond with hatred, anger, or bitterness, you say, "Father, in the Name of the Lord Jesus, I reject this. It will not have power over me."

Don't let anything or anyone produce the worst in you. Don't find yourself manifesting such ungodly attributes. Refuse to let your life be a vent for satanic expressions. That's why I like that song that says,

> *"Satan has no authority here in this place,*
> *he has no authority here,*
> *for this habitation was fashioned for the Lord's presence,*
> *no authority here."*

This is one of those songs that you sing and they help your life go in the right direction. You're the Lord's habitation, fashioned for His presence. Therefore, satan has no authority in any part of your life.

If you ever notice anger trying to boil over in you, you say, "No! I'm full of love!" Then you address the anger: "Anger, you have no authority in my heart, for I'm the Lord's habitation, fashioned for His presence!" When you do that, the love of God will well up and fill your heart, glory to God!

"TAKE NO THOUGHT"

I n his letter to the Philippian church, Paul the Apostle let us in on one of the unique blessings and benefits of mind management; he wrote:

"Be careful for nothing; but in every thing by prayer and supplication with thanksgiving let your requests be made known unto God. And the peace of God, which passeth all understanding, shall keep your hearts and minds through Christ Jesus" (Philippians 4:6-7).

The word "careful" is translated from the Greek word "Merimnao," and it means "to take thought" or "to be anxious about." That's why the New King James Version and several other translations render

Philippians 4:6 as *"Be anxious for nothing."* The Amplified Bible translation of the same verse says, *"Do not fret or have any anxiety about anything..."*

Thoughts come to us all the time. Your mind (and mental receptacle system) may be processing myriads of thought-signals coming through it even now as you read this book. You could be thinking about an extensive range of subjects and things: yesterday's events, tomorrow's plans, pending office work, a business transaction, your spouse's birthday, your kids' soccer practice, a dream you had, etc.

There can be a barrage of thoughts bombarding your mind at any point in time, but you ultimately decide and choose the one you want to dwell on. When you take a thought and ruminate on it, there's no telling what it'll do to and in you.

"To take thought" means to center your mind on something in such a way as to become concerned. Many times it refers to taking a thought that draws us away from what should be our focus. That's why we're admonished here not to take the thought that distracts and pulls us away from the Word and the peace it brings to our hearts and minds.

The Lord Jesus gave us the same charge in **Matthew 6:25-27**:

> *"Therefore I say unto you, Take no thought for your life, what ye shall eat, or what ye shall drink; nor yet for your body, what ye shall put on. Is not the life more than meat, and the body than raiment? Behold the fowls of the air: for they sow not, neither do they reap, nor gather into barns; yet your heavenly Father feedeth them. Are ye not much better than they? Which of you by taking thought can add one cubit unto his stature?"*

Notice the phrase "take no thought"; it's from the same Greek word "Merimnao" rendered as "be careful" in Philippians 4:6. The Lord Jesus asked them, "How many of you have increased in size or added to your years since you started taking thought?" He was letting them know, "You don't get better by worrying."

Let's read on:

> *"And why take ye thought for raiment? Consider the lilies of the field, how they grow; they toil not, neither do they spin: And yet I say unto you, That even Solomon in all his glory was not arrayed like one of these. Wherefore, if God so clothe the grass of the field, which to day is, and to morrow is cast into the oven, shall he not much more clothe you, O ye of little faith? Therefore take no thought, saying, What shall we eat? or, What shall we*

drink? or, Wherewithal shall we be clothed? (For after all these things do the Gentiles seek:)..." (Matthew 6:28-32).

These are the things people of the world are concerned about and run after. Their whole existence is about what they're going to eat, or drink, or wear, or drive, or spend, etc. They're concerned about having all these things just so they can be happy in this world. But the Lord Jesus charges us not to be like them, and He lets us know why. He says,

"...for your heavenly Father knoweth that ye have need of all these things" (Matthew 6:32).

In other words, "Don't worry about these things, because your Father knows you need them. Be like the birds of the air who "take no

"TO TAKE THOUGHT" MEANS TO CENTER YOUR MIND ON SOMETHING IN SUCH A WAY AS TO BECOME CONCERNED.

thought" for their meals and yet are constantly fed by your heavenly Father.

Then, in the next verse, He shows us what to give our attention to:

> *"But seek ye first the kingdom of God, and his righteousness; and all these things shall be added unto you"*
>
> *(Matthew 6:33).*

This is the first and most important thing you should be concerned with: to see God's Kingdom established and His righteousness manifested in your world. Don't be fixated on establishing your comfort, satisfaction, enjoyment, and happiness; let God's Kingdom be your focus instead. This should be your constant contemplation. Jeremiah said, "Let Jerusalem *(symbolic of God's Kingdom and His rule)* come to your mind" (Jeremiah 51:50). Let spiritual things of the Kingdom be uppermost on your mind.

Think Spiritually, Not Carnally

There are Christians who don't think spiritually but carnally all the time. They think only about their money, fame, position, and earthly connections; they're always concerned about how they're perceived by others. T.L. Osborn said those who are concerned about what people think about them are the slaves of the last people they talked

> DON'T STRIVE TO LOOK GOOD BEFORE OTHERS; BE CONCERNED ABOUT CHRIST INSTEAD.

to. How true! Such people are weighed down by the burden of trying to please others. Don't strive to look good before others; be desirous to please the Lord instead.

So be careful for nothing, but in everything by prayer and supplication with thanksgiving, let your request be made known unto God. Just tell Him what you want; He's big enough, and He knows everything about your life and the future. When this becomes your mindset, you'll understand that there's no use worrying about anything, praise God!

A Spiritual Principle And A Guaranteed Outcome

There's something about that admonition in **Philippians 4:6-7** I want you to notice; it comes with a promise:

> *"Be careful for nothing; but in every thing by prayer and supplication with thanksgiving let your requests be made known unto God. And the peace of God, which passeth all understanding, shall keep your hearts and minds through Christ Jesus."*

It says the peace of God, which surpasses all understanding, will mount guard over your heart and mind. This is a spiritual principle with a guaranteed outcome every time you put it to work. Understand that just as there are physical laws of gravity, electricity, mechanics, magnetism, and the like, there are also spiritual laws. And when you understand spiritual laws and act upon them, they'll produce results just as surely as the physical laws.

The principle here is that when you take no thought, but instead present your requests to the Lord in prayer and supplication with thanksgiving, the result is the peace of God protecting your heart and mind.

God's Word is God's wisdom; it's His thought clothed in vocabulary. When you learn to think God's thoughts by thinking His Word, then you come to the place where you live the supernatural life effortlessly. Now you can understand why Jesus says to us, "Take no thought." It's because, no matter what happens, there are spiritual laws to put you over. Even when trouble strikes and you feel pressured in your mind, you say, "No, I refuse to be concerned or anxious, in the Name of Jesus! I declare and I confess that I am a success, glory to God!"

A heart and mind that's full of peace and devoid of anxiety is one of the great benefits of managing your mind the way God's Word shows you to.

ATTITUDE—
YOUR MENTAL
DISPOSITION

10

I n the preceding chapters, we defined "the mind," "thought," and "the brain," and in discussing the brain, I emphasised how it works with the mind to give an individual his or her character.

It is my hope and belief that you've learned something that has been beneficial to you from what you've read thus far.

Now, we'll look at another key word from the definition of the mind, which is the word "Attitude."

Remember, the mind is the faculty of man's reasoning and thoughts. It holds the power of imagination, recognition, and appreciation, and it's responsible for processing feelings and emotions, resulting in attitude.

We've just discussed the processing of feelings

and emotions. Now, we'll look at the result of that processing—ATTITUDE.

> **Attitude is the disposition to act in ways determined by the mental processes of our feelings, emotions, beliefs or reasoning.**

This means you're responsible for your attitude— the way you act, pose, walk, talk, respond, etc.

Man's Information-Processing Center

By now you must have understood that the mind is the information-processing centre of the human person. In our definition of the brain, we said it is the primary center for the regulation and control of bodily activities, receiving and interpreting sensory impulses and transmitting information to the muscles and body organs.

I want you to hold that definition of the brain as we delve further into the study of the mind, and you'll discover that they do very similar things, except that one is spiritual while the other is physical.

The mind is the information-processing centre of the human person. It collects and processes all the information received through the nervous system of the outward man and through the spiritual senses of the inward man (human spirit and soul). The processing and eventual interpretation of information by the mind determines human behavior or attitude.

This is the reason for your attitude, positive or negative. It all comes from your mind and how you process the information you receive.

You may not always be responsible for how information comes to you, but you're certainly responsible for what you do with it, that is, how you process and act on it. And that's what matters.

So how do you process the information that comes to you? Today, we talk about crude oil, gold, diamond, and all kinds of precious substances beneath the earth, and all the beautiful things that come from processing them. But do you know there are nations walking on oil, gold, and diamond today that get nothing from them, because they don't know how to process them?

> YOU MAY NOT ALWAYS BE RESPONSIBLE FOR HOW INFORMATION COMES TO YOU, BUT YOU'RE CERTAINLY RESPONSIBLE FOR WHAT YOU DO WITH IT

It's the same thing with the mind. If you don't learn how to process your thoughts and mine the rich deposits of your inward man, you'll get nothing from it, and it'll reflect in the quality of your life. You must make the very important choice to get the best out of your spirit, through the diligent management of your mind.

An Exciting Reality

The exciting reality of the mind is that its contents and processes can be managed. This means they can be reorganised and re-programmed.

When you were born again, you were born after God, with His very life and nature in you. This means that you have an excellent spirit, for *"he that is joined unto the Lord is one spirit"* (1 Corinthians 6:17). However, having an excellent spirit doesn't necessarily mean you're walking in excellence. But you can walk in excellence, and that's the reason for the message in this book.

You see, the best and most excellent things of your spirit are expressed through your mind. Let's read some scriptures in connection with this.

Proverbs 4:23 says:

> *"Keep thy heart with all diligence; for out of it are the issues of life."*

The same verse from the NIV reads thus:

"Above all else, guard your heart, for it is the wellspring of life."

Keep or guard your heart with all diligence—above all else and with everything you've got—because it's the wellspring of life.

> THE EXCITING REALITY OF THE MIND IS THAT ITS CONTENTS AND PROCESSES CAN BE MANAGED.

Now, remember that your mind is the door to your heart, so if you're to guard your heart, where better to start from than your mind! That's what this scripture here is telling you—to mount guard over your mind, your thoughts, and your thinking process.

Then it says in verses 24-25,

"Put away perversity from your mouth; keep corrupt talk far from your lips. Let your eyes look straight ahead, fix your gaze directly before you."

"Perversity" here refers to deviation. So, in other words, "Don't deviate in your speech or talk; instead, let your eyes look straight on.

When God has given you His Word about your life—your work, family, marriage, children, finances, or whatever it is—don't lose His direction. Don't say the wrong things or speak outside of what God has said concerning you. Speak His Word and look straight on. This is what Solomon was talking about when he said, "Refuse to deviate!"

How wonderful it is to know that the best things of our spirits are expressed through our minds!

Renewal Of The Mind

The first and most important aspect of preparing your mind to glorify God is its renewal. This is the first thing you must do in learning to use your mind right.

In **Romans 12:2,** the Bible says:

"Do not be conformed to this world

(this age), [fashioned after and adapted to its external, superficial customs], but be transformed (changed) by the [entire] renewal of your mind [by its new ideals and its new attitude] so that you may prove [for yourselves] what is the good and acceptable and perfect will of God, even the thing which is good and acceptable and perfect [in His sight for you]" (Amplified).

You've got to have new ideals and attitudes, and be changed by the entire renewal of your mind. This is a complete overhauling of your mind, not just a change in some areas or aspects. And this doesn't just happen overnight; it's something you must do consciously and continually. In 2 Corinthians 4:16, Paul said his inward man was "renewed day by day." This is what should be happening with you as well; your inward man should be changed, transformed, renewed day by day.

I told you the exciting thing about the mind is that its contents and processes can be managed, re-organised or re-programmed. This is exactly what Paul is talking about here when he says to renew your mind.

Your mind must be renewed in content and processes. This is a taxing but worthy exercise, and the only potent instrument to achieve this effectively is the Word of God.

Now let's look at two other key scriptures.

#1) **Colossians 3:9-10:**

> *"Lie not one to another, seeing that ye have put off the old man with his deeds; And have put on the new man, which is renewed in knowledge after the image of him that created him:"*

This is talking about the renewal of the content of your mind. Your mind must receive new knowledge to replace the sense-knowledge you used to have or the worldly wisdom you walked in regarding any subject. This new knowledge is the "epignosis" of the Spirit—a new knowledge of God.

Go for and receive new knowledge. Learn spiritual verities through the Word and the agency of the Holy Spirit. Let the Word of God dwell in you richly in all wisdom and spiritual understanding.

Observe in the foregoing, two important factors:

• **removing, discarding or deleting the old information.**

• **receiving new information and knowledge through the Word of God and the Holy Spirit.**

#2) **Ephesians 4:21-23**:

> *"If so be that ye have heard him, and have been taught by him, as the truth is in Jesus: That ye put off concerning the former conversation the old man, which is corrupt according to the*

*deceitful lusts; And be renewed in
the spirit of your mind;"*

To be renewed in "the spirit of your mind" refers to being renewed in the "character or attitude" of your mind.

Look at the same scripture from *The Amplified Bible*; it says, *"...be constantly renewed in the spirit of your mind [having a fresh mental and spiritual attitude],"*

The *New International Version* says, *"...be made new in the attitude of your minds;"*

This means there's a new processing, a new way of looking at things, a new perspective. Remember, it's the mental processing of your feelings and emotions that results in your attitude. So, for you to have a new attitude, you've got to have a new way of processing your thoughts, feelings, and emotions through the power of the Holy Spirit and the Word of God. You've got to start seeing things from God's perspective.

When you do, your attitude will change in consistency with your new way of processing thoughts.

SEE IT FIRST FROM WITHIN

Whatever you want to accomplish in life, you must see it first and take possession of it from within; that is, from your mind. For example, if you're to be a goalscoring and exceptional footballer, you must first picture yourself in possession of the ball, controlling it and dribbling your way towards your opponent's defense. You must see yourself approaching their goal, beating the goalkeeper and scoring your goals. You must see it, dream, and ruminate it before you get on the pitch; otherwise, it'll be difficult for you to excel.

> ALWAYS BUILD IN YOUR MIND THE RIGHT PICTURES ABOUT WHAT YOU WANT IN LIFE

The same way, if you're a lawyer, you must see yourself addressing the court, with the judge, other lawyers, and the entire courtroom spellbound as they watch and listen to you present your case. You must see and hear yourself making such irrefutable arguments before you get into the courtroom. It all starts from the images of your mind!

One of the beautiful things you can do for yourself as a Christian is to always build in your mind the right pictures about what you want in life. It pays when you activate your faith-eyes to see beyond your present horizon, and envision yourself living out the very best of what God has prepared for you in this world.

God never created us to suffer or live the average life where we're barely getting by. He created us to excel and flourish in all areas of our lives. However, until you begin to see yourself that way—living in abundance, perfect health, victory, and success—it'll be difficult for you to experience it. You must first envision yourself living in that realm, living God's dream.

Your Future Is History With God

Romans 4:17:

(As it is written, I have made thee a father of many nations,) *(He's talking about Abraham here)* **before him whom he believed, even God, who quickeneth the dead, and calleth those things which be not as though they were.**

Remember when God said to Abraham, *"...your name will no longer be Abram, but Abraham because I have made you a father of many nations"* (Genesis 17:5 GW). Well, at that time Abraham had no child, and it was naturally impossible for him to, because he was old and his wife was barren. So when God told him, "I've made you a father of many nations," He was calling things that be not as though they were. In other words, in the mind of God, Abraham's future was history!

God had changed the man's name to Abraham to reflect his new identity and align with the vision for his life, and as far as He was concerned, it was a foregone conclusion. God didn't need to do anything more to make it happen. It was Abraham who needed to discover and align his mind with God's idea and plan for his life.

Abraham accepted his new name and began to introduce himself as "Abraham—father of many nations." But the lingering question was: Where were the children? How was he going to connect with this vision of God for his life and lay hold of that which God had given him?

How kind and gracious our Lord is. He knew Abraham was having difficulty connecting with this vision, and since he had no one to teach him, God had mercy on him and taught him to put his faith and imaginative power to work.

See With The Eyes Of Your Mind

The Lord had taught Abraham a powerful principle about the power of his mind (imagination) in **Genesis 13:14-15:**

> *"...Lift up now thine eyes, and look from the place where thou art northward, and southward, and eastward, and westward: For all the land which thou seest, to thee will I give it, and to thy seed for ever."*

Watch this very closely and catch what God was teaching Abraham here. He said to him, "From where you are, look northward, southward, eastward and westward, and all the land that you see from that spot I'll give to you and your seed forever!"

God was telling Abraham to see, not with the limited sight his physical eyes offered, but with the infinite range of his mind's eye. That's why He told him to stay in one spot and see all the land from there. This becomes even clearer as we read what God tells him in the next verse:

> *"Arise, walk through the land in the length of it and in the breadth of it; for I will give it unto thee" (Genesis 13:17).*

This is absolutely remarkable! God had told Abraham to stand in one place and look from there northward, southward, eastward, and westward, and all the land that he could see would be his and his seed's forever. Now he tells him to get up and walk through the length and breadth of all the land he could see!

Let's suppose for a moment that Abraham had looked with his physical eyes and seen all the stretch of land his eyes could possibly take in. Now God tells him to walk the length and breadth of all that land? It would have been practically impossible for Abraham to do that.

What God was simply saying to Abraham was this: "Son, see with your mind" And guess what? Abraham saw the whole world and took all of it; he left nothing out!

You'll see this when you read **Romans 4:13**:

> *"For the promise, that he should be THE HEIR OF THE WORLD, was not to Abraham, or to his seed, through the law, but through the righteousness of faith."*

Did you see that? God made Abraham a promise that He would give him everything he saw. Well, Abraham saw the whole world, and God fulfilled His end of the bargain and gave it all to him. That's how Abraham inherited the world!

But God had to show Abraham how to do it by using the power of his mind.

Help Your Vision

Now back to the question of how Abraham would connect with God's vision for him as "the father

IT'S IMPORTANT THAT YOU HELP YOUR VISION SO IT BECOMES CLEARER TO YOUR MIND.

of many nations." Remember, God had taught him in Genesis 13:14-17 how to use his mind and visualise what he

wanted. However, when it came to this issue of having an heir, Abraham just didn't seem able to see it.

Even though God had told him before this time, *"I will make thy seed as the dust of the earth: so that if a man can number the dust of the earth, then shall thy seed also be numbered"* (Genesis 13:16), Abraham didn't catch the vision or see the picture from that particular prophecy. God knew He needed something to help Abraham's vision, so one balmy night in the plain of Mamre, He told him to step outside his tent, look up in the sky and count the stars. Abraham looked up and started counting, but there were too many stars and he couldn't number them.

Then God said to him, "So shall thy seed be," and in that instant, that moment of awakening, the Bible tells us Abraham believed. He believed because his mind had now formed the picture, and he could literally see tiny little faces in those stars twinkling back at him from the sky that night.

God helped Abraham's vision by telling him to look up at the stars in the sky and see if he could number them. It's important that you help your vision so it becomes clearer to your mind. And you can do that by focusing your mind on things that strengthen or enhance your vision.

The Three Realms of Vision

You have three means or channels of vision:

1. The eyes of your spirit

2. The eyes of your body

3. The eyes of your mind

1. The Eyes of Your Spirit

What the eyes of our spirit see is not under our control but God's. You can't say, "Right now, I want to see something in the spirit realm"; no, you won't, because seeing into that realm is God's work. It's up to Him to make something appear to your spirit or to open the eyes of your spirit to see into the spirit realm.

Understand that when God put you in the earth, He made your spirit to function through your outward man—your body. Every spirit requires a physical body to function in the earth; and while you're here, you can't choose to function by your spirit without your body. That'll make you illegal to the earth.

This is why everything you'd ever do directly from your spirit would have to be through the Holy Spirit, and He would manifest Himself to you and deal with you in that realm without your body. This means the eyes of your spirit can only see what God shows them. You can't put them to work by yourself. That's why you've not yet seen some things you've always wished you could. It's because you simply couldn't "open your spirit-eyes" by yourself.

Ephesians 1:17-18:

> *"That the God of our Lord Jesus Christ, the Father of glory, may give unto you the spirit of wisdom and revelation in the knowledge of him: The eyes of your understanding being enlightened; that ye may know what is the hope of his calling, and what the riches of the glory of his inheritance in the saints,"*

You'll also find in Acts 2:17 that *The Amplified Bible* calls visions "divinely granted appearances." You can, however, use your other two sets of eyes at will. God gave them to you for your choice operations, and it's up to you when and how you use them.

2. The Eyes of Your Body

The eyes of your body are your physical eyes in your head. You can choose to use them whenever you want. Simply open them and you can see what's around you.

However, the sight or vision you get through these eyes is limited. They can only see things that are already existent in the physical realm; they can't see the invisible. This is where the eyes of your mind become so important.

3. The Eyes of Your Mind

The eyes of your mind are your creative eyes. In the mental realm, we're able to create whatever we want to see. Your physical eyes can only see what already exists in the physical; they can't make things become. The eyes of your mind, however, can produce what you want to see in the physical.

In my book, *"Recreating Your World,"* I teach

that your imaginative power is your creative ability. God gave us the ability to imagine as a special gift to help us create the world we want to live in. If you don't like the life you're living, you can change it. God has given you the tool (your mind) and the ability to make the change.

This ability is naturally God-given. With your mind, you can choose what you want to see. Seeing only what exists in the physical is living at the lower plane of life, and, sadly, that's where many are. But if you're born again, you have the God-nature and God wants you to lift your vision and see the unseen.

12

MEDITATION— YOUR MOMENT OF CREATION

Bringing Forth From Your Mind

Now let's talk about how to bring forth what you've seen or envisioned with the eyes of your mind. Creation doesn't end with you just simply imagining a thing and leaving it at that. After you've seen it, you've got to create it and form it.

Let's take our cue from God Himself. The Bible says,

> *"And God said, Let us make man in our image, after our likeness...So God created man in his own image, in the image of God created he him; male and female created he them" (Genesis 1:26-27).*

"And the LORD God formed man of the dust of the ground, and breathed into his nostrils the breath of life; and man became a living soul" (Genesis 2:7).

Understand what God did here: first, in Genesis 1:26-27, He created man from within, and then in Genesis 2:7, He formed man from the dust of the ground, according to what He had created from within Himself.

I'd suppose this would have taken some time. You say, "But God created man on the sixth day." Yes, but don't forget that one day with the Lord is as a thousand years and a thousand years as one day (2 Peter 3:8). That's because He lives in eternity. So God created and formed—in His own image and after His likeness —this excellent creature that He called man.

Now, you have an image, a vision you want to bring forth. Remember, your imaginative power is your creative ability; whatever you can imagine, you can create. So, it's important that you imagine. It's something you've got to learn to do for yourself.

But here's where many have misunderstood vision: they're waiting on God to give them one when they should be creating it. There're visions God shows you in your spirit, which you don't have any influence over (remember the eyes of your spirit), and there're those you must create with your mind. When God has given you a Word concerning anything, then you have the right to produce it, and its creation begins in your mind.

Your Times Alone

This is why it's so important that you have times of privacy to work on and with your mind. I call these times "moments of creation." How we need to have such moments alone, where we're not imagining how we're going to get back at those who offended us. Some people use their moments alone to bring up such unpleasant images, and end up creating all the wrong things in their lives. Then they turn around and wonder where their problems are coming from.

You ought to spend your moments alone creating what you want. When a negative picture comes to your mind, stop it and replace it with the right one.

True Meditation Is Creation

Isaac, the son of promise, had learned something from Abraham his father. The Scriptures show him as a deeply spiritual man who meditated often. On one occasion, Abraham asked his head servant to go get Isaac a wife, and when he returned with Isaac's wife, they found him meditating (Genesis 24:63-64). He had learnt the power of meditation, knowing that your moments of meditation are your moments of creation.

True meditation is creation, but not too many people have learnt to use their moments of meditation to create.

In the general sense, "to meditate" means "to focus one's thoughts on; reflect on or ponder over; to plan or project in the mind." However, in Scripture (Joshua 1:8), the Hebrew word translated "meditate" is

> YOUR MOMENTS OF MEDITATION ARE YOUR MOMENTS OF CREATION.

"hagah," and it means "to ponder, to mutter, to roar." This reveals the three stages or levels of meditation. Meditation therefore refers not only to pondering, ruminating, or reflecting on something; it also implies muttering that thought under your voice, speaking it out, and roaring it to yourself. In other words, you're saying something with your mind focused on it. You're getting your whole system to accept a certain truth.

We can see that Isaac had learnt the same lesson God taught his father. He knew what to do with his mind and his times of meditation. When everyone was fleeing from Gerar and running to Egypt because the economy was bad, the Lord appeared to him in one of his times of meditation and told him, *"Don't pack up and run off like everybody else; stay in this land and I'll give you everything"* (Genesis 26:2-3).

> SPEND YOUR MOMENTS ALONE CREATING WHAT YOU WANT. WHEN A NEGATIVE PICTURE COMES TO YOUR MIND, STOP IT AND REPLACE IT WITH THE RIGHT ONE.

Isaac stayed put and, even though there was a severe drought in the land, everywhere he dug, his wells sprang water. When others' crops failed, his flourished (Genesis 26:12-25). The Bible says he prospered, and continued to prosper, until he became so great and prominent in the land that the Philistines envied him (Genesis 26:12-14). He was a man of great prosperity, but he created it through meditation on God's promise.

Jacob's Creative Imagination

Jacob also learnt the same thing from Isaac his father. He had discovered the power of meditation and how to use his mind to create what he wanted. This was why, even though he suffered many things under his uncle Laban for many years, he came out very prosperous in the end.

Before we see how Jacob did it, let's first establish the backdrop for his extraordinary story. He loved Rachel, Laban's younger daughter, and wanted to marry her. Laban said it was fine with him, but Jacob must serve him for seven years before he could have Rachel as his wife. Jacob served the seven years, and at the end of the period, Laban reneged on their agreement, and tricked him into marrying Leah, the older daughter, instead.

But Jacob wanted Rachel so much, and Laban knew this and took advantage of it. He presented Jacob with another offer: "Serve me seven more years and Rachel would be yours" (Genesis 29:27). Jacob agreed and served Laban for another seven years, making a total of fourteen years before he eventually had Rachel as his wife.

Jacob continued serving Laban, who had over the

period reviewed his salary, not upward but downward, on ten different occasions! I mean, the man was just a mean, dishonest boss! Well, one day, Jacob went to Laban and said, "Uncle, it's time for me to leave. My wives are having kids and our family is growing larger. Better for us to leave now before we become a nuisance to you and to this place."

Read Laban's response: *"...If I have found favor in your sight, please stay here, for I have learned...that the Lord has blessed me on account of you...Just name your wages — I'll pay whatever you want"* (Genesis 30:27-28 NET).

Jacob agreed to stay a while longer and serve Laban, and now Laban tells him, "I'll pay whatever you want." But Jacob saw through the smokescreen; this was the same man who'd changed his wages ten times now asking him to name his price. He'd had enough of Laban's dishonesty, so he replied, *"I don't want you to pay me anything. Just do one thing, and I'll take care of your sheep and goats"* (Genesis 30:31 CEV).

Here was what Jacob asked, and this is where we begin to see his creative mind at work: Laban and his sons were to take away all the spotted, speckled, and striped animals from the herd, leaving only the pure-coloured ones. If those ones gave birth to any spotted, speckled, or striped young, they'd be Jacob's wages for his services as Laban's herdsman.

Both Jacob and Laban knew there was very little chance of that ever happening. But Laban, being the dishonest boss, was very happy with the deal. Now he didn't have to cheat Jacob anymore; he figured Jacob had cheated himself with this absurd deal he concocted.

Laban and his sons promptly took away the spotted, speckled, and striped animals and separated them from Jacob's herd by a distance of three days' journey, leaving him with the pure-coloured ones. Now they waited to see how Jacob would pull this off and have his own livestock and support his family.

Let's see how he did it.

How Jacob Created With His Imagination

"And Jacob took him rods of green poplar, and of the hazel and chesnut tree; and pilled white strakes in them, and made the white appear which was in the rods. And he set the rods which he had pilled before the flocks in the gutters in the watering troughs when the flocks came to drink, that they should conceive when they came to drink" *(Genesis 30:37-38).*

Observe closely what Jacob was doing here. He wasn't carrying out a ritual, as some have thought or suggested; he was helping his vision in the same way God helped Abraham's vision by getting him to count the stars.

Jacob got rods from poplar, hazel, and chestnut trees and made markings on them so they looked like the designs on the bodies of the striped, spotted, and speckled animals.

Next, he placed these rods where the animals came to drink and mate, because he was trying to help his vision of them bringing forth spotted, speckled and striped young, and he thought it could happen if they'd mate in front of the rods. So he set his focus on this.

This is how to help your vision—you meditate until your whole mind is inundated with the idea of what you want to see. That's why sometimes, when you want to meditate and you're in your closet with nothing in front of you, it'll be difficult to see anything.

Start by reading Scripture or some other material in the direction of your vision. I tell people, "If you want to have a productive fast, get some books you'll study during the period, so your mind can be well-focused. If you say you're fasting or meditating, and you're not

focusing on anything, then
your mind isn't creating any
picture. This is something
you've got to learn.

> MEDITATE UNTIL
> YOUR WHOLE MIND IS
> INUNDATED WITH THE
> IDEA OF WHAT YOU
> WANT TO SEE.

Jacob understood this; he knew that the things we see were not made of things that appear (Hebrews 11:3). Let's get back to his story now:

> *"And he set the rods which he had pilled before the flocks in the gutters in the watering troughs when the flocks came to drink, that they should conceive when they came to drink. AND THE FLOCKS CONCEIVED BEFORE THE RODS, AND BROUGHT FORTH CATTLE RINGSTRAKED, SPECKLED, AND SPOTTED" (Genesis 30:38-39).*

It worked! Those pure-coloured cattle actually gave birth to ringstraked (striped), speckled, and spotted young!

Now watch what Jacob did next:

> *"And Jacob did separate the lambs, and set the faces of the flocks toward the ringstraked, and all the brown in the flock of Laban; and he put his own flocks by themselves, and put them not unto Laban's cattle. And it came to pass, whensoever the stronger cattle did conceive, that Jacob laid the rods before the eyes of the cattle in the gutters, that they might conceive among the rods. But when the cattle were feeble, he put them not in: so the feebler were Laban's, and the stronger Jacob's" (Genesis 30:40-42).*

Isn't this amazing? I told you Jacob wasn't performing a ritual. He had started out by placing his marked rods before the cattle, so that when they saw the rods while mating, they conceived their young with designs like those on the rods. But now he no longer needed the rods. This time he put the spotted, speckled, and ringstraked calves and lambs before the adult ones so that as they mated, they'd conceive such as the ones they were seeing in front of them.

> *"And it came to pass, whensoever the stronger cattle did conceive, that Jacob laid the rods before the eyes of the cattle in the gutters, that they might conceive among the rods. But when the cattle were feeble, he put them not in: so the feebler were Laban's, and the stronger Jacob's"* *(Genesis 30:41-42).*

Don't think Jacob was cheating Laban here; all he was doing was helping his vision and ensuring he had the best possible outcome. So each time the strong cattle mated at the watering trough, he put in the marked rods so they would conceive striped, spotted and speckled young, and when he noticed it was the weaker cattle mating, he removed the rods so they produced their regular pure-coloured offspring.

What Jacob did was to use his imaginative power—his creative ability. You can create the vision you want in your mind. It's something you've got to consciously choose to do. Don't think, "Well, I can't see any vision until it appears to me." No, the vision that would appear to you without you working it is the one in your spirit; leave that to God. Truth is, you may never see a spiritual vision while on this earth, but that shouldn't stop you from being as successful as you choose to be, if you'll create the ones He gave you the ability to produce.

Not From Things That Appear

Laban and his sons couldn't figure out how Jacob came about having so many speckled, spotted, and ringstraked cattle when he wasn't even supposed to have any. They accused him of stealing from them, so he thought it necessary to open up to his wives—Laban's daughters—and show them how he made it happen.

Genesis 31:10-12:

> *"And it came to pass at the time that the cattle conceived, that I lifted up mine eyes, and saw in a dream, and, behold, the rams which leaped upon the cattle were ringstraked, speckled, and grisled. And the angel of God spake unto me in a dream, saying, Jacob: And I said, Here am I. And he said, Lift up now thine eyes, and SEE, all the rams which leap upon the*

***cattle are ringstraked, speckled, and
grisled: for I have seen all that Laban
doeth unto thee."***

Here, Jacob showed his wives the spiritual side of
things. He told them how he kept seeing a vision of
what should have been pure-coloured rams appearing
ringstraked, speckled, and grisled as they mated.
Notice, he didn't say, "I saw in a dream that I lifted
up my eyes." That would have meant he was sleeping
and then he had this dream. But he said, "I lifted up my
eyes and saw in a dream."
That's talking about a vision
of his mind that he created
while he was fully awake.
And when you see like this,

> IF YOU SAY YOU'RE
> MEDITATING, AND
> YOU'RE NOT FOCUSING
> ON ANYTHING, THEN
> YOUR MIND ISN'T
> CREATING ANY PICTURE.

God tells you, "Son, Daughter, you've got it!" The
things we see were not made of things that appear
(Hebrews 11:3).

13

SEE ALL THINGS NEW!

I n **2 Corinthians 5:17**, Paul wrote:

"Therefore if any man be in Christ, he is a new creature: old things are passed away; behold, all things are become new."

There's a powerful word here I want us to study; it's that word "BEHOLD." It means "SEE." Paul, by the Spirit, was saying, "See, all things are become new!" Not many Christians know that they have to see that all things have become new.

This is a charge, an instruction of the Spirit. He says to you, "See!" What are you seeing? Someone says, "Since I've been born again, things haven't changed." But that's not what the scripture says here. It says, "See, all things have become new!" If you've not been seeing all things as new, then you've been looking at the wrong thing. It's time to say to yourself, "No, this is not what I'm supposed to be seeing. All things have become new!"

Now begin to see yourself in that new light. Stop seeing yourself with the natural limitations or shortcomings you were born with. Stop seeing yourself as subject to the misfortunes that may have plagued your earthly family. You belong in a new family now—the family of God (Ephesians 3:14-15.) Now, see that all things have become new!

> IF YOU'VE NOT BEEN SEEING ALL THINGS AS NEW, THEN YOU'VE BEEN LOOKING AT THE WRONG THING.

Remember, you've got to help your vision. This is what we've learnt from Abraham, Isaac, and Jacob. The Lord used the stars to help Abraham's vision. Jacob used markings on wood to help his. Find the right pictures that help your vision and keep them before your face. Stay with the things that steer the focus of your spirit and your mind in the right direction.

Be In the Right Place

This is why it's so important that you go to the right church and are exposed to the truth of God's Word. When people go to the wrong place, their vision is altered, and they start seeing the wrong things, because the Word of God is not being taught. God's Word gives you the right pictures and visions. That's because God's Word is His mirror that reflects back to you your true image in the mind of God.

It matters what you see. I've been a pastor for more than thirty years, and from time to time, pastors come across people who would always want to tell them what's happening in the church that's not right. They think the pastor doesn't really know what's going on. But the truth is they're the ones who don't know what's going on, because they're looking at the wrong things. The pastor, however, has to keep his focus on what God is showing him.

Joshua And The Wall Of Jericho

So what do you want to see as a minister, businessman, parent, or student? If you keep looking at what negative-minded people are showing you, that's what you'll have. Let your focus be on what the Lord has shown you instead. We see a very instructive account in this regard from the life of Joshua.

> *"Now Jericho was straitly shut up because of the children of Israel: none went out, and none came in. And the LORD said unto Joshua, See, I have given into thine hand Jericho, and the king thereof, and the mighty men of valour" (Joshua 6:1-2).*

At this time, the battle for Jericho hadn't started and there was no fighting as yet. Joshua was only just planning to attack Jericho when the Lord said to him,

"...See, I have given into thine hand Jericho, and the king thereof, and the mighty men of valour" (Joshua 6:2).

But Jericho's fortified walls were still standing strong, and the entire city was in lockdown mode; nobody went in or came out, because of the children of Israel. Yet the Lord said to Joshua, *"See, I've given you Jericho, and the king, and all the men of valor."*

God's first instruction to Joshua here was simple: "SEE!" This meant that for Joshua to conquer and possess Jericho, he had to "see" it first from within; he had to use the power of his imagination. If he didn't see that God had given him the land, he never would have possessed it.

> IT DOESN'T MATTER THAT GOD HAS ALREADY DONE SOMETHING FOR YOU, YOU'VE GOT TO "SEE" IT TO WIN IT!

This powerful principle still applies today; it doesn't matter that God has already done something for you, you've got to "see" it to possess it!

How important it is for us to have the right mental

picture of whatever our desire is! Understand this: **the extent of your vision is the boundary of your blessing!** In other words, it's how far your vision can go that'll determine how much you'll possess.

What do you see today about your career, business, family, finances, ministry, academics, etc.? If you're not happy with the progress you're making or the direction you're going, it's because you're not seeing. It's time for you to SEE!

Your Set Time Is Here

What can you see? How far can your mind go? I remember a remarkable experience I had some years ago during one of our healing meetings. A young girl who couldn't walk because of a condition she had was brought before me in a wheelchair. As I laid my hands on her to pray, I noticed she was moving her limbs, as if bracing herself for a dash. And as soon as I said, "Be healed!" she took off running! I had to quickly reach out and restrain her, because I wasn't through with her just yet.

You may be wondering, "How did that happen?" Well, that young child had built a picture in her mind of herself running that day. To her, it was the set time for her transformation, and nothing was going to prevent her from receiving her healing. She had already pictured strength coming to her limbs, and she could see herself running again just like any healthy kid her age. Guess what? That was exactly what she got. She received her healing that day and started walking and running again, praise God!

BE RENEWED DAILY!

The Character Of Your Mind

2 Corinthians 4:16:

> *"For which cause we faint not; but*
> *though our outward man perish, yet*
> *the inward man is renewed day by day."*

When Paul made this statement, he wasn't giving a general comment about the Church. Study this portion of Scripture in context, and you'll see that he was talking specifically about himself and some other persons along with him who had experienced this in their lives.

He was letting the saints in Corinth know this should happen with them as God's children, because this was what happened with him.

Now, every Christian may not be able to say that

his inward man is being renewed day by day. But Paul said he was renewed on the inside day by day, glory to God! The renewing of your inward man should be a daily experience. Even though your outward man may be getting older, you've got to renew your inward man every day through the Word of God. I'll show you how that works.

Ephesians 4:23-24 says,

> *"...be renewed in the spirit of your mind; And that ye put on the new man, which after God is created in righteousness and true holiness."*

The "spirit" of your mind here refers to the "character" of your mind. Therefore, being renewed in the spirit of your mind refers to the education of your inward man. When one is educated naturally by going to good schools and reading the right books, he forms a new character, because of the information and enlightenment he receives.

That boy who was born in a remote village and knew nothing about the outside world could go on to become a secretary of state, or a prime minister, or the president of the nation, because he's been educated and has formed a new character different from that of the uncouth young lad that came out of that village.

In much the same way, your inward man can be educated to form a new character, which, as Ephesians 4:24 says, is created by God's Word in His likeness of righteousness and true holiness, glory to God!

Become All That God Has Created You To Be

Now that you know what you should be, begin to train and develop your inward man with God's Word to become all you should be in Christ. As a child of God, your primary focus in terms of your personal training and development should be your inward man. When your spirit is properly trained, you can see and hear as you should.

This is important, because, your senses of sight and hearing are basically the sources through which information comes to you. If you don't see clearly, you get the wrong picture, and if you don't hear right,

YOUR PRIMARY FOCUS IN TERMS OF YOUR PERSONAL TRAINING AND DEVELOPMENT SHOULD BE YOUR INWARD MAN.

you get the wrong message. But when you see and hear as you should, you have the right picture and message; you understand who you really are and can be all that you ought to be.

Colossians 3:9-10:

"Lie not one to another, seeing that ye have put off the old man with his deeds; And have put on the new man, which is renewed in knowledge after the image of him that created him:"

This is akin to what we just read in Ephesians 4:24. We're like God, and the real image of Christ is in our spirits. We have His life and nature, for as He is, so are we in this world (1 John 4:17). And as our hearts and minds are renewed in knowledge according to His image (His Word) in our spirits, we form His character and become more like Him in our thinking, words, actions, methods, and mannerisms.

Change Your World!

"And have put on the new man, which is renewed in knowledge after the image of him that created him:" (Colossians 3:10).

This scripture tells us something quite instructive about the nature of God—that He's a Creator. And since He created our spirits to be just like Him, He expects us to be creators as well. This means He wants you to make things happen and change your world.

Many of God's children around the world are

already doing new and big things that haven't been done before. You may even be one of them, but there's so much more you can do. As you learn to take from what has been deposited in your spirit and bring them to the fore through your mind, you'll be amazed at your abilities and how much more you can do.

There are enormous potentials deposited within you. Jesus wasn't lying when He said all things are possible to the believing ones. He knew what He put in us.

What a life He's given us! Meditate on this truth and see with the creative eyes of your mind. The Lord is asking me to tell you to use what He's given you. Remember, He gave you a mind with the ability to see things your physical eyes can't see. You can't create until you see with those eyes, so make up your mind to use them.

So much will happen in these last days; the glorious things that the Word of God has shown us will take place, but they'll happen only through those who are using what God has given. We're going to use our mental eyes to see and create what we want!

Therefore, see yourself making progress and doing big things for God. See with the eyes of your mind; focus them on what you want to see. If you can see it, you can and will have it.

Use What You've Learnt

If a different image tries to distort what you're seeing, reject it. If you see yourself failing, say no to that image! Keep your mind's eyes focused on the things that are consistent with God's Word concerning you.

> SEE WITH THE EYES OF YOUR MIND... IF YOU CAN SEE IT, YOU CAN AND WILL HAVE IT.

I've shown you how to improve your life through visions and produce outstanding results. Use your power of vision to create what you want in your job, business, ministry, family, health, finances—in anything at all that concerns you.

I believe you've learnt some things and have been reminded of others while reading this book. It's time to take all that you've learned with you, start functioning with them, and live the glorious and victorious life that God has made available to you!

To contact the author write:
Pastor Chris Oyakhilome:

United Kingdom:
Believers' LoveWorld
Unit C2, Thamesview Business Centre
Barlow Way, Rainham
Essex, RM13 8BT
Tel: +44(0)170 855 6604

South Africa:
303 Pretoria Avenue
Cnr. Harley and Bram Fischer,
Randburg, Gauteng
South Africa.
Tel: + 27 11 3260 971; +27 11 3260 972

Nigeria:
Christ Embassy
Plot 97, Durumi District
Abuja.

LoveWorld Conference Center
Kudirat Abiola Way,
Oregun, Ikeja, Lagos
Tel: +234-8023324188,
+234-802 478 9892-3, +234-8052464131

Please include your testimony or help received from
this book when you write.
Your prayer requests are also welcome.

OTHER BOOKS BY
PASTOR CHRIS OYAKHILOME

- **HOW TO PRAY EFFECTIVELY VOLUME 1**

- **PROPHECY: UNDERSTANDING THE POWER THAT CONTROLS YOUR FUTURE**
- **HOW TO MAKE YOUR FAITH WORK**

- **PRAYING THE RIGHT WAY**

- **THE GATES OF ZION**

- **THE POWER OF TONGUES**

- **DON'T STOP HERE!**

- **JOIN THIS CHARIOT**

- **7 THINGS THE HOLY SPIRIT WILL DO FOR YOU**

- **7 THINGS THE HOLY SPIRIT WILL DO IN YOU**

- **WHEN GOD VISITS YOU**

- **HOW TO RECEIVE A MIRACLE AND RETAIN IT**

- **THE HOLY SPIRIT AND YOU**

- **NOW THAT YOU ARE BORN AGAIN**

- **NONE OF THESE DISEASES**

- **THE OIL AND THE MANTLE**

- **YOUR RIGHTS IN CHRIST**

- **KEEPING YOUR HEALING**
- **THE PROMISED LAND**

- **RECREATING YOUR WORLD**

- **RHAPSODY OF REALITIES DAILY DEVOTIONAL**

- **RHAPSODY OF REALITIES TOPICAL COMPENDIUM (VOLs.1-4)**

- **HEALING FROM HEAVEN VOLUMES 1-3**

- **ATMOSPHERE FOR MIRACLES VOLUME 1**

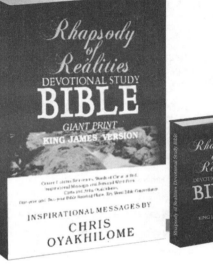
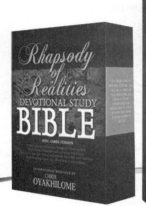

The **Rhapsody of Realities TeeVo** is a daily devotional for teenagers designed to inspire, encourage, and strengthen them. By providing answers from God's Word to questions of critical concern to the young person, this devotional helps teenagers discover their true purpose and programmes them for a life of out-and-out success.

TeeVo is packed with interactive, exciting and inspiring features for their continued spiritual upliftment and mental development. These include Powerful quotes from the author, Brain-teasing quizzes, Crossword puzzles, "Did You Know" fun facts, Captivating testimonies, and Wordscope—a reference page that gives detailed explanations of specific words. It's a richly-packed devotional, guaranteed to help teenagers enjoy an exciting ride with God's Word.

Call any of the numbers below to place your order:
Nigeria: +234 802 478 9892, +234 802 478 9893;
Ghana: +233 244211623, +233 548951736, +233 548951799, +233 548951800; **United Kingdom:** +44 1708 556 604;
United States: +1 980 219 5150, +1 281 759 5111, +1 281 759 6218;

Canada: +1 647 341 9091; **South Africa:** +27 72 268 5204

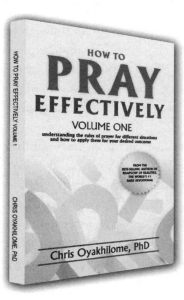

The Seven Spirits of God

...divine secrets to the miraculous

Explore the revelation knowledge you require to experience the fulness of the Holy Spirit in your life, and discover deeper dimensions of the Spirit that'll enable you walk in the miraculous and supernatural consistently.

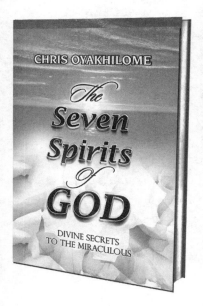

To order, please call

Nigeria: +234 802 478 9892,
+234 802 478 9893

Ghana: +233 244211623,
+233 548951736, +233 548951799,
+233 548951800

United Kingdom: +44 1708 556 604

United States: +1 980 219 5150,
+1 281 759 5111, +1 281 759 6218

Canada: +1 647 341 9091

South Africa: +27 72 268 5204

or visit:
www.loveworldbooks.org

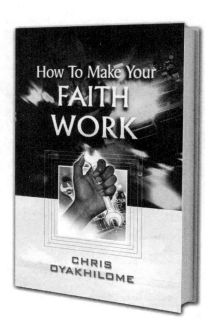

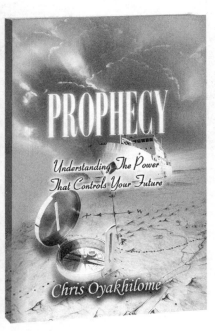

The LoveWorld Books Mobile App

Thinking of how to get instant access to wholesome Christian teaching from Pastor Chris' books?

Simply download the LoveWorld Books app to your mobile device to browse, purchase, download, and read all books by Pastor Chris. It's loaded with interactive, exciting features including

- a best-in-class epub reader
- your personalized bookshelf
- a digital bookstore
- i-capture and i-record functions
- photo and video galleries, etc.

Books are available as e-books and audiobooks, and are presented in engaging, interactive, and easy-to-read formats—just what you need to get your daily dose of inspiration...on-the-go!

Your anytime, anywhere access to Pastor Chris' books beckons. Download the LoveWorld Books app today!

Available in Google playstore and Apple store

 Google play  iTunes

PRAISE FOR GRAVE IMPORTS

"Eric Stone knows Asia up, down, and sideways, all of which are positions his characters find themselves in."
—SJ Rozan, Edgar Award-winning author of *In This Rain*

"...[A] terrific read. Stone's keen eye for the Asian landscape always finds the compelling image, the startling fact."
—T. Jefferson Parker, author of *L.A. Outlaws*

"In this intriguing tale of loss and redemption, Eric Stone takes the reader on a wild ride through the ruined temples, sordid back alleys, and the damaged soul of Cambodia ... A smart and compelling thriller."
—Dianne Emley, author of *Cut to the Quick*

"A multi-course Asian feast of a novel ... Dig in, savor the spice, and come back for seconds."
—Dan Fesperman, author of *The Prisoner of Guantanamo*

"The exotic and dangerous East comes to vibrant life ... Relax into your favorite easy chair. You're in for a wild and riveting ride."
—Gayle Lynds, *New York Times* bestselling author of *The Last Spymaster*

"...[T]he hustle is on in the underground market of rarified antiquities."
—Gary Philips, author of *Bangers* and *Citizen Kang*

"...[P]ick up Grave Imports *and let Stone export you to a whole new world."*
—*Crimespree Magazine*

GRAVE IMPORTS

| |GRAVE IMPORTS| |

THE SECOND RAY SHARP NOVEL
BY ERIC STONE

MADISON | WISCONSIN

Published by Bleak House Books,
an imprint of Big Earth Publishing
923 Williamson St.
Madison, WI 53703

This is a work of fiction. Any similarities to people or places, living or dead, is purely coincidental.

Set in Times New Roman

ISBN 13 (trade paper): 978-1-932557-47-3

FIRST TRADE PAPER EDITION

Library of Congress Cataloging-in-Publication Data has been applied for.

Printed in the United States of America

11 10 09 08 07   1 2 3 4 5 6 7 8 9 10

Cover and Book Design by
Von Bliss Design — "Book Design By Bookish People"
http://www.vonbliss.com

This book, too, is for Eva Eilenberg, my truest and trustiest partner in crime. And also for my sister, Nancy Stone, who I would love dearly and consider one of the greatest people on the planet even if we weren't related, and who was with me on my first trip to Cambodia.

||CHAPTER **ONE**||

The heads have all got different expressions, pretty much a look for each of my regular moods. But there's only ten of them and I've been irregularly moody.

At the moment they're propped against the wall by the window in my living room. Sometimes I turn them to look out at the sliver of Hong Kong's harbor that's visible through the surrounding buildings. Sometimes they're looking at me. That's what they're doing now, silhouetted by the morning sun glinting hard off the skyscraper glass.

I'm halfway through my second cup of coffee. The aspirin I took are working their magic. A friend dropped by last night to try and cheer me up. I don't know if it was her or the vodka that left me feeling this way, but I'm trying to get over it.

I talk to the heads. There are times when they are the best company I've got. Other times, they piss me off. "What're you guys looking at? Do something useful, why don't you? Tell me a fucking joke already. I could use a laugh."

They don't talk back—they're carved out of ironwood. I'm not that far gone.

"You look like hell, Ray, but at least you're smiling. Haven't seen that in a while." Bill Warner, my boss, comes into my office a minute or two after I get there.

"Susan came by last night. We had dinner and drinks."

"That tall Texan? No wonder you're smiling."

"Wasn't like that. Just friends, at least last night. She thinks I've been maudlin and need to get over it. She came around to give me a kick."

"Good. She's right, you could use it." He looks at the piles of paper and stacked files covering my desk and every other surface in the small room. "You want to get out of here?"

"I'd love to. Where're we going?"

He picks a foot and a half of annual reports off the visitor's chair in front of my desk and looks around for somewhere to put it. He sets it gently on the floor, then sits in the chair himself.

"Not 'we,' you. Acme Art Supply House, they're a big chain in California, they're looking to sink twenty-five million bucks into Golden Truly Million Artists Mansion Guangdong Limited. It's a simple due diligence job. They want us to tell them if it's a good idea or not."

"Hell, Bill, it's 1995. Can't they come up with a better name than that? Where do they get these names anyhow?"

"Golden Truly or Acme?"

"You've got a point. I guess Golden Truly whatever it is makes more sense in Chinese."

"It probably doesn't, but that's the job."

"So, where do I find the Golden guys?"

"They've got a couple of stores here in Hong Kong, one in Central, one in Mongkok. Their offices and warehouse are across the border in Shenzhen."

"They expecting me?"

"That's not how we do it. Take a look at them first; see what you can find out. Once you've got something to go on you can ask them directly."

I'd started working for Warner's company, Due Diligence International—DDI for short—about a month ago. Before that I'd been a journalist, deputy editor of Asia's largest circulation business monthly. So far, it seems like there's going to be a lot of similarities between the jobs.

One of the best ways to find out about a company is to do business with it. Golden Truly's shop in Central sells art supplies, but it also does framing. I call and ask if they make displays and stands for sculpture. They do, so I go by my apartment to pick up the heads on my way over there.

The heads, stacked into a five-foot tall totem pole, are supposed to come from Irian Jaya, the Indonesian part of the island of New Guinea. I found them in a flea market in Jakarta. The guy who sold them to me said they were made by former headhunters, who now have had to make a more socially acceptable living. A hotel concierge told me they're a fake. I don't care. They cost what they're worth to me. I've paid more for worse.

The cab driver makes a joke about eleven passengers in his taxi. I answer back in Cantonese, a wisecrack about ten fishballs and a guy with a big nose. My knowledge of the local language doesn't go very far, but I do know food and how to insult myself. He laughs, but then spits out a torrent of words that I don't understand. I throw up my hands and apologize for being an ignorant foreigner who only speaks a little. He apologizes for his English.

It's a nice ride as we try to chat. There are a few taxi drivers in Hong Kong who are pleasant to their fares.

He drops me two blocks down Stanley Street, past all the camera shops and the tourist-ridden but still charming Luk Yu Teahouse, in front of a small storefront with a beautiful array of handmade calligraphy brushes in the window. Below them are delicately carved lacquer ink boxes.

I'm admiring the display, leaning on my heads like they were a cane, when a narrow man comes out the door and stands next to me. "They are very beautiful, *lah*? Do you know Chinese calligraphy?"

He has a Singapore accent with a voice that squeaks out past thin lips under a hairline mustache. He's wearing soda pop bottle thick eyeglasses and what used to be called a "Mao jacket," but I don't think they're called that anymore.

"I admire it, I don't know it. Do you work here?"

"It is my shop, *lah*. Please to come inside."

The heads and I follow him in. He goes behind the counter and gestures to his shop.

There isn't much to point out. It's the sort of place in which you have to know what you want because the stock is all on dark shelves that stretch out toward the back. Other than the display in the front window, you'd have no idea what they sell.

"What do you want?"

I hoist the heads onto the counter. "I need to get a stand made for these, to hold them upright for display."

He picks them up and looks them over. He bounces them a little in his hands to judge their weight, then stands them on the counter so that they tower over us.

"Heavy, *lah*. Do you want them in a box, maybe Plexiglass, or to hang them on the wall?"

"No, just anything to hold them upright, so that they can stand on the floor."

"You can leave them with me, *lah*? I have ideas, I tell you later what I do and how much, okay, *lah*?"

I fill out a little paperwork and he tells me to come back or call tomorrow, and he'll let me know what he's figured out. It's not a bad day by Hong Kong's May standards. You can't quite poach an egg in the air. It's more like when you've got a dry cough as a kid and your mom puts a gently steaming humidifier in your room. Except it doesn't smell like Vicks. I decide to take a walk and get lunch before I head across the harbor to Golden Truly's other shop in Mongkok.

As I pick my way uphill through the dense, closed-in alleys of the Graham Street market, it smells of vegetables simmering lightly in the climate and overripe fruit, peanut oil sizzling in huge burnt woks, dried seafood, raw meat, diesel and a cautious note of orchids. It's loud with voices. Cantonese is a harsh sounding language that seems like it can't be spoken other than at high volume. It sounds like everyone's arguing, but they're not—they're having a good time haggling, just like in markets anywhere.

I make my way west through the small streets uphill from Queen's Road. Every so often at an intersection I catch a glimpse of the harbor through the towering glass buildings. It used to be that the waterfront was at the busy street just below me, but the land's been filled in and it's now a good quarter mile or more away. Another of the world's top ten tallest skyscrapers is going up, shadowing the short, squat, white barn-like structure that houses the Central Market.

It's lunchtime in Western District and I drop down to Des Voeux Road, to a small shop that's famous for its Chiu Chau-style fishballs and dumplings. I order a bowl of the light broth with rice noodles and an extra ration of fishballs, ten in all. In honor of my Indonesian heads, I suppose. I ladle in a couple of spoons of the rich, thick, oily chili sauce, sprinkle a fistful of chopped green onions onto the surface and try to make appreciative slurping noises when I suck the scalding, slippery mess into my mouth.

I've been here often enough that the owners no longer comment with surprise on the fact that I can use chopsticks, or that I like it spicy. They're not particularly friendly though, and I can read enough of the Chinese characters on the menu to know that I'm overcharged for lunch. But it's only the ten percent resident *gwailo* premium, not the fifty percent boosted from visiting foreigners or the hundred percent or more extra that the occasional Japanese diner gets charged.

When I leave I pat my stomach and in a loud and exaggerated way spew out *"mm-goy-lay, ho lahn ho seck-ah!"* in the general direction of the open kitchen, where three heavily sweating men dish out the food. No matter how many times I do it, it never ceases to amaze them that a foreigner would say, "Thanks, very fucking good food," and get all the tones right. They stare at me briefly then turn to talk with each other.

Cantonese is a very tough language to learn. There are seven commonly used tones—maybe eight or nine. I've heard there are twelve different tones in all. That's a lot of different ways to say *gow*. Say it one way and it means "dog," another and it's the number nine, another and it's a type of dumpling, yet another and it's the word for "old," stick the right sort of rising tone on it and you can call a guy a "prick." I know a British cop who speaks Cantonese fluently. Whenever we're together in a crowd and he's listening to the chatter around us, he looks uneasy.

I walk a block to the MTR entrance and descend the long escalator into the cool, dry Sheung Wan subway station. Hong Kong's subway is modern, sleek, but like everything else in the territory, it's also loud. There's a running joke among those of us who come here from quieter places, like New York: the government has placed noise pollution monitors around the city, and when the decibel level drops below a certain excruciating point, they dispatch a crew with jack hammers or pile drivers to pump up the racket.

As I'm carried down toward the platform, the roar of the air conditioning and the squeal of the brakes of a train and the mingled raised voices of thousands of commuters rise to greet and hug me. It feels oddly comforting. Maybe I've lived here too long.

I wait on the platform and look over the ads plastered on the wall. They're mostly for a new Amy Yip movie. She's the reigning artificially big-boobed Hong Kong B-movie queen. There's also a poster for Darlie Toothpaste. Its logo is a black man with a wide smile full of bright white teeth, wearing a bow tie and a top hat. Up until a couple of years ago the toothpaste was called "Darkie," but its manufacturer finally got tired of defending the brand. A few months after they'd announced the name change I was in the subway with a Chinese friend. There was a large ad in English sporting the new name, but with the same logo. My friend read the small Chinese print at the bottom and broke up laughing. When he finally settled down, he read it to me: "Don't worry, your favorite black man toothpaste is still the same black man toothpaste."

Language is cause for amusement, and misunderstanding, on both sides of the cultural divide. Tourists buy t-shirts with Chinese characters. The salesman will tell them the writing says "Great Fortune and Endless Prosperity" or that it begins with "Confucious say…" And the tourists believe that, and often enough it's true. But a Chinese photographer friend of mine has a lovely shot of two bulky Germans in matching plaid shorts with the Hong Kong skyline behind them. They're wearing identical t-shirts that say, "I'm a stupid foreigner and I can't read this."

And it cuts both ways. My photographer friend's English isn't very good, his girlfriend's is non-existent. They met me for dinner one night and she was wearing a lapel pin that said, "Liquor in the front, poker in the rear." She had no idea what it meant and wanted me to explain it to her. I tried, but she didn't get it—or didn't care because she figured no one else would get it either.

Names can cause problems, too. At birth, many Hong Kong Chinese are given names in both their native language and

English. If not, they pick their own when they need them. Hitler Wong works in a local hotel—I've met him. He doesn't know much about history, but he does know that the name belonged to a powerful man, and that's good enough for him.

I once met a teenage girl who was getting ready to go to university in the U.S., in Michigan. She needed an English name and she liked the sound of Easy. Even worse, her family name was Poon. I tried to discourage her from taking the name, but she'd submitted her application and was planning to stick by it. I hope she's getting what she wants out of college.

Two trains and about ten minutes later I pop out of the ground at Mongkok. Hong Kong's public transportation has got to be about the best in the world.

Mongkok is the most densely populated place on the planet. Unbroken waves of humanity sweep along the sidewalks. I surf the crowd to the entrance of a shuttered shop on Nathan Road. Nothing stays closed for long around here, the space is too valuable. But for the moment, the stoop of the closed shop is about two square feet through which people aren't moving. I pause there to get my bearings and plan my strategy to maneuver through the throngs.

The art supplies shop is on the first floor, what we Americans would call the second floor, of a building around the corner on Argyle Street and down a couple of blocks. I ease into the current and am carried swiftly along, straining to stay at the inside of the sidewalk so I can make the right turn up ahead. It's a little easier walking close to the buildings because the people who can avoid it, do. The path leads under the dripping window air-conditioning units, and pedestrians don't want to get wet. I try to imagine that the cold drops of water and occasional streams are refreshing. It doesn't work.

My hair feels wet and oily; the shoulders of my shirt are soaked and stained by the time I get where I'm going. There are people who go about their business in the heat and humidity and pollution of Hong Kong and still manage to look relatively fresh and clean by the end of the day. I'm not one of them. I'm one of the frumpled ones. The sort who usually looks put upon by the environment. I'm used to it. I gave up trying to be anything else not long after I got here.

One crowd is jostling to get into the elevator in the building's lobby while another is shoving to get out. It's only one floor, so I take the stairs.

It's arctic cold in the store. Maybe that helps keep the paint and ink fresh. Maybe it's meant to discourage browsing by anyone not dressed in a down parka or fur and wearing mucklucks. There are more employees than customers. There's one stationed at each end of every aisle, wearing a scowl and a blue Chinese quilted cotton jacket. They eye me suspiciously when I walk in and pause in the entry to look the place over.

I walk over to the aisle of brushes. I don't paint, I don't do calligraphy, but the tools fascinate me. This is one of the best selections I've ever seen, arranged by size.

At the start of the aisle are small kits with near-microscopic brushes that look to be only one or two thin stiff hairs in size. Several of the kits come with what look like small surgical clamps to hold the writing implements. There are brushes the size of slender toothpicks with ornately turned tiny handles.

Moving up the aisle the brushes get bigger. By the end they're hanging from hooks in the ceiling and are as much as five and six feet long and a full foot in diameter. Some of them have plain handles, others are beautifully whittled works of art themselves, dragons and cranes finely etched into their polished wood surfaces.

At the end of the row, the largest brush hangs by itself, set against a creamy swath of raw silk. It has a magnificent bright red lacquer handle that tapers leisurely down to a fat, hard and shiny black bristle. It comes to a point sharp enough to pierce the thick hide of an art critic. I'm admiring it when I sense a person behind me.

"It is beautiful *señor*, no?"

I turn to look but I don't see anybody. I look down and she's looking up at me from about two feet below. She's Chinese, with a friendly rounded face, deep set eyes with arched brows, and a broad grin splayed across her mouth. Her hair's about shoulder length. It's bobbed in a way that's popular across the border in the People's Republic, but with enough stylistic flourish to make it plain it's been cut here.

"It is beautiful, yes." I look her over more carefully. She's about thirty, in jeans, a man's button down collar cotton shirt and wearing what look like low-top hiking boots. She's holding a reporter's notebook, one of those long skinny ones that easily fits in a pocket. It registers, what she said to me.

"Señor? Funny, you don't look Mexican." She'd said it with a distinct south of the border—the U.S. border—accent.

"Funny *señor*, *no se*. I come from Tijuana, Mexico. You know it?"

"Yeah, I know it. I come from Los Angeles. What're you doing here?"

"Getting back to my roots, apparently."

"You got a name?"

"Marisol, or Wen Lei Yue, take your pick. You've got one, too, I guess."

"Ray. That's a complicated couple of names."

"Not really. But if you want my life story you'll have to buy me a cup of coffee."

"You trying to pick me up?"

"Not like that. I recognized you. A colleague pointed you out once at a press conference. I wondered what you were doing in here. I'm trying to avoid going back to the office."

"What office?"

"OJ. You want to ask any more questions you'll have to do it over that cup of coffee."

OJ is what everyone calls the *Oriental Daily Journal*. It's the blood, babes and bathos Chinese tabloid in town. It was the only paper that would publish the story I had written a few months ago about the Russian mafia, the white slave trade, and Ed and Marta. OJ had given big play to the sex and violence angle, fulminated for a few days over the outrageousness of it all, and then let it drop.

I don't like to think about it. A woman I cared for got killed. Another, who I loved, left me. I killed a couple of people who probably deserved it, and caused the deaths of a few others. Maybe some of them didn't deserve it at all. The whole thing drove me out of journalism. Writing about it hadn't done anyone any good.

And drinking to forget it hadn't done anyone other than vodka companies much good, either, and it wasn't even all that effective. Memories I don't want, doubts, worry, and confusion still rattle through my brain all too often.

There's a coffee house on the first floor across the street. We don't say much until we're seated in front of stupidly delicate, tiny floral cups filled with a watery excuse for coffee. I take a sip of mine, push it aside and move the glass of ice water closer.

She smiles at me over the rim of her cup. It almost looks large in her small hands. "Coffee not strong enough for the big American?"

"Enough already. So, should I call you Marisol, Lei Yue or Ms. Wen?"

"You can call me Marisol if you ever see me in Mexico. Other than that, Lei Yue's fine unless you make any dumb jokes about 'lay you.' Then it's going to have to be Ms. Wen."

"I guess you know me from the story I brought you guys."

"That was a nasty story. Good work. I was really sorry when it got buried. I asked around. People said you quit your job because of it."

"Yeah, I hoped it would stir things up. It didn't. It never does. People talked about it for a day or two, 'My my, *tsk tsk*, we ought to set up a commission to investigate,' then they forgot about it.

When I lost my illusions about journalism, the power of the press, that sort of crap, I lost interest."

"What're you doing now?"

I start telling her about Bill, how he used to be a spook and how he'd tried to keep me out of too much trouble with the Russian mob, and how he quit the C.I.A. and started his company and what a relief it was when he offered me the job. I get about halfway through it when she holds up a hand to stop me. "That's better?"

"Not so far, but it's no worse either, and it pays better."

She changes the subject. "Do you do calligraphy, or paint?"

"Neither one. I like looking at the brushes and I was working." I tell her about the job, leaving out the company names.

"I'm sorry, but that does not sound exciting or useful at all."

"Exciting? No. Useful? Sure it is. If the American company invests in the Chinese one it means more jobs and money at both ends. What's wrong with that?"

"Nothing I guess, but from what I've heard about you, I'd think you'd get bored."

"I could do with a little boredom. I don't need any more excitement for a while. You read the story. It was cleaned up for the papers, even your rag. I'm not going to go into the details. I don't like thinking about it."

"I'm sorry I asked."

"What's with you? Tijuana? OJ? What's the deal?"

Lei Yue's story is that her parents got out of Hong Kong before the Japanese got into it at the start of the Second World War. They made it onto a freighter that crossed the Pacific to Mexico. California was the land of opportunity, but it turned them back at the border. So they stayed in Tijuana, bought a decrepit cart off an *al pastor* taco vendor who was raising money to head north himself and started selling noodles and wonton on the streets. By the time their first child was born they owned a small restaurant near the bullring.

In 1962, the year Lei Yue was born—the last of nine sons and daughters—they bought a larger restaurant, with a bar and a back room where they opened an illegal gambling parlor. Business was good and their youngest daughter was the first family member to make it across the border. She went to college at U.C.L.A., got a degree in journalism and five years ago moved to Hong Kong after having worked on papers in the U.S.

"So, what do you cover for OJ?"

"Whatever I want. I'm in general features. The editor doesn't know what to do with me. I think I scare him so he let's me do what I want. He likes it when I'm out of the office."

"My last editor was like that, too. Good position to be in."

"Maybe we can help each other out from time to time."

"I don't see why not, but I can't tell you a lot of what I find out. Our clients are confidential."

"I'm sure we can work it out."

"I'm sure you are. We'll see."

After swapping numbers I go back across the street to look around again. I don't know what I'm looking for and nothing stands out. It looks like it's a large, well organized art supplies store. None of the sales staff approach me. When I buy a small notepad it's rung up efficiently enough.

Back at the office I do a computer search on Golden Truly, but I don't learn anything of interest from that either.

| |CHAPTER **TWO** | |

The Singaporean is opening the shop in Central when I walk up. His name's Tommy and he has a good idea for how to display my heads. I give him the go ahead to make a thin metal stand and pay him half the money in advance.

I'm turning to leave when he beckons me closer with a crooked finger. "Mr. Sharp, do you fancy Khmer sculpture, *lah*?"

I don't know anything about it other than "Khmer" means it comes from Cambodia. But the guy's lowered voice and nervous look make me curious. What's there to be cagey about? "Why not? Sure."

"Please then, come with me." He emerges from behind the counter and heads into the street. I follow and he locks the door behind us. He doesn't go far, just to the next door down the block; a heavy, rusted metal slab with two bright new stainless steel locks set into it.

Tommy sorts through his ring of keys and finds the two that open the door. Despite its weight and the rust, the door swings inward easily, silently. He switches on the light and we're in a small room. He turns and locks the door behind us. This is getting even more interesting. He smiles at me.

"Do not be alarmed. You will like what you are going to see, *lah*."

What is it about people sticking unnecessary sounds at the ends of their sentences? Canadians have their "ay," Singaporeans have their "lah." He bends down to a large, polished padlock that secures a garage door. He undoes it and heaves the door up on its rollers. "Wait here, I will open the lights."

He disappears inside and I move to stand at the threshold of a small warehouse, a "godown" in the local colonial English. The fluorescents flicker on.

In front of me is a carved stone panel. It's about ten feet tall and three feet wide and looks like it might have been a door. It's busy with a battle scene. Armies march up and down it, and what appears to be cavalry, mounted on armored elephants, crush soldiers underfoot. It's gruesome and magnificent. The detail is astonishing. There must be hundreds of individual figures. The faces on the combatants are all different, and even the elephants seem to have their own characters. There's a ragged seam running across it near the middle. It's been broken and repaired

"This is a very nice piece do you not think, *lah*? It is Khmer, Twelfth Century."

"It's a lot more than merely nice. Where'd it come from?"

"A citadel in the west of the country. Close to Angkor. Are you interested in art such as this?"

"Interested, sure. I doubt I can afford it though."

"Yes, this is our most expensive piece: two hundred and fifty thousand dollars."

I do the math in my head, thirty-two thousand U.S. No way I could ever afford it, but it seems cheap for what it is.

"Please to look around. If you have any questions, please ask, *lah*. We do have many less expensive pieces."

It's like being left to wander the back rooms of a museum. There are more doors, though none as spectacular as the first. There's a wall hung with lintels that were chipped from above entryways. They've been cracked and damaged, though a couple look fresh and perfect. One I particularly like has monkeys battling humans, watched over by a pantheon of gods. Two of the gods look like they're betting on the outcome. Maybe it's an early theory of evolution.

Along the opposite wall are the women, dancers, a dozen of them. About half have been chipped out of larger panels, the others are stand-alone statues. I approach them and am transfixed. Tommy creeps up next to me and whispers in my ear, as if afraid to disturb them.

"They are very beautiful women are they not, *lah*? They are the heavenly dancers, *apsaras*. They are very sexy girls."

They are at that. Dressed in flowing skirts or baggy pants that seem as soft and translucent as silk, even though carved from limestone. Their delicate arms and long-fingered hands look as if they are sensuously in motion. They're playful and ethereal at the same time, like goddesses that might climb down from the clouds to play with us mere mortals. They have individual faces and expressions, lips fat with promise. Their breasts are amazing; as varied as the rest of them, but all perfect. Firm and ripe, big, small, medium, all rounded and youthful, defying gravity through the ages and capped with perky nipples. Their waists are slender and smooth, their bellies slightly pooched and hips cocked in a way that suggests easy carnality.

If one of them sprang to life, I'd be very happy. If this is what the women of Cambodia look like, I need to go there, soon.

But when I tear my eyes away and look around the room, there's a churning in my gut, a snapping in my brain. They don't belong here. They've been stolen, kidnapped, ripped from their homes and brought to this place for the pleasure of people with more money than morals.

"What'd you call them? *Apsaras*?"

"Yes, they are nymphs, *lah*, the heavens' dancing girls."

"How did you get them? Is it legal to sell them?"

"It is no problem here in Hong Kong, *lah*. When they leave Cambodia they are legal. I do not buy them in Cambodia."

"That's a neat distinction."

"Yes, my customers desire the *apsaras* most of all."

I move away to look at the rest of the warehouse. I'm trying to think of ways to find out if this is simply Tommy's own side business, or if Golden Truly's involved.

The light drops off as I walk toward the back, but there's a skylight and a fall of pale sunshine filtered through the filthy glass is spilling onto the round, bald head of a large sculpture.

It's Buddha, and he looks mad. I don't blame him. From the chipped limestone at his neck, it's apparent he's had his head crudely sawn off. He scowls across the room, displeased with what he sees but unable to do anything about it.

His mood's contagious. I get mad, too. I want to call the cops and close this place down. I want Tommy to go to jail and Buddha and the *apsaras* and the lintels and the doors to go back home to Cambodia. And it's all mixed up in my head with all those stolen women I got mixed up with a few months ago. And I want Sasha to be alive. And I want Irina to love me again. And I want to do something right, good, useful. But this time I've got to be careful. It could all go wrong again.

I keep my mouth shut until we're back out on the street. I'm afraid if I say anything in the warehouse it'll be the wrong thing. Tommy locks up then turns to me. "Please let me know if you or any of your friends are interested in my Khmer art. I can make good prices, *lah*."

I take a breath before talking. "That's a good business, beautiful stuff. It's gotta be a lot of work to get it here. I'm surprised you can keep your prices low."

"My partners have very good connections, *lah*. They procure only the best."

"Yeah, I guess it's gotta be a lot better than the art supplies and framing business."

He shrugs and smiles, then turns to unlock his shop. We enter and he goes back behind the counter, facing out. "So, Mr. Sharp, your heads. I will have them for you in about a week, *lah*."

"Great, thanks." I'd forgotten about them. "At the moment I'm interested in your Cambodian art. I have friends with a lot of money who might want to know more."

"You are welcome to bring them to my shop, Mr. Sharp. Perhaps if they make a purchase we can make an arrangement between ourselves, *lah*."

"It's a nice offer, but I think they'd want to see more. They're the kind of people who always want a big selection to choose from. Do you have any more?"

"My partners have a godown in China, across the border in Shenzhen. Perhaps I could arrange a visit."

"Okay, I'll talk to my friends, see what they want and let you know."

"That will be fine, Mr. Sharp. I will talk with you soon I trust."

I tell him I'll get back to him soon. It's a long, very hot and sweaty walk all the way back to the office. No one in their right mind walks this far in Hong Kong's heat and wet, but I want the time to think.

Ringo, the receptionist, frowns when I come in. I can see why when I catch a glimpse of myself in the mirror on the wall above the sofa. I'm drenched, my hair matted to my head, my shirt transparent from my sweat.

I stand politely away from her desk. "Yeah, I know, *cheeseengwailo*. What do you expect from a crazy ghost person, Ringo? I like to walk and I'm not going to let Hong Kong stop me." She shakes her head and bends down to a pile of papers.

Warner's in his office and he frowns, too, when I walk in. "Christ, Ray, we don't have enough clients yet that I can afford to put a shower in the office. Can't you get over this habit of yours? You're neither a mad dog, nor an Englishman. It's so, so…"

"Uncolonial?"

"That's only part of what it is. Don't sit down. How's it going with Golden Truly?"

"It's going, and it's not good."

Warner perks up to attention in his chair.

"I think they're involved in smuggling Cambodian antiquities. The guy who owns the shop in Central's got a small warehouse next door. He's selling art that's been looted from the temples around Angkor Wat."

"That's not illegal, at least not in Hong Kong."

"Yeah, but getting it out of Cambodia is. Sooner or later selling it, even here, is going to be. It's also plain wrong. Would you want to do business with a company that's involved in it?"

"What makes you think it's not just a sideline for the guy in Central? How're Golden Truly involved?"

"I'm not positive they are, yet. He mentioned his partners in China; they've got another warehouse in Shenzhen."

"So, what next?"

"I said I've got friends with money who might be interested in what they've got in Shenzhen. He said he might be able to arrange a tour of the warehouse. I'm thinking I'll tell him they can't make it, but that they've asked me to take a look."

"Won't he be suspicious?"

"As you said, it's not illegal. He's eager."

"Worth a try I guess. Good work."

"Maybe I'll go home, take a shower and change."

"That's definitely worth a try, I guess. Don't walk back here afterwards."

| | CHAPTER **THREE** | |

When I get back to the office I phone Tommy. "I called my friends. They're excited about what you showed me."

"I am not surprised, *lah*. We have excellent quality. When would you like to bring them to my shop, *lah*?"

I'm beginning to wince every time he says "lah." I'm going to have to control that when I see him in person.

"They're pretty busy. They asked if I could find out more and tell them about it, maybe take pictures. Would that be okay?"

"Certainly. Would you like to visit our godown in Shenzhen as well?"

"Sure. Better to give them as much choice as possible. When do you think you can arrange a visit?"

"Perhaps Saturday. I will have to call my partners. Can I return your call, *lah*?"

He does, about an hour later. Saturday at eleven-thirty in the morning will be fine. I get the directions, thank him and get off the phone to make plans. If my previous experiences in China are any indication, it can't hurt to have an interpreter. I make another call.

"Wen Lei Yue." She barks out her name in a very crisp manner.

"Is it supposed to intimidate callers when you answer the phone like that?"

"It's efficient. What do you want?" The words sound gruff, but there's an audible grin behind them.

"Maybe I don't want anything."

"You calling to chat? I don't have time. Don't stalk me, you're not my type."

"You're not my type either, don't worry."

"What, I'm too short? Not big enough boobs?"

"Maybe I should hang up; call back and we can start over."

"No need, what do you want?"

"I need a translator."

"Call a service."

"I might have a story for you. A good one."

"I'm listening."

"It's embargoed, forbidden, off the record, no story until I tell you it's okay. Okay?"

"Why should I agree to that?"

"Because it probably won't be all that long and you'll like it."

"So I agree, for now. What's it about?"

"Smuggling stolen artifacts out of Cambodia and into Hong Kong."

"That's not a big story."

"It could be though. What I've got might be the tip of the iceberg."

"Why do you need a translator?"

"I've got to go to Shenzhen for a day. I've got an appointment to see a warehouse of stolen art."

"Are you going to buy me dinner?"

"You know a good restaurant?"

"Yeah, plenty. Deng Xiaoping's cronies from Sichuan Province set the place up; they brought all the best chefs with them."

"Your family's Cantonese, you guys don't like spicy food."

"Maybe you forgot I grew up in Mexico."

"Okay, I'm buying dinner, and the hotel. Two hotel rooms, don't worry."

"When?"

"Saturday. Meet you at the KCR at nine in the morning."

That's two days from now. Plenty of time to get a visa if I pay extra. You can get anything in China, if you can afford it.

I need to know more about Cambodian art. I call Susan. One of the magazines she writes for is *Asian Arts and Antiques*. Maybe she knows an expert. She doesn't, but she knows a writer, Randolph Giles, who thinks he's an expert. She reckons he knows enough. We make plans for dinner that night. She calls back a little later to tell me he insists on meeting at Jimmy's and that it'll be on me.

I think I'd like Jimmy's if it was in London or Los Angeles. In Hong Kong, well, I'm sure it's a personal failing on my part but it rubs me the wrong way. It's one of those clubby, stuffy places that reeks of stale cigar smoke and the kind of brow sweat that enormous, overcooked roasts and joints of meat bring out in a certain sort of aging, plush English gentleman.

It wasn't so long ago that the restaurant wouldn't admit women, and the elderly Chinese waiters, while professionally courteous, make it all too plain that the change in policy was unwelcome. I once joked with one that if the Queen herself showed up, they would no doubt want to search her trademark oversized handbag on her way out to make sure she hadn't nicked one of their heavy crystal ashtrays. The waiter hadn't cracked a smile; he simply asked if I wanted ice in my drink, "as is the barbarous American custom." I did.

I get there early and I'm halfway through a double vodka on the rocks when Susan and the art writer show up.

Giles fits right in. He's probably my age, mid-forties, but I guess he's always looked old. He has that sort of face, that sort of posture. Susan makes the introductions and he flops a puffy hand into mine for a moment before snatching it away, looking as if he wants to wash it. He's English, and his thin lips and weak chin are set into an expression like he's bitten into a particularly sour lemon. I dislike him instantly. It's going to take a massive effort to avoid antagonizing him, at least until I get the information I want.

They sit. Giles orders a Pimm's Cup. Is there any more colonial cocktail than that. I turn away to talk to Susan to avoid grimacing in his direction. Susan kicks me under the table and orders a beer. We chit chat about nothing in particular until their drinks come.

His voice is a high-pitched whine, like a distant siren. It's soft enough that I have to lean toward him to hear what he has to say. That causes him to lean back and me to tilt even further forward. He's too polite to scoot his chair away from the table to escape, so he's barely audible.

"Miss Watkins informs me that you have an interest in Khmer art."

I've never heard anyone refer to Susan by her last name, it sounds strangely inappropriate coming from him.

"Yes, I've come across some for sale. I have friends who might be interested. I told them I'd check it out."

"This, I presume, is through Thomas, the Singaporean chap in Central. He does on occasion offer very fine pieces. I have purchased several smaller artifacts from him myself."

Now I like him even less. I don't do a very good job of keeping it off my face and that makes him uncomfortable.

"Mr. Sharp—Raymond, if I might—you are aware, no doubt, that the collection of Khmer art outside of Cambodia is perfectly legitimate. The country, if I do say so, is a terrible mess, a quagmire that is unlikely to improve for many years, if ever. It is a well-established fact that these artifacts are better cared for outside of Cambodia than they would be within the country itself."

"Another example of the enlightened West taking on its role as self-appointed caretaker of the world's treasures."

"How do you mean, sir?"

"You know, like the Elgin marbles or the Rosetta Stone in the British museum."

"Indeed sir, those treasures would likely have been lost to the world, or at least terribly mishandled, if left in their countries of origin."

I'm tempted to get nasty, but even I realize it won't get me what I want out of this meeting. I move my right leg out of the way before Susan can give it another kick.

"You may have a point, Mr. Giles." I have to pinch myself hard when I say it. "In any event, what can you tell me about the trade in Cambodian antiquities?"

"Yes, indeed, well, perhaps a bit of history will help us to get started." He clears his throat, takes a swallow of water and I steel myself for a lecture. "There have, of course, been inhabitants of the region for thousands of years, but for our purposes I shall start with the Funan culture which dominated the area from the first to the sixth centuries A.D. It was a maritime power that traded with Siam, Burma and India and was thus exposed to a great many Hindu influences.

"By the seventh century A.D., the Funan had been taken over by the Chenla Empire, which had arisen in the hilly areas of what is now northern Cambodia. In turn, the coastal regions were conquered by the Silendra dynasty of Java, a powerful Hindu kingdom."

I sip my drink and when it's done I wave the glass at a waiter in the hope of attracting another. I'm trying not to fall asleep, as it is painfully obvious that the only way I'm going to get anything useful out of Giles is to let him prattle on at his own pace.

"In 802, Jayavarman II, a Khmer prince, returned to his ancestral home near what is now Angkor Wat, and declared himself a divine king. He built his palace and temples on the plains of Angkor. The kingdom became fabulously wealthy. Much like the Nile Valley in Egypt, the plains were created by floodwaters, in this case of the lake Tonle Sap. When the waters recede after the rainy season every year, the shallows become one of the world's richest fishing grounds—the soil is soft and fertile. The climate permits a year-round growing cycle.

"After Jayavarman, subsequent kings built new monuments to themselves, new palaces, temples and even cities, each more magnificent than the ones before it. The Khmer Empire reached the height of its power in the eleven hundreds. King Suryavarman II commenced the building of Angkor Wat and others of the significant temples. The empire stretched into what is now Malaysia, Thailand, Burma and Vietnam.

"But Suryavarman overextended himself, failing terribly in his attempt to conquer what is now northern Vietnam. After his death, the Cham people of Vietnam attacked and sacked Angkor in 1177 A.D. The defeat discredited Hinduism in the eyes of the Khmer. The gods Shiva, Brahma and Vishnu had failed to protect the empire."

The waiter returns hoping to take our orders but Giles, intent on his history lesson, waves him away.

"Four years later, a new king, crowned Jayavarman VII, soundly routed the Cham and declared Mahayana Buddhism to be the religion of the Khmer. He built new temples and palaces and the wondrous city of Angkor Thom. But alas, this age did not last long.

"The king died in 1218 and the empire declined under the stewardship of his heirs. For a time the kingdom returned to Hinduism, then to Theraveda Buddhism. Eventually, in 1431, the Siamese, from what is now Thailand, invaded and looted Angkor.

"For the next five hundred and forty-four years the country was batted about by the Thais, the Vietnamese, the French, and then bombed nearly into oblivion by your chaps. Then the Khmer Rouge took power and destroyed almost everything else. Then the Vietnamese chased them away. But the buggers still make trouble in the forests. Now the king is back. The U.N. held elections, but that hasn't changed much. The government is friendly to the Vietnamese. In much of the country there is disorder."

"So I've heard. Let's order dinner. Then you can tell me about the art."

I order a steak, rare, which means if I'm lucky it'll be about medium. It comes with a small baked potato, canned vegetables and a plate of innocent lettuce that's been flooded with gelatinous orange goo that is meant to pass for salad dressing. It's all palatable enough, if one's palate is numbed with large amounts of alcohol. I order another double.

Susan's never been here before so I have to steer her away from the grilled fish. Battered and fried haddock and chips are okay.

Giles lives up to his stereotype and orders the tiffin.

"I thought that was Indian for a light lunch."

"It is indeed. But the chappies here do a marvelous curry. It is ever so slightly zesty, but not so much as to give cause for alarm."

It astounds me that some people fail to be embarrassed by themselves. I'm sure there are plenty of ways in which I am a stereotypical Yank, even a stereotypical expatriate male one, but if I ever caught myself living the caricature I'd have to go into hiding, or kill myself.

Susan kicks me under the table again before I can say anything. She looks like she's about to bust up laughing, but she pulls herself together, dabbing at her lips with her napkin and getting up to go to the bathroom. I can see her shoulders shuddering as she walks away.

I gird myself for another lecture and ask Giles about Cambodian art.

"Ah yes, the art and antiquities, it is marvelous work, simply, magnificently marvelous. As you may well have inferred from our brief history, the esthetic is a splendid mix of Hinduism and Buddhism, the subject matter both sacred and profane. Leaving aside the architecture—as there is no trade in that unfortunately, the monuments have been left to deteriorate—the finest pieces are statuary or fantastically realized limestone friezes that date from the eleventh to the thirteenth century.

"There are several notable motifs. I, myself, am partial to the *naga*; it is the snake, or serpent. It has five, seven or nine cobra-like heads. Originally, it was a symbol in Hindu fertility cults. In Buddhism it has come to be the god of rain and the protector of the law."

I lift a hand to interrupt. Giles looks annoyed but it's beginning to sound like I ought to take notes. I have a pen. A tent card offering vile sounding drink specials is on the table. No one should consider ordering those anyhow, so I snatch it to write on. When he sees that I've written "naga – snake – rain – law," he nods, then continues.

"The *garuda* is often supposed to be the enemy of the *naga*. It is a great bird, much like the phoenix in Western mythology. Throughout the temples and palaces there are also many *linga*, erect phalluses that rest upon a base of a *yoni*, the female sexual organ. They were regarded by the kings as symbols of their divine power. They were generally carved from limestone, but a few were molded from precious metals, or even hewn from crystals.

"The *apsara* are perhaps the best known, but I find them rather, dare I say, disreputable. They are often referred to as "celestial dancers." That is little more than a euphemism for temple prostitutes. I prefer the *lotus*. It represents purity and the divine birth of the Buddha into an impure world. There is also Lokesvara, the bodhisattva of compassion. And lastly there are the guardians, the *singhas*, or lions; Kala, a terrible monster; and the demon Rahu who swallows the moon when there is an eclipse.

"All of these motifs are represented in various Khmer structures, both in Cambodia and Thailand. The greatest repository are what is colloquially known as Angkor. It is in truth hundreds of structures in an area of hundreds, perhaps more than a thousand, square miles."

Susan's returned to the table and what Giles is saying has made her look unhappy. "What's the problem?"

"I told you, I'm supposed to go there and do a story."

"So, what's wrong with that?"

"There's no way I can cover the place in three days."

Giles reaches over and pats her on the hand. "There there, Susan dear, not to worry. I am certain you will pen a very fine basic introduction."

He blathers on about things she already knows. I'm about to order up another drink when dinner finally arrives. Giles' tiffin, bright yellow and sprinkled with withered, brown caramelized onions, doesn't look or smell like anything I'd ever want anywhere near my mouth. Susan's fish and chips might be a bargain if they came wrapped in newspaper and at a quarter the price. I saw off a piece of my steak and chew on it for a while, regretting the whole time that Hong Kong had been colonized by the British.

After a couple of bites my jaw's had enough of a workout. I set down my cutlery and start asking Giles questions. He doesn't like to talk while he's eating. That's too bad.

"So, what are the desirable pieces?"

He slowly finishes chewing, then washes it down with a large gulp of water, before looking up from his plate to answer.

"That of course depends. As I mentioned, I am particularly fond of *nagas*, but the best of them are very large, consisting of dozens of carved blocks and quite long. I have several very fine smaller specimens in my collection, but the size of the truly best pieces prevents them from being collected by anyone other than museums and a few select individuals. The same is true of Lokesvara. The Bayon, at Angkor Thom, has the finest, but they are quite large, made up of numerous blocks and would be nearly impossible for a private collector. If left intact, the larger reliefs are also quite impossible for anyone other than a museum or a very wealthy private collector with a sizeable exhibition space.

"As you may imagine, *apsaras* and *lingas* are very popular. The obsession with sex is widespread. They are also smaller, easier to transport, and there are a great many more of them. *Lingas* made from materials other than stone are very rare indeed. I have never encountered one for private sale. Recently there was a rumor of a very fine, carved quartz *linga* on the market, but I have not been able to verify its existence.

"Heads of the Buddha are also popular. The Khmer Rouge chopped many of them off of the statues and they have since found their way to market."

"What's all this sell for?"

"Of course it depends on the piece. I have seen small *apsaras* taken from larger friezes selling for as little as a thousand U.S. dollars. A few years ago a good head of Buddha would cost two to three thousand, now it would be more than five. *Linga* come in all sizes and the price can range from a hundred to many thousands of dollars. But increasingly, one must be cautious of fakes."

"How do you know the difference?"

"An expert would know. There are dealers that can be trusted, others that cannot."

"What about Tommy?"

"Yes, you have already seen his selection, he is one of the more reputable dealers. I trust him implicitly."

"Are there others?"

"In Hong Kong, no. Should you find yourself in Bangkok, there are several legitimate dealers in the River City Shopping Center. It is the center of the trade."

"It's legal in Thailand?"

"No, but the law is seldom enforced."

I ask Giles more about the legal status of the trade in Cambodian antiquities and spend the next ten minutes getting an earful of justifications that I've already heard and already dismissed. I want to get out of there, but he insists on dessert.

"They have marvelous puddings here, simply marvelous. I am inordinately fond of their spotted dick, perhaps you would care for a serving."

I can't help it. I recoil in horror. And it isn't just the name. Spotted dick is a dense, spongy pudding made of suet, the hard fat from around the kidneys and loins of sheep or oxen, a lot of sugar, and dotted with raisins. They fatten English school kids with it.

I'd have an espresso if it wasn't so weak here. I order another vodka instead. Susan has tea. We both try to avoid watching as Giles digs merrily into his nostalgic feast.

Twenty very long minutes later we pack the Englishman into a taxi. I invite Susan back to my place for a nightcap.

"You're not going to have anything more to drink are you? Fat lot of good you'll do me then."

"It's not that kind of invitation anyhow. I didn't do you that kind of good the other night. I don't think tonight's going to be any different."

"Why not? You used to think I was hot stuff."

Susan moved to Hong Kong about a year ago, fresh out of journalism school. A friend at the *Wall Street Journal* gave her my name and number when she was looking for work. I didn't have any for her, but we became friends. I introduced her to my pal Mike and they'd hooked up, then broken up. After that she and I became other kinds of friends, too, but only on occasion.

"I still do, but I'm not feeling like hot enough stuff myself. I thought I told you all this already."

"You did, but I thought I cheered you up."

"Not enough, I guess."

"How long's this celibacy thing going to last?"

"Not permanently I hope. I'm still working too much out in my head."

"I don't think I need to hear all this again tonight."

"Yeah, it's still got me all messed up. No sense dragging you into it. Like I said, I don't know if I'm part of the solution or part of the problem."

"I can't help you there. I don't get it. Prostitution's a guy thing; a guy in Asia thing. It didn't seem to be a problem back in the U.S."

"I'm not sure I get it either, but I want to, and for the time being it's fucking me up."

"I read a detective book once in which the detective said, 'Don't sleep with anyone who has more problems than you do.' I think maybe he was right."

"I'd still be a virgin if I took that advice. Half the time you don't know about their problems until it's too late, the other half they're with you because of their problems. And then my own problems get in the way of seeing what's really going on anyhow."

"You know, it was easier being your pal when you were a simple guy who didn't think so much. Let me know when you figure it out. If you need an ear, I'll listen, but I'm not sure how much good it'll do you."

"You do me a lot of good. You make me wish I'd figured it out already. Can I have a raincheck?"

"Doesn't work that way, Ray. We'll see when the time comes."

It's an awkward peck goodnight. But that's all I've got for her.

| |CHAPTER **FOUR** | |

The Kowloon-Canton Railway gets you to the border in about forty-five minutes. On a Saturday morning it's filled with golfers, whore-mongers and people bringing the latest electronic gadgets to their families in China. Golf in Hong Kong is ludicrously expensive—in the People's Republic, it's cheap. Same goes for prostitutes. What's expensive in the P.R.C. are VCRs, stereos, televisions, video cameras and similar gizmos. I like to think of the train from Hong Kong to China as the free market express chugging straight into the station of the world's largest, so-called, communist country.

At the border you get out, flash past Hong Kong immigration and walk the bridge over the bubbling, odiferous Shenzhen Creek. There, you present your passport or Hong Kong I.D. card to the bored Chinese border guards and stroll out the other side into China.

Or at least what passes for China in these parts, these days. There are borders where you immediately know you're in a different country. Crossing from San Diego to Tijuana is like that. It's a short stroll across an arbitrary line, but everything changes; nothing looks, sounds, smells or feels the same when you cross it.

Walking from Hong Kong to Shenzhen was like that as recently as five or six years ago. Now it's hard to figure out why you even need a passport. It all looks the same. If it wasn't for the border guards and the fact that you hear a bit more Mandarin being spoken, you'd never know you were in the People's Republic.

The first time I crossed this border was in 1978. I was here as a freelance journalist masquerading as a tourist. There was scarcely a town to cross into. The train station was hung with huge portraits of Chairman Mao and Hua Guofeng, his successor whose reign didn't last long. Giant red cloth banners, splashed with yellow characters of quotes from Mao, draped from the ceilings. Loudspeakers blared patriotic songs and a chipmunk-like chatter of revolutionary fervor. Everyone around was dressed in matching drab, blue, shapeless outfits.

The train I'd been on back then clanked slowly past farmland being worked by masses of uniformed peasants and oxen. Political officers, recognizable from the red bandannas tied around their necks, read to the workers from the Little Red Book through squawky megaphones.

But that was then. Now, emerging into the crowded street, choking with unmuffled motorbikes, exhaust spewing trucks and construction dust, the only splash of red I see is the six-story tall Coca Cola billboard on the building across the way. The only amplified sound I hear is a cacophony of Hong Kong pop music, blasting from stalls that sell pirated cassette tapes. The arriving crowds beat up on each other for position in the taxi line. A lot of the taxis are stolen from Hong Kong.

Lei Yue tugs on my sleeve. "It almost makes you miss communism."

"Almost."

"What now?"

"I've booked us into the Shangri-La. We can drop our bags and get a cab to the warehouse."

"How're we going to get to the hotel?"

"It's a couple of blocks. If we can get across this street without getting killed, we can walk."

Several close calls later we're in the cool, tall, quiet lobby of the five-star hotel. Lei Yue had stayed here before, when she was interviewing the chief of the Shenzhen development board, the biggest cheese in town. She knows the manager, Lam, who is obsequious, on the verge of overbearing. She yells at him when he winks and suggests we might really want one room. He gets a sheepish look on his feral face and hands over two keys.

The elevator is plastered with posters for this, that or the other development company promising golden opportunities to the hotel's guests. Shenzhen is more than just another city. It's the country's first, richest and most booming Special Economic Zone. Unlike the Soviet Union, where the communist party reformed itself out of power, the Chinese communists have been smart. They've bribed the people with economic progress while keeping a tight hold on politics.

Deng Xiaoping is chairman of the All-China Bridge Association. That's the only title he's kept. But he's still the most powerful man in the country and a wily bastard at that. He's the one who figured out that if you give the people refrigerators and food to fill them; and TVs and mindless programs to watch on them; and let them earn a little extra here and there so they can enjoy the rattle of change in their pockets; they'll keep their mouths shut. Every now and then things go wrong, like they did around Tiananmen Square in Beijing in 1989. But so long as people are happily bought off, they get over it quick.

So Deng and his cronies from Sichuan Province designated the wretched, sleepy, little fishing village of Shenzhen to become competition for Hong Kong, an enclave of unbridled capitalism. They roped off a sizable chunk of land, got rid of the farmers and fishermen, forbade entrance to Chinese citizens who don't have the proper permits, and said, "this is where development can happen."

And it has. Shenzhen is probably the world's biggest construction site. It's a high-rise, Wild-West-style boomtown with a population of well over a million. Economically, it's even less restricted than Hong Kong.

We drop our bags in the rooms, then settle into overstuffed chairs in the lobby. We hadn't talked much on the train. I'd sipped bad coffee from a crumbling Styrofoam cup while Lei Yue scribbled in a notebook. I fill her in on what I'd learned from Giles, but she looks impatient.

She's been doing her own research. "It's a lot uglier business than I thought, Ray. It's not just harmless assholes like your Giles guy."

"What'd you find out?"

"The trade in Cambodia is run by leftover Khmer Rouge. They've given up being revolutionaries, now they're crooks."

"They were always crooks; they only called themselves revolutionaries."

"Yes well, there's also the Thai army, the Vietnamese, and the Chinese, too."

"The P.L.A.?"

"Yes, the People's Liberation Army, defenders of China's revolution. They're in on it."

"I think they're in on anything crooked in the country."

"That's true, I think. The Khmer Rouge steal the artwork then transport it to the border with Thailand. They sell it to Thai generals—the same ones involved in illegal logging and gem smuggling, and probably opium, too. The generals sell it to the antique dealers in Bangkok.

"In the other direction, the Khmer Rouge also sell to the Vietnamese, maybe a rogue army group or freelancers, who transport it to China and sell it to the P.L.A., who bring it down here and into Hong Kong."

"I thought the Vietnamese and the Chinese were enemies."

"This is big money. No one cares about politics."

"So you think it's going to be P.L.A. guys we're meeting with at the warehouse?"

"Probably."

That makes me nervous. Heroes of the Revolution or not, I've had experience with the army in China. I think they're gangsters. Maybe not all of them, but too many to make me comfortable.

It takes us a half hour in traffic to get out to the industrial park. The taxi driver has pictures of both Buddha and Chairman Mao hanging from his rearview mirror. When a bus turning into an intersection narrowly misses us, he puts a hand over his heart, then to his lips, then touches one of the photos. He does it quick enough I'm not sure which one. It doesn't matter. Mao, Buddha; cover all the bases.

At least the men we're meeting aren't in uniform. Mr. Chen and Mr. Li are dressed in perfectly tailored Armani. They've both got large, glistening Rolexes on their wrists that don't look like the cheap fakes you can buy on any street corner in the area.

They greet us in a small reception room at the entrance to the warehouse. A glass-topped, intricately carved wood table is set with tea, sugar cookies and slices of orange. We make introductions and sit. Our cups are filled by an elderly tea lady who doesn't look at us. Before we can even take a sip we're motioned up and out the door. Other than their names and, "Welcome," our hosts haven't said a word.

The door opens into a warehouse stacked with pallets of art supplies. We walk to an aisle of ten-foot-high stacks of paper and turn to the right. There's another door at the end. It's made of steel and takes three different keys and a shove from a shoulder to open. Bright lights come on as the door swings inward.

It looks like half of ancient Cambodia's in there. I guess the other half is in Thailand. Lei Yue reaches out and squeezes my hand. I grip back unconsciously hard until she yanks hers away, making me aware of the pressure.

Chen—or is it Li?—sweeps his arm in the air to indicate the room, gesturing for us to take a look. I get out my notepad and pen, but I need to walk around and take in the whole place before I can make any sense of the individual pieces.

There's everything Giles talked about and more. There are dozens of Buddha and other heads, large friezes and lintels, a couple dozen whole body statues of Buddha and six enormous heads made up of large interwoven stones. There's a forest of *linga* in sizes ranging from a small pocket rocket to an imposing six feet tall, three or four Vegas extravaganzas' worth of *apsaras*, and a tangle of *nagas*, several of them slithering nearly the length of the large room.

And that's only half of it. The other half is stacked from floor to ceiling with wooden crates. Lei Yue and I walk back to Chen and Li.

"It's a remarkable collection. Do you have certificates of authenticity? My friends are very careful people." Lei Yue translates. Chen, who's slightly older and stands with a stiffer bearing, does the talking.

"Thank you. Please, you must understand the circumstances; we have no proof of authenticity. If your friends are truly interested they are welcome to send an expert for examination. I can assure you that everything you see here is genuine, from the temples in Cambodia."

"If my friends want something special, can it be ordered?"

"Yes, that would be possible. It will be more expensive and we cannot guarantee how long it will take to get the piece, but it can be done."

"May I take pictures of the pieces I think my friends might be interested in?"

The two of them nod their heads together and whisper briefly. "Yes, of course."

A small flash won't be nearly bright enough to expose the whole place, so I balance my camera on a box to take a long exposure. Then I ask Lei Yue to stand next to the pieces I'm photographing, to give a sense of size.

She stands in front of the biggest of the *nagas*. Its seven rearing heads with bared fangs and spread hoods fan out several feet above her, and two or three feet on either side. It's a frightening scene. The snake's thick limestone body disappears into the darkness beyond the flash's reach, extending maybe thirty or forty feet.

"How tall are you anyway?"

"No jokes *cabrón*."

"I keep forgetting you're Mexican. Maybe I am an asshole, but that's not how I meant it."

"I'm three foot eleven. What of it?"

"Don't be so touchy. I need to know so I can work out the height of these things from the pictures."

"It is not easy being a dwarf, you know. People do not take you seriously."

"I do. You seem like one of the most serious people I know. Just shorter."

"Thank you, I think. It is only my legs. The rest of me is normal." She stands a bit straighter and preens.

I haven't really looked at her that way before this, but now I do and actually, Lei Yue is better than normal from the waist up. I don't say anything, though. It doesn't seem like a good idea. I like her. She's smart and fun. But I'm not going to let it get complicated.

Three of the multi-block Buddha heads are about five feet tall, a six panel wide frieze is about ten feet high. Lei Yue fits perfectly into a medium-sized frieze of voluptuous *apsaras*. I move past the *linga* forest but she stops.

"Hey, what about these?"

I turn around to look at her. She's gently patting the top of a three foot tall, thick, perfectly carved phallus. I try not to blush, but I don't quite pull it off.

"Oh yeah, well, get out of the way and I'll take a picture. I don't think I'll need you in it."

She winds her way into the middle of the maze of limestone penises and turns, her arms wrapping two five-footers like they were a couple of good friends. "But you've gotta admit, it'll be a better picture with me in it."

I really can feel myself blush this time. She smiles and gets a teasing look on her face. "Come off it, Ray. I can really embarrass you if I want. Take the damn picture and make sure you give me a copy."

I look over at Chen and Li. They've got their backs to us. If they've got any thoughts about a dwarf fondling their antique dicks, they aren't letting on.

So I take the picture. Then she spots another one, the tallest and fattest, about twice her height. She goes over to it and barely manages to wrap both arms around it, her face peeking out from behind with an exaggerated salacious grin. I take another picture.

"Happy?"

"Hey, little people need love too."

"Is that what it is?"

"I guess it will have to do until the real thing comes along."

"I've felt that way before, just not about a bunch of stone dicks."

"I'll take it where I can get it."

"Enough with the clichés already, okay?"

"*Por que, cabrón*, do you prefer cynicism? I can do that, too."

"I'm sure you can. Let's finish the picture taking and get out of here. And stop calling me an asshole, even if it is in Spanish."

"I'm not calling you 'an asshole,' I'm calling you 'asshole,' it's a term of endearment." She laughs and slaps me on the ass as she walks past. I ignore her. I don't know what else to do.

After taking pictures of everything in groups, I shoot the more spectacular pieces by themselves, making notes about each one. Chen and Li ignore me, waiting by the door talking to each other. When I'm done I have Lei Yue get prices and ask if they have anything else.

They say they have a couple of particularly fine items that they keep locked up. They lead us to a small office with a desk, two chairs and a large, ornate, freestanding safe. It looks like the sort of thing the James Brothers would have blown open during a train robbery.

Li spins the dial, hiding it from us by standing in front of it. Pulling down and out on the lever, the door swings open into the room with a loud creak. He reaches in and pulls out a small wooden crate, about two feet long and six inches wide. Li sets it on the desk and then goes back for another that's about two feet square. Chen moves forward to open the lids.

The thinner box contains a *linga* nestled into crushed velvet. It isn't like any sex toy I've ever seen. It's about eighteen inches long and four inches wide, intricately carved from what looks like quartz crystal. It's set at the base with rubies and emeralds. Sparkling stones, possibly diamonds, are embedded in it, running the length of the shaft to the perfectly formed head.

Lei Yue nudges me. I look down and she gestures for me to bring an ear closer. "If it vibrates, I'm in love."

All I can do is roll my eyes. "Ask them about it; when, where it's from, what they're selling it for. Anything you can find out."

I move to pick it up while she's talking to Chen and Li, but Li steps forward and waves me away. So I examine it from a respectful distance. It catches the fluorescence from above and rainbows it back around the room. It looks like the light is emanating from within the thing itself. It's a little fuzzy around the edges, as if it is vibrating, but it's a trick of the shimmering in my vision.

Lei Yue tugs on my sleeve. "They think it's from the thirteenth century. It was found in a burial mound near Angkor Thom. It's made of quartz. The rubies and emeralds are from Cambodia, but they aren't sure where the diamonds come from. There's no set price; there's going to be a private auction in Hong Kong a week from now. They think they'll start the bidding at around a million U.S."

The piece in the other box is just as impressive. It's an *apsara* figure, about a foot tall. The others I've seen were hewn from rough stone. This is intricately carved from a finer substance. The body and features are so realistic that it looks as if a perfectly formed tiny woman had been dipped into a vat of bubbling gold. She's heavily bejeweled. Her necklace is pearls. She's got rubies and sapphires on her fingers, jade bracelets and anklets, and a large, sparkling diamond in her belly button.

She was found in the burial mound with the *linga* and will go up for sale at the same auction. Chen and Li won't let me photograph the two items. They close the boxes quickly and put them back in the safe.

Outside, the cab driver's waiting for us, snoozing. His meter's ticking, but we'll add that to the flat fee we've already agreed on. We wake him up and he takes us back to the hotel. It's early enough to go back to Hong Kong, but I feel like poking around Shenzhen. Lei Yue goes down to the hotel pool, and I decide to take a walk with my camera.

| |CHAPTER **FIVE** | |

Even in Shenzhen, there's still a little of old China. About five blocks from the hotel I come across a street market, a "wet market." It's noisy and crowded. Around the vegetable stalls the street is slippery with discarded leaves and stems, ground into the pavement by the foot traffic. There's a moldy, herbal odor. The fruit stalls are abuzz with flies and emit a cloying, slightly vinegary smell. The fish send out a sharp prong of ammonia that slices into my nostrils. The poultry squawk and protest and shit out a dusty, sweet, coppery cloud. Then there are the meat stalls with their rich, deep, moist earthen stench of blood and fear. Fans keep away the insects but blow the noxious fumes at passersby.

At the far end of the meat stalls are dogs, cats and more exotic fare like pangolins and lemurs, raccoons and small bears. A dizzying sour steam rises off the simmering surface of a cat stew at a sidewalk café. Cages of kittens mewl behind the chef, the ground in front of them slick, glistening bright red in the sun.

I know there's nothing wrong with eating anything, at least the non-endangered animals. It's traditional, and in poor countries it's necessary. Too many people in China can remember the last big famine, or have family members who can. It would be stupid to write off anything potentially nutritious.

I grew up with dogs, roamed the hills of Los Angeles with them, played ball with them, watched TV with them half in my lap. I wept when a favorite pet of my youth got too old and the humane thing to do was have him put down.

But the meat isn't bad. The first time I ate dog was in an *Akha* village in the hills of northern Thailand. Four of us and a guide had been hiking through heat and humidity all day. We collapsed onto the ground in front of a rattan hut in the late afternoon. They had a solar panel in the village and a small refrigerator stocked with overpriced beer. It could have cost three times as much and still been one of the best brews I've ever had.

One of my hiking companions was an attractive Swiss woman I'd met three days earlier in a café in Chiang Mai. A scrawny young dog trotted straight up to her and nuzzled the sweaty crotch of her blue jeans. She let out a happy squeal and with one hand pushed the dog away while petting it with the other. It lay down and rolled over so that she could scratch its belly.

Two young village guys walked up smiling. They pointed to her and to the dog and made happy faces. No one spoke anybody else's language but it looked like they were making conversation. "You like dogs? That's great, we like dogs, too." Everyone was smiling and getting along.

But there was the inevitable miscommunication. Sure, they liked dogs; only they liked them differently than she did. One of the guys grabbed the poor beast by the scruff of the neck and pulled it away from her side. The other picked up a large rock and smashed it once, hard, on the head.

It couldn't have been more than five minutes later that the dog was skinned, gutted and turning on a spit over a fire. Served with chilies, shallots, lime juice and cilantro, with partially husked sticky rice, it was good eating. After hiking all day I had a hearty appetite. The Swiss woman never spoke to me again.

I don't know about cat, though. It smells so awful when it's cooking that I've never tried it.

On the other side of the market are a couple of blocks of restaurants and salons. It's between meals so a lot of the restaurants are closed. The barber shops are open but I don't see anyone getting a haircut. Young women wearing white smocks and a lot of makeup sit in plastic chairs on the sidewalk, clustered around the red and white barber poles, smoking cigarettes, their legs casually flung in front of them. They don't look much like barbers to me.

They don't want their pictures taken, either. I pick up my pace when a couple of them start yelling at me.

I get to a large traffic circle and look all ways through the exhaust and construction haze. A few blocks down I can see several tall wooden poles; the masts of old sailing junks. There's a small fishing harbor here, near the mouth of the Shenzhen river where it cuts through the Mai Po Marshes and into Deep Bay. I head that way.

My grandfather was in the merchant marine when he was young, then the Navy. He used to take my cousin and me down to the docks at San Pedro when we were kids. We'd walk around, taking in all the activity on shore; he'd talk our way onto the ships. We'd eat shrimp cocktails and fish and chips from the rough wood stands near the fishing boats. I've liked walking around harbors ever since.

There's a gate before I get to this one, but it's open and there's no guard in the small lean-to next to it. I walk in past the only propaganda poster I've seen so far, a large billboard with a smiling Deng Xiaoping being handed a bouquet of roses by a gang of grinning kids. It's one of the only pictures of him I've ever seen without a cigarette.

Closer up, the sailing junks look sad, shopworn. They'd look good, romantic even, bobbing on the water out in the bay. But they're run aground on mud flats and listing heavily to one side or the other, abandoned, their timbers rotting in the salt air, pollution and harsh sun. I can hear rats scurrying around inside.

The mountains of Hong Kong's New Territories rise up on the other side of the thin, black, oily trickle that's all that remains of the Shenzhen river. I can see the rows of razor wire, the high electric fence, and the border posts that stretch along the top of the peninsula to the south.

To the west, the river has been kept open to allow passage of small Chinese naval launches and patrol boats. I can see them moored to a new dock a few hundred yards away. They cruise the northern waters of Deep Bay, looking to cut off people swimming for the better life in the British colony to the south.

I think it's P. J. O'Rourke who said, "I'd rather live in a country that people are trying to sneak into than sneak out of." There's a lot of basic wisdom in that. The Chinese border guards don't catch all that many hopeful immigrants; the sharks are more effective. Still, enough get through to make it a popular swim.

The harbor may have been picturesque, once. Now it's run-down and smells bad. I take a couple of pictures anyhow and turn around to walk back into the city.

There's a guard in the lean-to. He looks surprised to see me. He's a pimply teenager in a wrinkled, baggy P.L.A. uniform. He stops me on my way out and says something I don't understand.

It takes a little while for it to sink in with him that I don't speak Chinese. I'm pleased by that. Most people assume foreigners don't speak anything other than English. He makes smoking gestures and points to me. I only smoke on rare occasions, usually involving a lot of booze, but I often carry cigarettes with me for this sort of situation. I don't have any at the moment. I shrug my shoulders and spread out my hands, point to my mouth and wave a hand in front of it. I say "no" in Cantonese, but from the look of him the soldier's a northerner. I don't know if he understands.

He really wants a cigarette, though, because when I make it clear I don't have one he points his rifle at me. It's an old rifle and not too impressive looking, but I don't know all that much about firearms. With his finger on the trigger I have to take him seriously. I put up my hands.

He nudges me toward the lean-to and then motions me to sit on my hands on the bench. He keeps an eye on me while he speaks into a walkie-talkie. When he's done he clicks off and moves back to put space between us. We wait. I wish I had a cigarette.

I don't think I've done anything all that serious. Maybe I shouldn't have walked past the gate, even if it was open and unmanned. This is China. It's one of those places where it's easy to screw up even though you have no idea what it is that you might've done.

It's no more than about five minutes before a small truck pulls up in front of the lean-to. Two soldiers jump out of the canvas covered back and cover me with their rifles. Their guns are a lot more impressive. They're modern, sleek and clean, with banana clips sticking out of the bottom. An officer—I assume he's an officer because his uniform fits better, is newer and has discreet flourishes—gets out of the truck's cab and approaches me.

He talks briefly to the young soldier who'd arrested me, then sticks out a hand, palm up, in front of my face. I'm not sure what he wants. It could be a bribe. If it isn't, and I try, that'll make matters worse. He snaps his fingers impatiently. Maybe he wants my papers.

I fish out my wallet making sure to fan a few bills partially out of the back section, remove and unfold the photocopy I keep of my passport and hand both to him. I figure he'll take any money he wants, if that's what he wants. He doesn't. He points at my camera and I hand that over too. He looks at it, peers through the viewfinder then drapes the strap back over my neck.

He barks an order at one of the soldiers, who hands his gun to the young one. He gets out a pair of rusted handcuffs and snaps them onto my wrists in front of me. They point me toward the back of the truck with their guns.

The truck bounces and heaves through town and quickly out onto a potholed rural road. We drive for about forty minutes, into farm country, the horn bleating to shove people and animals out of our way. I try to think of what I can do, but there isn't much. Cooperate, don't give them any excuses for hurting me, hope to find a high-ranking anybody who speaks at least a little English.

We pull up in front of a small brick building in the middle of a field of "Chinese broccoli." For a few weeks every fall, poisonous, insecticide-drenched truckloads of it make their way to market in Hong Kong from fields like this. Year after year twenty to thirty people, the very young and the very old, die from eating it. Often as not people drown the vegetable in thick, sweet oyster sauce to mask the flavor. I avoid it altogether, whether it's deadly *choi sum* season or not.

There are two rooms in the small, dirt-floored building. The main one has a window, a couple of desks, a file cabinet, a bare bulb dangling from the ceiling and a small fan wired into the light fixture. There are framed photos of Chairman Mao and Deng Xiaoping. The other room's a cell, with a splintery wooden bench, a cracked chamber pot and one greenish fluorescent tube hanging in the hall beyond the bars. That's where they put me. At least they take off the handcuffs.

I lie down on the bench and follow the progress of a parade of red ants making their way up the opposite wall and across the ceiling. It's hot and I'm getting groggy. I'm startled by the clank of metal. A young woman soldier, shapeless in a baggy green P.L.A. uniform, is knocking a large steaming tin mug against the iron bars. She gestures me over with a chin wag and hands me the mug. It burns my hands and I put it on the floor. I look up at her and say "*shieh shieh*." "Thank you" is about all I know in Mandarin.

She smiles at me before she turns to go. She'd have a nice smile if she didn't have such bad teeth and a nose that pancakes down over her upper lip. She's the tea lady, of course. Despite forty-six years of Communist Party enforced "egalitarianism," and torrents of propaganda based on the idea that "women hold up half the sky," women are still second-class citizens in China's classless society.

The "one-child policy" ensures the continued popularity of female infanticide. The population balance of whole provinces is being thrown out of whack. There are places where there are nearly two surviving boys for every girl. Kidnapping rings get rich stealing girls to sell for brides. Maybe free market reform will take care of this, too. Maybe if girls become rarer, they'll become more valuable and their parents will stop killing them at birth.

Maybe being an army tea lady isn't so bad. Maybe it's better than the alternative, especially for an unattractive farm girl.

The mug of water is still too hot to drink. I push it with my foot over to the bench and sit back down. I wish I had a book, a pen and paper. I spend a couple of minutes looking through my camera, maybe there's an interesting angle or two. There isn't.

There's no window in the cell, but I sense that it's becoming dusk outside. A few mosquitoes start buzzing around and that doesn't make me any more comfortable. By now I figure Lei Yue's beginning to wonder where the hell I am. She'll have no way of knowing. I went out for a walk and disappeared.

It's too damn easy to fall down on the wrong side of the law in a lot of developing countries. It's weird—China's a dictatorship run by one political party. You'd think that would mean everything's consistent in the place. You'd think that would mean there are laws and set ways of doing anything so you'd always know where you stand.

But it doesn't mean that at all. It's way more arbitrary than that. A different soldier might have found me in a restricted area and merely yelled at me to get the hell out of there. Another might have shot me without asking any questions. If I'd had a cigarette for the guy who did stop me, maybe he'd have let me go. Who the hell knows?

I've run into this sort of lunacy a bunch of times in Asia, Eastern Europe, Western Africa and Latin America. The first few times it was scary as hell. But then I realized—there isn't much you can do about it, other than stay home where it's safe. I'm not willing to do that. Safety's got its attractions, but if the price is boredom, it's not worth it. Maybe I've been lucky so far. I got punched in the gut once in a police station in Senegal, but that's the worst it ever got.

Maybe it's blind optimism, but I'm not too worried now.

I recall reading that prisoners are supposed to do mental gymnastics to keep from going nuts. That, and physical exercise. I spend a while trying to remember everything Giles told me about Cambodian art and history. I can summon up most of it, but not enough to keep me busy for long.

Quotes from Chairman Mao seem appropriate, but that doesn't take much time either, I don't know many. I spend a little more time on batting averages and figuring out compounded interest on my meager savings account. I'm running through Bob Dylan songs in my head, which is taking quite a bit longer than I thought it would, when the tea lady comes back with dinner.

It's a chipped ceramic bowl of rice topped with seven strands of anemic looking *choi sum* that've been brushed with oyster sauce and a couple of fatty chunks of pork. "*Lat jiu jiung?*" I ask for chili sauce just to talk. I can't really do much of it in any flavor of Chinese. She obviously doesn't understand.

I used to think Chinese was Chinese, but it's not. There're seven or eight different Chinese languages and hundreds of dialects. Mandarin and Cantonese have similarities, but probably fewer than Spanish and French.

"*Moh guangdongwah.*" She doesn't speak Cantonese. At least she knows that's what I'm speaking. She leaves me with a sad smile. I give her one back.

I choke down the meager dinner even though it's November and people are already dying from *choi sum*. I'm not sick, old or young and I'm hungry.

A while later, about the time I'm nearly done listing all the vegetables and fruits I can think of, the two soldiers from the truck come for me. They take me into the main room and park me in a chair in front of one of the desks.

The soldier seated in front of me looks stern, about my age, in a knife-edge-sharp, gray-green uniform with a stiffly blocked hat sporting the usual red star, but outlined in gold. He's obviously an officer and he's shuffling through papers, including everything that was in my wallet. When I sit down he looks up.

"I am Captain Cheng. What were you doing at the naval base, Mr. Sharp?"

"Walking around. I'd gone for a walk. I like boats; I saw the masts of the junks and thought I'd take a look."

"How did you enter the base?"

"I didn't know it was a base. The gate was open and there wasn't a guard I could see."

"Do you read Chinese, Mr. Sharp?"

"No, sorry."

"Did you take photographs in the base?"

"A few, of the old junks."

"Please open your camera and give me the film."

I'm not about to argue. I do what he says. He puts the film in a drawer. Luckily the pictures I took in the warehouse are on another roll I'd already taken out and left in the hotel room.

"Where do you stay, Mr. Sharp?"

"The Shangri-La in Shenzhen."

"You will stay here tonight. In the morning we will go to your hotel room. If there is anything you are hiding, Mr. Sharp, it will be better if you tell me now."

I'm not exactly hiding Lei Yue, but I don't want to get her into the middle of anything. If we're going back to the hotel in the morning I'll be able to contact someone. I assure him I've got nothing to hide. He waves me back to the cell. I doze off. I have terrible dreams. I can't remember them, but I know they're terrible.

When I wake up, it's to a loud fizz, then a bang. It's like a champagne cork popping in reverse. I shake my head to clear it and the sound goes off again, with a whine in between the fizz and the bang. I don't know how long I'm awake, with only the regular strange sound to count the time by.

Maybe it's ten minutes, maybe an hour, before a couple of guards come to get me. They cuff my hands in front and gesture to the door with their guns. They prod me through the office and out the front door and into the back of a beat-up Toyota pickup truck. There's nothing covering the bed of the truck and I can look around.

It's early morning, mist still rising off the *choi sum*. The edges of the field are lined with people dressed in what look like pajamas. It's a screwy assortment, too. One old woman's wearing flannels covered with yellow smiley faces. An old man's in purple silk that looks like a Hugh Hefner discard, as if Hef had donated an old set of his lounging attire to Goodwill and it ended up in China. They're all lighting bottle rockets, shooting them into the air with the screaming corkscrew fizz, whine and pop I've been listening to since I woke up.

I look at the guard who's sitting in the back of the truck with me and gesture toward the people in the field. I don't know if he speaks any Cantonese, but I shrug my shoulders, widen my eyes and ask him *mut yeh*?

I don't understand his answer. When he realizes I don't get it, he puts his rifle down, points at the sky and starts flapping his arms and making squawking sounds. Now I get it, birds. They're scaring away the birds.

China has a bad history when it comes to scaring birds. In the 1960s when there was an increase in the population of sparrows, Chairman Mao ordered everyone in the country to spend time outside with pots and pans. Whenever they saw a sparrow about to alight, they were supposed to frighten it back into flight. Eventually millions of sparrows died, exhausted, falling to their deaths when they couldn't flap their wings anymore. Then there was a plague of insects, the bugs that the sparrows used to eat. The insects ate up even more of the crops than the birds had. A lot of people starved to death.

The Chairman knew a lot about making a revolution. He didn't know jack about running a country.

I'm hungry and thirsty. I could use breakfast, coffee, and a shower. But I get a long, dusty, uncomfortable ride back to the city.

| | CHAPTER **SIX** | |

Lam, the general manager, isn't happy to see me. A foreigner led in handcuffs by three armed soldiers through his hotel lobby can't be good for business. He's quite flustered.

"Oh my god, Mr. Sharp, what is the problem, where have you been all night, Miss Wen has been very worried, what do these soldiers want with you? What is happening, Mr. Sharp?"

I plant my feet to stop. It surprises the soldiers holding onto my arms and one of them drops his rifle. It clatters loudly onto the polished granite floor and all the businessmen treating their paid overnight company to breakfast in the lobby café turn to look.

I start to explain, but Captain Cheng holds up a hand to stop me. He steps up to Lam and it looks like he's going to slap him with one of those "snap out of it" open-handers. Instead he growls at him in a low, menacing voice. Whatever he says, it causes Lam to clam up fast and scurry away.

My escort leads me to an elevator, scares a couple of other guests out of it, and takes me up to my room. Cheng points at the bare wood desk chair and has me sit on it while he supervises the search. Like a lot of lower rank P.L.A. soldiers, my guards probably aren't too long off the farm. They tear the place apart.

The bed is torn almost to shreds, the carpet ripped up in places, a wall panel pried open. They lift the lid on the toilet tank and drop it by mistake. It cracks in half. I hope I don't end up having to pay the damages.

There isn't much for them to paw through. I'd only planned to be in Shenzhen for a night, and I pack light. But all of it's exotic to them. You'd think they'd never seen clothes like mine before, or shoes or toothpaste or shampoo. My small bag has a lot of pockets, zippers and compartments. I try to tell them that the stiff thing they feel inside one of the sides of my soft briefcase is a rod to help it keep its shape, but they take a bayonet to it anyhow. They're disappointed when it isn't contraband.

They're winding down and I'm wondering what's going to happen next when the door opens. Lam's standing in it, his passkey in his hand, his jaw hanging limp and his eyes wide. Lei Yue explodes past him shooting nearly visible high energy bolts of fury from her eyes and spewing a torrent of bilingual abuse from her mouth.

"*Chingate cabrónes, doo lay loh moh, mut yeh, chingones, que paso lay chau gau?*"

The three soldiers stop, their mouths drooping open and their eyes taking on that deer caught in headlights look. I'm laughing. I can't help it.

Lei Yue fixes me with a hard glare. "What's so fucking funny? I've been worried."

"Yeah, well, thanks, but it's a good thing these guys don't understand Spanish or Cantonese. You might've made things worse. They didn't need to get it anyhow, I'm sure they caught the tone."

"Well, they are a pack of motherfucking asshole smelly pricks and I want to know what the fuck's going on."

"I guess the demure bit was just an act."

"What demure…Oh fuck off."

Cheng's recovered by now. He starts talking rapidly to Lei Yue with a gruff tone but a low voice. She listens for a little while, then cuts him off with a bark. I can't quite believe it; she seems totally in control of the situation. The other soldiers pick up their guns and ease them around in her direction, but another bark from her stops them. They lower the guns to their sides, pointing at the floor.

She pulls a wrinkled business card out of a pocket and hands it to Cheng. He reads it carefully and looks sheepish handing it back to her. She barks at him again. He turns to his underlings and speaks softly to them. One of them takes out a key and unlocks my handcuffs, then they both march crisply out of the room. He turns to me and puts out a hand. I'm rubbing the sore spots on my wrists and I ignore it.

"I am so sorry for you to have any inconvenience, Mr. Sharp. Please do enjoy your stay." He turns and follows his minions out the door.

Lei Yue is grinning. Lam is scowling at the mess that's been made of the room.

"What the hell was that all about? What's on that card you showed him?"

She hands me the card. It's a fine, silky, paper stock, lightly embossed with an impressive symbol. It's in Chinese and I can't read it. On the back is a small note written in pen.

"It is the business card of the chief of the Shenzhen Development Agency. On the back he has written that whoever I show this card to is to give me any help I ask for."

"That's all it takes? Those guys are the army."

She taps the card in my hand. "So's this *hombre*. He's a general."

Lam insists on buying us breakfast and fluttering around while we eat. He's finally called away to deal with an emergency in the laundry room.

"I thought we'd never get rid of him. What is it that's so annoying about hotel managers?"

"Hey, don't knock it. He came and got me so I could come to your rescue. He's also being pretty nice about those *cabrónes* tearing up one of his hotel rooms."

"I'll send him a note. What'd you end up doing yesterday?"

"I hung out at the pool for a while, made calls, talked to people. Had a great Sichuan dinner. I'm sorry you weren't here for it."

"Anything interesting?"

"Other than dinner?"

"You know what I mean."

"The warehouse we were at is owned by a company called Golden Truly blah blah blah Art Supplies."

"I knew that."

"Is that the company you're supposed to be checking out?"

"Yep, but you didn't hear it from me. Find out anything more about Chen and Li?"

"Definitely P.L.A., at least Chen. He's a colonel. Li's a director of Golden Truly. What did you do to get picked up by the army? Does it have anything to do with any of this?"

"No, I don't think so. Just stupid, wandered around the harbor with my camera."

"You can bet Chen knows about it by now though. He's connected. It might make him suspicious."

"Why? What's it got to do with his warehouse?"

"You were walking around the harbor. I'm pretty sure a lot of what they're selling comes in by boat. Probably Cambodia to Vietnam by truck, then by boat to Hainan Island to here."

"I saw a few wrecked old fishing junks, didn't look like they were going anywhere."

"There's a naval pier closer to the bay. Maybe you didn't get that far."

"I saw it. It didn't look like much."

"There's probably more going on than you could see. The Chinese military is good at keeping a low profile."

| |CHAPTER **SEVEN**| |

"**G**ood work, Ray. I doubt our clients will want to get into bed with Golden Truly. We've saved them a lot of grief."

Warner's beaming as he waves my report in the air in front of my desk. "I think we'll leave out the picture of the little woman with the big dicks though. You have any problems?"

I tell him about being arrested. He sits down and scowls. "That does present a problem. Normally, what I'd have you do now is make an appointment with Golden Truly management and go talk to them straight, see what you can get from that. Tie up any loose ends. But now I don't think we can risk it. Our friends to the north don't tend to believe in coincidences."

"How do you want to play it, then?"

"Don't sweat it, I'll go. I doubt they'll tell me anything interesting anyhow."

"So, what do you want me to do now?"

"Write up what you've got, leave it at that."

"I'd rather keep digging for a while, if you don't mind."

"Why?"

"Old journalism habit, I guess. Once I get started I don't want to stop until I know everything I can. Besides, you never know what else you're gonna find out. Could be useful. At least I'd like to go to the auction, see who else shows up."

"Think you can get in? What if your being detained in Shenzhen has them worried?"

"Sure I can get in. Why not? They think I'm a buyer, or have friends who might be. As for the other thing, who knows? My poking around at the docks didn't have anything to do with them. Maybe they'll believe that, maybe not. Maybe they want to see what I'll get up to next."

"Why not. It can't hurt to find out as much as we can."

Tommy sounds pleased to hear from me. "Mr. Sharp, I am still working on your heads. Did you enjoy your visit to Shenzhen, *lah*?"

"Yes, it's an impressive collection. Mr. Chen and Mr. Li showed me two items in particular that one of my friends might be interested in. They said there's going to be an auction here for them. Do you know anything about that?"

"Yes, I know of the auction. Perhaps your friend would like to attend, *lah*? I can arrange for him to do so if he will call me."

"He's pretty secretive. He might prefer to send me as his representative."

"That, too, might be possible, Mr. Sharp. But you must appreciate that this is a very exclusive auction, *lah*. For you to attend, your friend will need to provide you with a letter of authorization, his proxy as it were, and financial references."

"I'll see what he wants to do."

"Please do this with dispatch, Mr. Sharp. The auction is to be held this coming Friday evening."

"I'll get back to you."

Warner's got superb connections. Within a day I have a letter on stationary from one of Hong Kong's top law firms granting me the proxy to bid up to two million U.S. dollars on behalf of one of its clients who wishes to remain anonymous. And another from Heng Seng Bank affirming that the funds are available.

I've also got very firm instructions not to use the letters for anything other than gaining entrance to the auction. I'll be in very deep shit if I actually enter a winning bid.

Friday night I feel underdressed in my finest tailor-made suit when I walk into the Mandarin Hotel's Chinnery Bar. It cost me nearly seven hundred bucks, U.S. bucks. That's about what the guy who greets me spent on his shirt. He looks at my shoes. I'm glad I polished them. It was a last minute decision.

The Chinnery is where we're all meeting. The plan is to then whisk us off to a secret location for the auction. It's all very hush hush. I can hardly see the assembly of men through the thick blue haze of Havana cigar smoke. I'm sure it's only the finest tobacco, but it takes all I've got to keep from doubling over in a fit of coughing. I'm not sure who's here for the auction. I'm the only one who isn't in a tuxedo.

A waiter—at least I think he's a waiter, he's in a white tux— comes up with a tray of rich, golden brown liquid in snifters.

"What is it?"

"It is our finest house stock Grande Fine Champagne XO cognac, sir. I am certain it will meet with your approval."

"Would it be too much to ask for a beer?"

"What beer would you prefer, sir?"

"Whatever you've got on draft will do."

"I'm afraid, sir, that we only have bottles of beer."

"Okay, have you got any Guinness? I haven't had dinner. I can use something nutritious."

"I shall bring you a Guinness then, sir. By the way, perhaps you would be interested to know that there are canapés at the table next to the bar."

I am interested. I follow the waiter to the bar where he orders my beer. The bartender hands it and a glass to him and he takes a while pouring it slowly down the side of the glass, then hands it to me. I could have done that for myself, but I doubt I would have poured such a perfect head. He's earned his tip.

The snack table looks lonely. Everyone's mouth is already busy with their cigars and cognac. I sidle up to a large platter of fire engine red smoked salmon on top of thin-sliced dark bread, topped with a slight puff of sour cream and sprinkled lightly with small pebbles of shiny black caviar.

When I first moved to Hong Kong I was impressed by spreads like this. I knew journalists who moved from hotel party to hotel party and practically subsisted off the appetizers. I've eaten more than my fair share of it. Now I'm sick of it. But I'm hungry.

I've nestled a third one into my mouth when a man comes up and stands next to me. I notice him by the glistening tip of his cigar in my peripheral vision. I turn toward him while chewing.

"I don't much care for Chinnery myself. The work seems so pompous, don't you think?" He points with his cigar at the wall above the food table.

There's a painting. It's all somber yellows and browns and dull gold and black. It's a landscape, one of the islands that are part of Hong Kong. It's dated 1842 and it's signed George Chinnery, the painter the bar is named after.

"Looks rather stiff to me, like he thought he was going to do a Rembrandt thing with the light but he wasn't good enough to pull it off."

"Neither, perhaps, was Rembrandt himself. I have seen one of his paintings after it was given a good scrub. It was positively garish."

"Some things are better left alone." I stick my hand out at him. "I'm Ray Sharp. You here for the auction?"

He puts his snifter down on the table, puts his cigar out into it and thrusts out a hand with a surprisingly strong grip. He nods at the beer in my other hand. "Where did you obtain that? I could do with something wetter and colder than brandy. I'm John, John Montgomery."

"I thought it was cognac."

He raises an eyebrow. "Dare I say, Ray, quite honestly now, I have no intention of giving offense, but it is positively delightful to meet a fellow who does not know the difference. I congratulate you. It is, of course, no more than a meaningless distinction that has been foisted upon us by the French."

He's a strange man. He's a couple of inches shorter than me and of medium build. His tuxedo is classic, perfectly tailored and he seems as comfortable in it as James Bond always does in his. He's sporting diamond cufflinks and an incongruously large military-style wristwatch. His thinning salt-and-pepper hair is cut short in an unfashionable way that looks as if he doesn't want to bother with it. He speaks with a clipped, very upper-crust British accent. He must have gone to all the right schools. I decide to have fun with him.

"I don't get it, John. You don't like Chinnery. You don't give a shit about the difference between cognac and brandy, but you know what it is. You wear an army watch, but you speak posh and look like you were born in that tux. What the hell kind of Brit are you?"

He has a solid, manly laugh, fluid and easy, nothing forced about it. He claps me on the back.

"Ah, it is pleasing to not be so easily, what do you Yanks say, pigeonholed. Let me go to the bar in search of a beer. I will return and then we can talk. I think we still have time before they lead us to auction."

He's back soon with a beer for himself and one for me. He looks me over in a way that makes me a little uncomfortable, like he's taking inventory.

"Once more, Ray, please do not permit me to offend you, but may I ask on whose behalf you are here?"

I take a long, slow sip of beer. "How'd you know?"

"Simple really. I like to think that I am acquainted with everyone in the region who has an interest in Khmer artifacts. You could, perhaps, be a new eccentric wealthy American on the scene, but I don't think so. You are dressed in a very nice suit, but nice within its price range. From the look of it, I'd say it's from one of the better Shanghai tailors in Tsim Sha Tsui and cost you perhaps a thousand U.S., including an extra pair of trousers. If you could afford to bid at this auction on your own behalf, your suit would be much more expensive. And your shoes. They appear to be comfortable, but not custom made. Perhaps I am wrong, but I don't think so."

"No, you're right. Got me. But I can't tell you who I'm bidding for. They wish to remain anonymous. You here to bid for yourself?"

"I have not yet seen the items on the block, so I am not at all certain that I will enter any bids. But perhaps."

"Okay, so what's your story?"

"Of course, yes, but I am afraid that will have to wait." He nods his head toward the door. "It seems that they are calling us to the auction."

The auction turns out to be upstairs, around the indoor, classic Roman-style swimming pool. The room is steamy, hot and moist. Even Montgomery loosens his tie. There are perhaps twenty of us men in dark suits, all but four of us Hong Kong Chinese. I recognize about half of them from my work as a business journalist.

There are at least as many cool, attractive waitresses in tiny lamé bikinis, clicking softly around on high heels, carrying trays of refreshing drinks. A raft with a table and chair is tied up at one end of the pool. Two beefy men stand by it, holding machine pistols. They look alert. The two boxes I'd seen in Shenzhen are on the table.

There are two rows of folding chairs on one side of the pool. I take a beer from a stunning Eurasian waitress with bright green eyes and long, flowing rich black hair. She's alluringly under-dressed in a couple of small scraps of cloth the same color as her eyes. Montgomery takes a beer as well, and we sit next to each other at the end of the second row of chairs.

"Ray, have you participated in many auctions before?"

"No, this is my first."

"A word of caution, once it gets underway you must sit per-fectly still. At an auction of this small size the slightest movement, a nod of your head, a raising of your glass to take a drink, could be misconstrued as a bid."

"Thanks for the warning. I'll have to keep my tics in check."

"It appears that there are only two lots to bid on this evening."

"Yeah. I saw them last week in Shenzhen. I went up to visit the warehouse. They're pretty impressive."

He looks at me, wanting to hear more, but the lights dim and a voice tells everyone to please be seated. There's a little shuffling for position and then a spotlight hits the boxes on the table. A slightly built, middle-aged Chinese man, in what looks like a waiter's tuxedo, walks out from behind one of the Romanesque columns around the pool and steps onto the raft. He speaks in flawless, British English, with a flat, mid-range voice. He sounds like he's been to TV news anchorman school and gets right to the point.

"Gentlemen, welcome. Tonight we have only two lots on which to bid. The starting bid on each is one million U.S. dollars and fur-ther bids may only be submitted in increments of ten thousand U.S. dollars. As usual, settlement must be immediate upon the successful conclusion of bidding and in the form of an authorized bank draft or wire transfer. We have a secure computer station available."

He opens the latch on the square box and gestures to one of the bikini girls to come pick it up. The one who served my drink steps up to take the box. She holds it out in front of her and walks slowly past us, followed by a moving spotlight and shadowed by one of the armed guards.

It's the *apsara* that I'd seen last Saturday. The glare off it is searing as it sparkles in the beam. The auctioneer describes it as it passes.

"Our first item is this superb twelfth century *apsara* figure. It was recently unearthed in perfect condition from a royal tomb in the vicinity of Angkor Thom. It is approximately thirty centimeters tall and finely carved from excellent grade Burmese jadeite. It is plated with twenty carat gold to a thickness of 3.175 millimeters. The necklace consists of twelve, perfectly spherical, unblemished white pearls. The rings are highest grade ruby and sapphire, flawless, bright medium-color. The bracelets and anklets are perfect semi-transparent Burmese jadeite with no inclusions. And the diamond in the navel is approximately six carats, D-flawless and by modern standards would be considered to have a triple-zero ideal cut."

The bidding goes quickly to a million and a half dollars, then settles into discreet, silent nods, chin wags, waves of a finger and even one mere raising of eyebrows that I happen to catch when I'm cautiously looking down the row I'm sitting in. Montgomery isn't bidding, so I figure I can get away with sitting on my hands, my face locked into a lowered position, moving only my eyes to follow the action. By a million seven the bidding has settled into a polite battle between an elderly and a middle-aged Chinese man. The older one, whose face I think I recognize from one of those small, black-and-white dot engravings in the *Wall Street Journal,* wins it at one million, seven hundred, and sixty thousand. The loser is occasionally the richest man in Hong Kong, depending on the current fortunes of the stock market.

While the winner goes to the computer terminal to make his payment, we break for drinks. I fetch beers for Montgomery and myself. They're free, but I drop a large tip on the tray being held by the woman in the green bikini. At least it seems like a big tip to me, but it only buys me about a quarter of a smile, a slight tug on the corners of her mouth. She switches on the whole thing and flashes it past me at the losing bidder, who's walking up on my right.

Montgomery's chuckling when I hand him his glass. "Didn't impress her with your charm or your tip, I see."

"She seems to go for older guys."

"No, just rich ones. Sorry."

"She's not my type anyhow."

"What, you don't like your women beautiful, cold and calculating?"

"Does anyone?"

"If you can afford it, it's convenient."

"I guess I'm old-fashioned. I like a little inconvenience. It keeps things interesting."

He tilts and lifts his glass toward me. I clink it with mine.

"So, John, you were telling me what you do."

"Ah, yes, I suppose it ought to be gratifying that I am not recognizable."

"Not this again. The last spook I met's now my boss. What is it? M-I 5?"

"No, nothing so glamorous, I'm afraid. Sorry to disappoint you. I am what you Yanks would refer to as a 'front man,' although a highly compensated one to be sure."

"Who do you front for?"

"Wellfleet."

"I didn't think it used that name anymore, not since Chau bought it."

"It doesn't. It's now Chau Keong Holdings, Wellfleet's the trading division."

"So what's Chau want you for? He made such a fuss over a Chinese company buying out one of the original big British firms."

"Much of our business is with Europe, or you Yanks. He seems to think I speak the language of our customers. My little patch of the empire's all secondary in any event; property's the only thing that really interests the new owners."

"What do you mean?"

"You of course know of our recent winning bid to construct the new container port on the east side of the New Territories. Shipping is only the excuse to buy up the land. There certainly will be docks, but there will be quite a few more blocks of flats, and of course a shopping complex, all with waterfront views and accordingly high prices."

"If you're the front man, why haven't I seen you before? I used to be deputy editor of *Asian Industry*. I would have thought we'd have run into each other."

"I am relatively new in the post and I am better known in Europe than here."

"It must pay well if you're here bidding for yourself."

"It does, but I'm not. I, too, have outside backing."

"Chau?"

"That, too, is my secret."

We exchange business cards. I get one from him with his private line. We haven't really told each other anything, but I think we each figure the other might come in handy sometime.

The tuxedoed Chinese auctioneer comes back to the raft and bangs us all into our seats with his gavel. This time, a tall blond woman in a gold bikini parades the box past us. I look around, the woman in not much green is sitting next to the losing bidder from the last lot, she has her hand high on his leg, her bright green fingernails contrasting nicely with the rich brown of his suit.

"Gentlemen, our second lot is from the same tomb as the first. It is a magnificent *linga*, fashioned from flawless quartz crystal. It is forty-six centimeters in length, with a diameter of fourteen centimeters. It is set into a cup of twenty carat gold, encrusted with flawless mid-range color rubies and emeralds approximately twenty-four carats in total. Embedded within the shaft of the *linga* are eight, D-flawless, triple-zero round cut diamonds with a slight yellow cast. They are estimated at approximately eight carats each. As with our last lot, the bidding now commences at one million U.S. dollars."

You always hear that sex sells, and I guess the world of stolen Cambodian antiquities is no different. The bidding quickly gets up above two million, slows as it approaches three and finally ends at three million, six hundred, and thirty thousand. I haven't made a move. Montgomery had been in on it until a little over two million, but then he sat on his hands.

After the last gavel rings down, Montgomery turns toward me. "Ah yes, well, easy come, easy go. Perhaps the next auction."

"I don't know about you, John, and I know it's not my money, but nothing in the millions sounds easy to me."

He smiles and I can't tell if it's with amusement, sympathy or empathy. "Are you remaining for the after party?"

"Here?"

"Yes, we've been invited to continue drinking and to mingle with the hired help."

Two of the waitresses have attached themselves to our sides and are whispering seductively in our ears about more drinks and whatever else we might desire.

In other circumstances there's probably a lot I'd desire. But it's not my crowd. I feel out of place enough already.

"It's tempting, but a little too rich for my blood and I'm tired." I gently remove the soft, warm arm from around me and place the hand on Montgomery's shoulder. "I'll leave you three alone now. I might give you a call next week."

"Please do."

I leave before the scene breaks out into much more than flirtation and the teasing removal of black ties.

| |CHAPTER **EIGHT** | |

walk up the hill to the Foreign Correspondents Club where I've got a lifetime membership at the cheap journalists' price. The auction left me with a bad taste I need to wash out of my mouth. The company of hacks is preferable to that of the captains of industry. There's probably not one person in the F.C.C. who could afford to spend millions of dollars on stolen art.

On a Friday night the place isn't cozy, it's heaving. Even the women seem to be pumping testosterone into the atmosphere. I shove my way to the bar, through a knot of sports writers in town for an international rugby tournament. I've had enough beer for the time being. I order a double vodka, cold and neat. I take it and wind along the edge of the crowd, looking for a seat.

There's a small table with two chairs squeezed into a corner at the back of the room. There's a highball glass in front of one of the chairs but no one there. I take the other one.

The glass on the table is half full of whisky and there's a business card carefully perched across the top of it. The card says: "Gone to piss, please don't fuck with my drink," and has the name and address of a bar in New York. I'm thinking I might enjoy this person's company.

I do. I've known Mike for a few years. He was back home in New York recently and picked up a pocket load of cards from a bar he likes. He gives me a couple. I'm sure they'll come in handy.

"Hey, Ray, you're not the hot babe I was hoping for."

"Holding the seat? I'll make myself scarce when she gets here."

"Nah, no plans, just fantasies. You seen Susan lately?"

Susan was the one who'd broken it off between them. She didn't like feeling tied down. I can't say I'm sorry.

"The other night. We had the usual awful dinner at Jimmy's with a stiff Brit she works with."

"Why'd you subject yourself to that?"

"Cambodia. I needed to learn about stolen art. Know anything of interest?" Mike had worked in Cambodia when he first got to Asia. He doesn't go there anymore, not since getting caught in the middle of a firefight between the Khmer Rouge and government troops. He still might know something, or maybe he'll have some connections.

"I know a guy you can talk to in Bangkok, but you'll have to be careful. He's the nervous type. The type who could get dangerous if he gets too nervous."

"Who is he? Why's he so jittery?"

"I guess he shouldn't be, he's a general. Retired, but still plenty connected. He runs a freight-forwarding company, some electronics factories, some nightclubs, massage parlors and shops in River City. He sells Khmer relics, imports them, too."

"Why's he going to want to talk to me?"

"He owes me a favor, a big one. But I can't collect; journalistic ethics. I'll call him and tell him you're coming."

"What sort of favor?"

"You're better off not knowing. Don't ask him either."

"That sounds ominous."

"Only if you know too much."

"I'll play dumb."

"That's why I'm not telling you. You won't have to."

"I'm not even sure if I need to go to Bangkok."

"If it's stolen Cambodian art you're interested in, you do. When you're ready to go, I'll call General Tran."

"Vietnamese?"

"Yep. He left Saigon in 1975. He's naturalized in Thailand. You'll like him. He's full of great stories and he's one hell of a host. And best of all, since you're not a journalist anymore you can accept his hospitality. Carefully though. I mean it."

"Trying to scare me off? He sounds interesting."

"Within limits, sure."

I agree to call Mike if and when I'm heading to Thailand and we settle into a night of heavy drinking. I tell him about the auction, and he tells me I'm nuts for having turned down my chance at the after party.

"Oh man, I've heard about those things. That old guy, the one who lost the first bid, the guy who took your girl in green, did you recognize him?"

"He wasn't all that old, maybe sixty or so, and she was hardly 'my' girl."

"Whatever. It was Ip Shau Kee, wasn't it?"

"Yeah, so?"

"You know the stories. I'd love to see him in action. They say that every year he sets up the winner of the Miss Hong Kong Pageant in a suite at the Mandarin and doesn't let her out for a month."

"Yeah, I know the story. Then he gives her a signed blank check the day he kicks her out. If she refuses the check she never has to work another day. If she writes in a reasonable amount, anything up to a million Hong Kong, that's what she gets."

"Yeah, but you've heard about Miss 1990, haven't you?"

"Yeah, right, she wrote in ten million bucks and he let her have it, but he had his goons beat her up. I don't believe it."

"Believe it. I've seen the scars."

I still don't know if I believe it. People get scars in a lot of ways. Then again, the guy's got a reputation for being particularly ruthless in business. Who knows what the hell else he's capable of? The only time I ever met him, in a fast moving reception line, he had a firm handshake and a cordial nod.

It's getting late and I'm beginning to consider leaving when I get a hard poke in the ribs that turns me around.

"*Buenos noches borracho cabrón*, buy a lady a drink?" Lei Yue looks like she's already had a few. She's slurring her words. She's wearing a big grin and half-wearing a blood red, shiny dress that's threatening to fall off entirely.

Mike taps me on the shoulder. "Aren't you going to introduce me to your lady friend, Ray? How's she know you're a drunken asshole?"

I'm about to make the introduction, but she steps around me and thrusts a hand at him. "Marisol Wen, you can call me Lei Yue. If your chump pal here isn't going to introduce me or buy me a drink, maybe you'd like to."

"Ray never said anything about you. You're a handful."

"I'm a lot more than that, pal. And at the moment I'm in a lousy mood, too. Do us both a favor, buy a lady a drink."

Mike shoots me a look like he's drowning and needs me to jump in after him.

"Hey, Lei Yue, be nice to my friend Mike. Take my seat. What do you want to drink?"

She wants shots of tequila, at least three. The best they've got, which isn't very good, but it will have to do. Forget the lime and salt.

I go get it, and a double vodka for myself and a double whisky for Mike. It looks like it's going to be a long night. I set the drinks down and look around for an empty chair. By the time I find one and drag it back to the table, Lei Yue's downed one of her shots. Mike is staring at her wide-eyed over the rim of his glass.

I sit down with Lei Yue between us. She throws back another shot then puts a hand on each of our legs and talks to the wall in a low, steady, disgusted sounding voice.

"You think I wanted to be a fucking *enano*? It's not fucking easy, not with all these *cabrónes. Chingao!* Why'd I fucking come here anyway? I'm not anything here. I'm not fucking Chinese, not fucking Mexican, no one thinks I'm a fucking woman; I'm just a dwarf, just a fucking *enano*. If I was a *puta* I could make big bucks from the fetish crowd. There's plenty of those *cabrónes* who'd pay me."

Mike's looking at me behind her back and I can't tell if he's amused, terrified or both. I reach down and squeeze Lei Yue's hand. She stops talking and looks at me.

"What happened?"

"I got fired. The fucking assholes fired me. I'm fucked. I'm going to have to go back to Tijuana and be a waitress, or perform in donkey shows or something else fucked up."

"Hold up, will ya? One thing at a time. Why'd they fire you?"

"After we went to Shenzhen I went back to the office and pitched the story to my editor, Lo. Not about the company you're investigating or anything, but about smuggling of Cambodian art in general. So he tells me he's not interested, there's nothing new about it, and he puts me on some bullshit story about women rugby players.

"Okay, fair enough, Lo's got shit-for-brains but I'm used to that. But then this morning I find out he's given my story to Martin Lim, the golden boy of the newsroom. I find out because Lim wants to take me to lunch and pick my brains.

"So I'm pissed off, mad as hell, but it's a good story and it ought to get written, so I say yes. What a fucking *cabróna* I am. Turns out his idea of lunch is he's picked up takeaway, gets me into a taxi and tells the driver to take us to a love motel in Kowloon Tong. What's with that?

"I start screaming at the fucker. The driver pulls over and kicks us out. We're on the sidewalk about a block from the office and he's looking all hurt, like he can't understand why I'm so upset. Finally he tells me that Lo's told him I'd been saying I need to get laid, and that I'm a good little spinner."

"What's a spinner?" Mike rolls his eyes upwards and shakes his head at me when I ask. Lei Yue doesn't seem happy at being interrupted, or with the question.

"What the fuck do you think it is? Use your imagination. I don't know if I'm glad you can't think of me that way or if it makes me madder.

"So anyway, I leave that fuckwit Lim on the pavement and head back up to Lo's office. He's in a meeting with the publisher, but I push in and start screaming at him. I guess I also tore up a bunch of papers on his desk. I'd have liked to have kicked him in the *cojones,* but he was sitting down and I couldn't get to them.

"So he gives me the boot, right then, no severance, no nothing. He calls security and a couple of big guys come and haul me out. What the fuck are you smiling for?"

"I can't help it. Sorry. I wish I'd been there to see it. I'd have liked to have held Lo down so you could get to him."

She looks at me and her eyes soften and begin to tear. She squeezes my hand hard, nods her head and cries softly. Mike eases out of his chair, nods his head toward the bar and heads out in search of less complicated company. I stroke her hair lightly with my other hand, not sure how comforting I can be, or how much I want to be. I like her. That's as far as it goes. Getting involved in any way seems like a bad idea.

Maybe I can get her a job. My company's starting up. It's only me and Warner, a research assistant and the receptionist secretary so far. Lei Yue's a journalist, she's bright and she speaks fluent English, Spanish, Mandarin and Cantonese, maybe more. Maybe I can talk Warner into hiring her.

Or maybe that's a bad idea. I don't know. But I'm going to have to think of something to say because she's getting those light hiccups that some people get when they stop crying. I look around for a napkin to give her to dab at her eyes but I don't see anything.

I'm wearing a long sleeve shirt. When she looks up at me I make a show of rolling the right sleeve down and flapping it at her. She smiles, then buries her face into it. Her eyes are only a little red when she looks up at me again.

"Thanks. I feel like a fool. I shouldn't unload all that on you. Just what you need huh, a drunk, pissed off dwarf feeling sorry for herself, crying in your beer."

"Vodka actually." I lift my glass to her and take another sip. "You've still got a shooter of tequila to get through."

She bends her head to it and sniffs. Her head shoots back up fast. She isn't looking any too happy. "I think I've had enough for one night. This is crappy tequila anyhow, only good for margaritas and people who don't know any better."

"So now you're not just a pissed off dwarf, you're also an affronted Mexican?"

"You sure know how to make a girl feel better, don't you?"

"It's getting late. I need to go home. Can I get you a taxi?"

"I don't know. I don't think so. I live across the harbor and I don't want to be alone. Look, don't worry about telling me to fuck off, we hardly know each other, but you live here on the island don't you? Have you got a couch I can sleep on? I won't be a pest, promise."

I've got an unopened bottle of really good tequila in a cupboard in my kitchen. A friend brought it to me from the duty free shop in Dubai. I pull it out and wave it at Lei Yue, who's examining my book shelves.

"Where'd you get that? I haven't seen anything that good in a long time."

I hand her the bottle. "Open it, feel free. I don't drink it."

"I will, but only a little. This should be sipped, not slammed."

"That's good; you've slammed enough for one night."

We sit and drink and talk and it's comfortable, friendly, easy. I feel a little guilty that I'm not attracted to her. I don't know if she wants me to be or not, if she's attracted to me or not, but in principle it seems like it might make her feel better. Or maybe it would make her suspicious. I don't know, but it doesn't come up.

When I get too tired to hold my head up much longer I tell her I need to go to sleep. I offer her my bed, telling her I'll take the couch. She refuses. I get her a blanket and pillow, show her where the things are that she might want during the night, and am soon asleep without the usual squirming for the right position.

| |CHAPTER **NINE**| |

L ei Yue makes good coffee. Better than I do. I'm halfway through my second cup, contemplating a third. She's at the table in the kitchen leafing through the *Economist*. I remember thinking I might be able to get Warner to hire her.

"I've got an idea."

"Does it hurt?"

"I might be able to help you get a job."

"Making coffee? I can go home to Tijuana to do that."

"Nope. How do you feel about the glamorous world of corporate investigations?"

"Your company? What would I do there?"

"What do you think? You're smart. You're a journalist, so presumably you know about research and investigation, and best of all, you're multi-lingual. My boss speaks English, Russian and a little Mandarin. I speak English, and Indonesian, and I can swear pretty good in Russian and Cantonese, but not more than that. You'd come in handy."

"I like being a journalist."

"So did I. Funny thing is that this work's sort of the same thing. You conduct research, interview people, poke around and then write it up. It's just for a smaller audience and you don't get a byline."

"Neither do the people who write for the *Economist*."

"What?"

"They don't get bylines either. I wonder if it's frustrating."

"I don't know, probably. I need to go into the office this morning. Why don't you come with me and I'll introduce you to my boss, Bill Warner."

"The spook?"

"The ex-spook."

"Once a spook, always a spook; isn't that what they say? Okay."

A couple of hours later Warner walks into my office, where I'm writing up everything I've found out so far about Golden Truly. "Ms. Wen starts Monday."

"What's she doing?"

"Same thing as you. We're beginning to get a lot of inquiries about work in China. You're right; she'll be great. Disarming, too."

"Is she still here?"

"No, she left. She'll call you later. What happened at the auction?"

I tell him and he asks a lot of questions. "It's a shame you can only identify about half the people who were there. Part of what's going to make this company work is collecting as much as we can about everyone important. See if you can find out who the others were."

"They didn't give out a guest list. What about Montgomery? Do you know him?"

"I know of him. He might be M-I 5. Wellfleet would be a good cover."

"Wouldn't it keep him too busy to get much spying done?"

"He's privy to a lot of useful information. Did you ask him about Golden Truly?"

"No."

"Do. Give him a call. He's a good connection to have no matter what. You never know when a guy like him might come in handy."

"Maybe I ought to go to Bangkok. I don't know how connected Golden Truly is to this Cambodian art racket, but it can't hurt to find out more about it."

"I'm not sure the client gives a damn, Ray. They already know enough to make up their minds about doing business with these guys."

"Seems to me there's a lot more of the picture to get. There's a lot of bigshots connected to this. I'd like to keep at it for a while."

"This isn't a series of features for a magazine, Ray. We give the client what he wants and move on."

"Yeah I know, but I think there's more to it. It isn't illegal here yet, but it will be. It already is in Cambodia and Thailand. Shouldn't we be putting together files on this sort of thing for future reference, or something like that?"

"That's pretty weak. Why're you so hot to go to Bangkok? You horny? You can take care of that here."

"Fuck, Bill, it's not that. This is nagging me. I'm not sure what the hell it is, but I don't feel like I can let it drop until I know more about it."

"Hell, is this what I get for hiring a journalist? I'll think about it. Now call Montgomery."

He picks up himself after one ring. "Montgomery."

"That's crisp. Aren't you enough of a bigshot to have a secretary?"

"I give her Saturdays off. I like being alone in the office."

"How was the after party?"

"You don't want to know. You'll be too sorry you missed it."

"Well, maybe next time."

"To what do I owe the pleasure? I don't suppose you simply rang to hear the salacious details of last night."

"Do you know anything about a Chinese art supplies company called 'Golden Truly'?"

"A little. They are one of our shipping customers. Why do you ask?"

"It's a due diligence job. An American company is looking at them for a joint venture."

"I can't tell you much. We have a lot of customers. Our Chinese subsidiary deals with them directly, we don't. I suppose if they had presented us with any problems I would have heard more about them."

"Have you ever been to their warehouse in Shenzhen?"

"No. I've had no reason to do so. Should I?"

"I was there last Saturday. The art supplies were all up front, but there was another, larger part of the place behind a locked door. It was filled with Cambodian antiquities. I saw the two items at last night's auction there. They were in a vault in an office."

"That is interesting. I wonder if we have been shipping more than art supplies for them. It would be quite disturbing to discover that we are unknowing participants in a smuggling ring."

"You didn't seem to have any problem with it at the auction."

"It's a legal formality. There's no law against it once it's here. Shipping it is questionable. And even worse, if our bills of lading are not complete or correct, it may present us with legal problems no matter what the cargo. Are you looking further into this matter?"

"Yeah, for a little while at least, but I've already got what our client needs in the way of due diligence. I'm not sure how far I can take it."

"This could be a matter of some concern to Wellfleet. We have customers all over the world. They would not be happy to know that one of our subsidiaries is falsifying records. It might also be a violation of maritime law and certainly of trade procedures. I would like to employ your company to delve as far as possible into this. I'll need proof, or our Chinese subsidiary will simply deny it. Would that be possible or appropriate?"

"I don't see why not. My boss'll have to work out the details. Should I have him call you?"

"Please, right away." He hangs up.

I walk into Warner's office. "I spoke to Montgomery. He wants to hire us." I repeat my conversation with the head of Wellfleet and as I'm leaving his office Warner's reaching for the phone, visions of a very big new client dancing behind his eyes.

As I'm about out the door he turns me around with a "Hey, Ray."

"Yeah?"

"Fly business class to Bangkok if you want. Stay in a nice hotel."

| |CHAPTER **TEN**| |

fly economy anyway and stay at the Swiss Park, where I always stay. The hotel's cheap, comfortable, efficient and conveniently near the fun, noisy parts of town, but down a quiet side street. It's late Saturday afternoon when I arrive, during a brief lull in the traffic. It only takes an hour to get in from the airport. I pay the extra 30 *baht*, about a buck twenty U.S., to get an air-conditioned private car and driver rather than a steaming taxi. It would be worth 20 times as much.

Bangkok's a complicated place. It's horrible in many ways that are immediately apparent on the surface. And wonderful, even charming in beautiful in ways that make themselves known only when you scratch that surface.

It's as filthy, smelly, impoverished, rundown and ugly as any other gigantic third world city. At first glance it's a simmering stew of feculence. And I mean "simmering" as close to literally as is possible for a place to get. The city bubbles under a dense, wet blanket of foul air, held in place by the hottest average temperature and the highest average humidity of any major urban area on the planet. It's a great climate for flowers. The scents of orchids and incense are as much notes of the Bangkok broth as the exhaust and pollution.

Still, block after block of three- to six-story buildings are covered in grime and soot that's been steamed into place by the climate. Overhead exposed electric wires snap and crackle. The air pops with staccato sound waves that continually explode from unmuffled motorbikes and *tuk tuks*—three-wheeled, two-stroke-engined mini-taxis that seem to have been engineered specifically to spew noise and exhaust.

And Bangkok's traffic is, well, there are really no words that can fully convey how terrible it is. When I was writing for a business magazine I did a story on Thailand's economic prospects. One of the frightening statistics I came across was that nearly 98 percent of the country's reported car crashes happen in Bangkok, but they account for less than two percent of traffic fatalities. That's because no one is moving fast enough to hurt anybody.

A couple of years ago things picked up for a few months. A local entrepreneur got the bright idea of sending out a fleet of motorcycle taxis that could knit their way in and out of all the immobile cars and trucks. But now they're stuck in traffic, too.

The city is building an overhead light rail system. It's supposed to make things a lot better, and it might, if all the corruption and cost overruns and general inefficiency don't stop the project before it's done. At the moment though, all the construction is making things worse.

And there's plenty more construction, as well. All over town, with no slight nods to city planning or zoning or even common sense, new buildings are rising. From the few vantage points that overlook the city you can see tall, spindly cranes—looking like the long necks and small heads of grazing dinosaurs—sticking up from the skeletons of skyscrapers in varying states of reverse decomposition.

There's so much building going on that there's a concrete shortage. But you wouldn't guess it from the choking cement dust in the air.

A little over 300 miles to the east, a crashed Lao Aviation 737 jet sprawls at the end of the runway in Vientiene, Laos. A couple of years ago a Thai general, wanting to make a quick killing in Bangkok's booming construction market, secretly filled the hold of the plane with bags of raw cement. The plane never got off the ground. Eleven people died. The cargo was off-loaded, taken by barge across the Mekong River and by truck to Bangkok.

That's progress for you. None of this would be happening if Thailand's economy wasn't going nuts. If foreigners weren't flocking to the country to invest. If the stock market wasn't going apeshit. If the banks weren't passing out cheap, unsecured loans like candy on Halloween. If Thais, carpet-bombed with media images of the over-ripe life in the U.S., in Japan, in Western Europe, in Hong Kong and Singapore, weren't clamoring for what it looks like everybody else with money has got. They want McDonald's and MTV and Nikes and Sonys and Toyotas. They line up to buy buckets of chicken at KFC, despite the fact that on every other block in Bangkok, in every rural market, street vendors sell a far superior and cheaper local product.

And who are we to say they can't have these things? If they want these things, and we've got them, why should we, why would we, say "no" to potential customers?

And if they're making a mess of their country in the meantime, isn't that their own business? We made a mess of ours. In the same stage of its development was New York any better? Was London? It's only now, now that we've got all the goodies, now that our lives, our societies, are bursting at the seams with an over-abundance of stuff, that we're beginning to give a damn about what that means for our environment, our traditions, our health, our families, our souls.

And what about the Thai soul? In the midst of all the greed and filth and noise and ugliness, the Thai soul is what makes the place so damned attractive, so seductive, so beautiful in spite of everything. One of the first things that almost every visitor to the place comments on is how friendly everyone seems.

Thai people are peaceful, gracious and graceful, except when they're not. They're accommodating, fun-loving and helpful, except when they're not. They're demure, respectful and accepting of others, except sometimes when they're not. I guess in a lot of ways they're like anybody else.

Thailand is a very conservative, tradition-bound country. People are friendly but shy, quiet. They're horrified by loud, aggressive behavior. They're not very physical, not touchy-feely. They keep their feelings and thoughts to themselves. To do anything else is considered rude. It unbalances the delicate equilibrium of society.

But as a foreigner, especially a man, it's easy to get a different idea. When those truckers got to the big city and delivered their bags of Laotian cement, you can bet they went out and got laid. Thailand is the world's favorite brothel. Anyone who's interested is greeted with open legs, puckered lips and an inviting smile.

There's a widely accepted but little publicized theory that's popular in development banks—investment flows fastest to countries where prostitution is easily available, relatively cheap and at least tolerated.

When I was a journalist I interviewed the president of a major garment manufacturing company. He laughed when he told me that he had customers who could get better quality work, cheaper, from Bangladesh, India, even Malaysia, but who insisted on doing business in Thailand. He said they were all happy to pay the "pussy premium."

Foreigners, businesspeople and tourists, flock to Thailand for all sorts of reasons: its art and culture, its beaches and mountains, its fantastic food. But sex is also high on the list of attractions. Anything is available. There are bars where you can sit down and order a drink, and after bringing it to you the waitress will duck under the table to give you a blow job while you discuss a deal with your companions. There are swank clubs that sell the services of well known models, actresses and musicians. There are skyscraping massage parlors with as many as five hundred numbered and color-coded women to pick from behind a huge glass window. There is every kind of sex show and service imaginable. There are straight clubs, gay clubs and clubs where no one cares who's what and it would be rude to ask.

And it's not just foreigners who indulge. There isn't a city, town or village in the country without a brothel or at least a few prostitutes. It's been going on for thousands of years, long before any foreigners ever set foot in the place. A bad harvest? Sell a daughter. An especially voracious tax collector? Sell a son. Estimates are that only about five percent of the sex trade in Thailand involves foreigners. The main thing the visitors have done is raise the prices.

And the higher prices don't matter much to visitors, because it's still cheap compared with most places.

The police like the higher prices because prostitution is, at least technically, illegal in Thailand. The more it costs, the more money that's in it for them in bribes and extortion. It's easier to keep sex workers under their thumbs. If it's legal, what's there to threaten them with?

The government likes it because all the tens, maybe hundreds, of thousands of sex workers get paid in cash that they plug back into the economy when they go shopping. And since they're in an illegal trade, they tend to keep a low profile and not make much trouble.

Their families like it because of the money that they send home. A week of sex with a moderately well off foreigner in Bangkok can bring in as much money as a whole rice harvest on a small farm.

And rural life, especially in Thailand's poorest, northeastern Issan province up near Laos and Cambodia, is hard, very hard. A lot of people come to the conclusion that back-breaking, fourteen- to sixteen-hour workdays to barely eke out a living on a hardscrabble farm is a lot harder, and as soul-destroying, as drinking and flirting and dancing and fucking with strangers in the big city.

There're plenty of ways that people can come up with to tell themselves that prostitution beats the alternatives. Thailand's a poor country. Prostitutes, at least the successful ones who deal with foreigners, make a lot more money than other people. They can buy things they want. They can live more comfortably, eat better, dress better, enjoy more leisure. If they're ambitious they can get a better education and work their way out of it. If they're smart they can save and invest. There isn't a country on the planet where it isn't better to have more money than less money.

It's also a devoutly Buddhist country with a strong belief in reincarnation. A person gains merit through self-sacrifice on behalf of others. They'll need that if they want to be reborn into a better life than the one they're in now. If a young woman sells herself into the sex trade she's helping her family in this life, and so she's helping herself in the next. Even if her parents sell her into it, the suffering she's enduring will make things better next time around. Even if she gets AIDS and goes home to a terrible death, it's merely a portal to a better life.

And for that matter, in Thai Buddhism, a woman can only rise so high through reincarnation anyhow. If they want to get much higher and break out of the cycle, sooner or later they have to be reborn as a man.

And *sanùk* makes it all easier to live with. It's one of the great blessings and one of the great curses of Thailand that there is a deep cultural belief in fun, in *sanùk*. Life isn't worth living without fun. It's hard to disagree with that. But maybe the Thais take it too far. They find *sanùk* in anything, in everything. They lay it on thick with a trowel, sometimes thick enough to hide horrors that lie beneath the surface. It's their opiate and it makes for great, cheery, enthusiastic prostitutes, among other things. And it's seductive as hell, except for when it's not.

Bangkok's a giant cesspool with the most beautiful lotuses you've ever seen floating on top of it, fertilized by the shit underneath. You can hop from flower to flower, not looking down, not taking deep breaths, and you might think you're in paradise. As much as I hate the place, that's how much I love it, too.

||CHAPTER **ELEVEN** ||

I t's Noi who makes Bangkok great.

She's graceful, lithe and strong. She moves with confidence, a regal bearing. But you wouldn't know any of that unless you saw her move. She's as plain and dull looking as the dusty pavement she sets up on.

Every morning at ten she comes up the street from the direction of *Klong Saensaep*, one of the foul canals that criss-cross the city. Swaddled in a fading, threadbare sarong, sheathed in an ill-fitting homemade rough cotton blouse, Noi seems to float along above the dirt and broken pavement underfoot. It's a neat trick because she does it on large, scarred, thick, flattened peasant feet that spill out to the sides of flip flops hewn from old truck tires. Her posture is perfect, unbent, straight. That's remarkable because she carries a thick wooden staff across her shoulders behind her head. Heavy buckets, covered with damp towels hang by wires from each end of the pole.

She glides to the same, small patch of shade on the sidewalk across from my hotel every morning. Maybe she rents the space from the travel agency it's in front of. She settles herself into the rocked-back-on-her-haunches squat that people all over Asia are so comfortable in and that westerners never seem to be able to master. She's dignified, comfortable, calm, at peace. Looking at her settles something inside me. That's part of it.

She sells fish, whatever fish was freshest in the market earlier that morning. The fish is coated with a thin sheen of coconut, lime and chili paste, wrapped in a banana leaf and smoked over a low fire. People come from all over Bangkok to buy it. If you ordered it in a fancy restaurant and it came on fine china with a few artfully arranged vegetables and you paid twenty-four dollars for it, you'd walk away a satisfied customer. She sells it for about fifty cents a piece, a big piece. That's another part of it.

Before her, it was her mother who squatted on the sidewalk and sold the fish. Before that it was her grandmother, whose recipe it is. That's more of it, the continuity, the cool flow of life that has endured through the generations, through all sorts of hardship. It's the regular, everyday people you see—on the street, in the shops, at the foodstalls, in front of their homes—that make this place great.

Whenever I see Noi I eat a piece of fish and we talk, to the extent that we can. She doesn't speak much English and I don't speak more than a few words of Thai, but she's one of those people who's good at communicating, who makes you feel understood and who makes herself clear with gestures and expressions and words you can pick up through context.

She's twenty-six, unmarried, and has two daughters who she swears aren't going to sell fish on the street. Not that there's anything wrong with that, but there's a better life to be had if you plan for it, if you work hard and save and get an education.

I'm not sure how she's going to save much selling fifty cent pieces of fish. I tried overpaying a few times but she wouldn't accept it. I did buy a couple of Thai-English children's books for her kids. She thanked me for those.

I've seen her maybe twenty or more times now. I feel like we're friends, of a sort. She came up to my hotel room once. A passing taxi had splashed her with mud. I offered her a place to clean up. I sat with her pole and buckets in the lobby while she went upstairs. When she came down I treated her to lemonade in the lobby bar. She was nervous the whole time. Before that I'd considered asking her out to dinner. I never have.

Noi's one of the lotus blossoms that floats on the surface of the city. One of thousands, tens of thousands. It's people that give a city its life, its depth, its soul, and Bangkok's got plenty of them.

My cab driver, on the way into town, offers me some of those people. Thailand's a poor country; too many of its people are for rent. He's got brochures for massage parlors, nightclubs, escort agencies, bars, hotels, private clubs, guided tours, shows, girls, boys, transvestites, pre-op transsexuals, post-op transsexuals, hermaphrodites, you name it. But I want to get to the hotel, take a shower, maybe a nap. General Tran's driver is picking me up at eight.

I'm waiting out front when the black Mercedes pulls up. I've been talking with the Indian tailor whose shop is next door. He wants to make me a suit, two suits for the price of one when I tell him no. His family also owns a condom factory. Maybe I know a distributor in Hong Kong? I don't.

The driver, a small man with quick hands and a heavily muscled neck that squats on top of a bright orange track suit, hands me a note. "Welcome, Mr. Sharp. If you have no objection, my driver will bring you to Chao Phaya, where I will greet you. I think you will enjoy it."

It takes forty-five minutes to get there. I try making small talk with the driver, but I just get grunts in return. I can't really blame him.

Driving in all this traffic would be enough to reduce me to the same. We take the bridge by the Royal Palace over the river to Thonburi. It's lit with a supernova of small, twinkling bulbs for a festival. It's bright enough that I wish I had my sunglasses. The driver's wearing his, but he's been wearing them all along anyhow.

Ten minutes past the bridge we turn into the driveway of a twelve-story building clad in gold reflective tiles and topped with huge neon letters in Thai. Two Hollywood premiere-type spotlights criss-cross the front, bouncing blindingly back off the glistening surface. We curve around to the side, stop, and a very tall white man in a purple tuxedo opens the car door for me.

I step out blinking and a heavy metal door swings out. The white guy gestures me toward it with an open palm. Inside there is a podium, behind which is a much taller than usual Thai woman. She's wearing a rich, burgundy dress that looks as if it simply fell around her like a mist and a headset with a microphone set in front of thick lips that match the dress. She steps out from behind it and hands me five fingers. They're cool and dry, along with a faint whiff of a light citrus perfume. Her presence is refreshing, like a fine, cooling fog has been spritzed into the air around me. Her voice is soft but clear, I'm not sure if I'm hearing it or if it's telepathy.

"Mr. Sharp, welcome. General Tran awaits you in his suite. Please forgive your arrival by the side entrance. We do not often have Caucasian guests and unfortunately a few of our Asian guests are, I am so very sorry to say, prejudiced."

They can hate me for all I care at the moment. My libido's been on the fritz lately, but I'm not dead. Too soon she takes back her hand and uses it to point me in the direction of an elevator. It opens as I approach. Another tall white guy, this one in a cream yellow tuxedo, is standing at attention by the panel of buttons. As soon as I'm in, the doors close and he pushes twelve. He has a broad back that doesn't invite conversation.

"Helluva place, huh? I guess they don't get too many of us white guys. What're you doing working here?"

I can't see his front, but I guess it doesn't want to talk any more than his back does. We ride up in silence. The doors open and he waves a hand at me to leave. I do and am greeted by a woman who looks like the twin of the one downstairs, only she's sheathed in translucent, shimmering white. There's a halo of light around her. I can't tell if it's emanating from inside the dress or from down the hall behind her.

There's a familiar haze entering my brain. It's obscuring the introspection I've been afflicted with the past few months. Mike warned me to be cautious around General Tran. None of this is helping. Maybe that's the idea.

"Welcome, Mr. Sharp. I am Thanee. I will take you to the general, but please, if there is anything at all that you would like, please do ask. It is my pleasure to ensure that you have a lovely stay with us."

I stammer in reply. I don't even know what I say. I'm sure it's stupid. She has a tinkling little laugh, it bubbles into my head. She leans in to take my hand, which she clasps to her breasts as her lips follow her laugh to my ears, lightly tickling them.

"Please, do not concern yourself about anything, Mr. Sharp. Whatever you wish, you have only to ask."

At the moment I can't think of anything. I'd be happy standing here like this for a while. Maybe a long while. But she kisses me softly on the cheek, her lips lingering a breath or two longer than they might with an elderly relative, then turns to lead me down the hall.

It's a long hall, deeply carpeted, with light gray walls and warm pools of light that seem to well up in front of us, then recede when we pass. We walk by three doors on each side before coming to the door at the end. I notice a small video camera high in the corner where the wall meets the ceiling. We stand under it briefly and then there's a soft click and the door cracks open.

Thanee pushes it all the way open and steps inside, gesturing for me to go ahead. I can feel her close behind as I enter through a short hall and into a very large room. The first thing I see is Bangkok, spread out before me under its blanket of smog. Twinkling red, green, white and yellow lights seem to move in erratic patterns, like fireflies flittering through a swamp. It makes my eyes glaze over. You don't get a lot of high, big views of this city, and this is one of the best.

I pull my focus back into the room and look around. The room is enormous. Directly in front of me is a "conversation pit;" two sofas and four plush armchairs arranged in a semicircle around a coffee table set with a botanical garden's worth of tropical flowers, platters of artfully carved fruit, small bowls of nuts and a couple of bottles of champagne in buckets.

Far off to the right, in an alcove surrounded on three sides by floor-to-ceiling windows is a formal dining table, set for royalty that might drop in for dinner. To the left, across a ballroom-sized, highly-polished dance floor set with a dazzling inlay of tropical hardwoods, is a large, magnificent Chinese silk screen, finely embroidered with a graphic orgy scene. It's big enough that I can easily make out the details.

There's only one man in the picture, a trim but muscular, almond-colored man with jade green Asian eyes and a wisp of a mustache. He's got *nagas* tattooed up each leg, their hoods spreading from his hips to embrace him on both sides, their tongues flicking out to nearly meet around his belly button. He is being attended to by a dozen women of different races and sizes, all beautiful and all faintly Asian. He's got a huge penis, not quite comically so, but just short of that. It's being lovingly ministered to by a jet-black woman with teenage-boy fantasy curves, long curly hair and perfectly oval eyes. She's being assisted by a Scandinavian ice-princess and a porn magazine's notion of Mata Hari. The other women are amusing themselves and each other within reach of the man in the middle. There's a soft bubbling sound and indistinct voices coming from behind the screen.

I've never seen anything like this. Never even imagined it. It's a dreamscape, the ultimate playroom built for a horny billionaire. It makes me feel small, a little timid. Part of me's thinking, 'this guy's got too much money.' And another is thinking, 'I wish I was rich.'

I walk toward the screen. It's something to focus on, to help me catch my bearings. I'm admiring the work and wondering what to say about it if anybody asks my opinion, when the man in the tapestry steps out from behind it wearing mirrored sunglasses, a plush black robe that looks as if it's made from the finest raw silk, and a grin.

"Ah, Mr. Sharp, I am glad that you have arrived. Please forgive my informality, but I came to know the ways of Americans while I was in the army. Perhaps I am mistaken, but I am under the impression that you do not object."

I stick out a hand to shake. "No problem, General. This is an incredible place. I've never seen anything like it. It's a bit overwhelming."

"Thank you; perhaps later I will have Thanee give you a tour. Please now, let us sit and talk for a few moments. What is your pleasure to drink?" He gestures toward the conversation pit.

I ask for a vodka on the rocks and by the time the general and I sit down a silver bucket with a chilled bottle of Stoli Cristall has been set down beside me, a cut crystal glass and a small silver ice chest on the table in front of me. I could grow to like this.

The general, seated with one leg crossed over the other at the knee, his tattooed legs exposed nearly to the thigh, is so at ease in his loose robe that I feel rude for being dressed.

"Mr. Sharp, Ray, if I might, our mutual friend Mike speaks very highly of you."

"We go back a few years. He's a good guy, a great reporter."

"Yes, but perhaps a little too ethical for my tastes. I would like very much to be his host. I have no desire to corrupt him, certainly no need to, but he does not see this as I do."

I can't think of anything to say to that, so I shrug my shoulders.

"You were once also a journalist, were you not, Ray? Were you also such a paragon of virtue?"

"I don't know that I'd call it that, General, but I suppose so, yeah. It always ends up being more trouble than not if you aren't."

"But now you are no longer with the press, so you are willing to accept my hospitality. I suppose in a sense, you are here as Mike's surrogate."

I raise my glass. "I guess you could say that. Here's to Mike. My new work is different."

"You are now an investigator, I understand. What do you Americans say, a 'private dick'? I have read Raymond Chandler. It is most amusing. Is that what your work is like? Do you carry a gat?"

"No gat. I do corporate investigation, due diligence, nothing as exciting as what Marlowe got up to."

"Yes, Mike let me know that you have some questions, perhaps a favor to ask of me. I do not wish to seem rude, it is perhaps not very Asian of me to be so direct, but we should talk of these things now so that we can then put them aside and enjoy our evening."

"I'm working on an investigation that has led me to look into the smuggling of Cambodian antiques. Mike tells me you might know about that."

He puts his glass down, uncrosses his legs and looks at me for several long tense moments. Mike had cautioned me, and the way he's looking at me makes me think Mike was right.

He picks his glass of champagne back up, takes a slow pull at it with his eyes closed and puts it down again before speaking. His voice is measured, firm and neutral.

"Can I be certain, Ray, that you are not investigating my business?"

"To be honest, I don't know. I'm investigating the activities of a Chinese company that sells stolen Cambodian art in Hong Kong and probably ships it other places, too. I don't know if you're involved in that or not. If you are, you're part of my investigation. If you aren't, I'm just looking into this one company. Maybe it's an old habit from journalism, but I want to learn everything I can. If

I find out enough, even facts that don't seem like they're going to be important, I get a better picture of what's going on."

"I appreciate your candor, Ray. I know the company you are investigating. They are one of my competitors. I have no objection to assisting you in this matter. What is it that you would like to know?"

"I'm trying to learn as much as I can about the trade, how the pieces are stolen, how they're smuggled, by who, for how much, who the customers are, what's being done to stop it. Once I know all that I'll try to trace it to the company I'm investigating."

"I can certainly add to your picture. But let us not dwell upon this tonight. It will be better attended to tomorrow. In the morning I will send one of my associates to pick you up at your hotel, she will answer your questions and take you on a tour."

"That'll be great, thank you." He looks at me like he expects me to continue the conversation, but it sounded like he just ended it. "Is this your apartment?"

"It is one of the perquisites of ownership. I am the main shareholder in this establishment. My home, where my wife and children live, is in the countryside between here and Ayutthya, Thailand's old capital. You will pass it tomorrow. If you care to, I will instruct my associate to bring you to my home for lunch. I have my own art collection there. I imagine you will find it of interest."

"I imagine I would, but I don't want to be any trouble."

"It is no trouble. I will let my wife know that you will be her guest for lunch. I can, of course, trust in your discretion regarding anything we may indulge in or that you witness here."

It's hard to imagine that he's the sort to be overly concerned with what his wife, or anybody else for that matter, knows of his business or not, but I'm not about to rat anybody out for no good reason. I lift my glass in a silent agreeable toast between us guys.

"It is settled then, Ray. Now, let us not speak of business any more tonight. Perhaps you would care for some dinner?"

I am hungry and I have the distinct impression that General Tran is not a person I should say "no" to unless it is absolutely essential. As we get up to go to the dining table, he suggests that I might wish to change into more comfortable clothes for the remainder of the evening. His suggestions have the ring of command, polite and soft-spoken, but still an order. I nod my assent.

Thanee materializes by my side and takes my hand. She leads me behind the screen where there is a large Jacuzzi. Three naked women lounge in its froth. They look very much like the black, blond and Asian women pictured on the screen. They smile invitingly as I pass by. The black woman licks her lips and winks. I try not to stumble as Thanee tugs lightly on my arm to pull me along.

We go down a long hall that doesn't seem to have any doors. We stop about halfway. Thanee faces the wall, then waves a hand over her head. A large panel glides silently open and we step into a room. It's dark at first but the entire ceiling slowly illuminates with electric twinkling stars and a bright crescent moon, casting a beautiful, calming-to-the-eye glow.

There's an enormous, much larger than king-sized, heart-shaped bed with a blood red, raw silk cover and a dozen or more satin pillows. A wet bar, crystal bottles with different colored liquids glistening in them, is set into the headboard. At the foot of the bed is a small Jacuzzi, a light steam drifting off its surface. A deluxe dentist's, or perhaps gynecologist's chair, covered with soft beige leather, is in a corner of the room. There is a door open through which there's a large bathroom, all glistening exposed plumbing, a walk-in shower built for five or six friends and an intimate tub for no more than three or four.

Thanee slides open a closet filled with robes and asks me to pick one. There's a variety of colors and sizes, some in fine silk, others in deep pile terrycloth. I select a long, blue silk robe. She takes it from the hanger and lays it on the bed.

I'm not at all sure of the protocol, but I sit down on the bed and bend to untie my shoes. She stops me, kneels in front of me and takes over. It makes me feel uncomfortable and I put out a hand to stop her and pull her upright.

"No, please, Mr. Sharp; this is my job and my pleasure." I tamp down my feelings and let her get on with it.

When she's done with my shoes she moves up to undo my belt and unzip my pants. I stand and she finishes undressing me, her hands pausing along the way to caress and stroke me into a state that's going to be embarrassing unless it subsides before I walk back out to the dining table. I enjoy it for a little while, even though I'm thinking I shouldn't. I pull her hands away.

"That feels great, but maybe later okay?"

"Whatever you wish, Mr. Sharp."

"I think we're getting to know each other a little better than that. Call me Ray."

I put on the robe and avoid looking at her and the bed and shower and bathtub and the strange chair and try to think about something else. Cambodian art sort of works but quickly gets me thinking about the *apsaras* and that doesn't work at all so I force thoughts of Giles, the dreadful Brit Susan introduced me to, into my head. That's enough to make anyone flaccid.

We walk back into the main room, past the women in the Jacuzzi who I avoid looking at. General Tran is seated at the table. I sit down across from him. Thanee glides away.

"I hope you don't mind, Ray, I have taken the liberty of ordering for us."

"No problem. It looks fantastic."

And it does. The array of Thai salads and seafood dishes tastes wonderful, too. It takes a lot of willpower to not gorge myself. When we're finished the general pushes away from the table and returns to his leather armchair. I sit down across from him.

I say "no" to a cigar, "yes" to a brandy. The general offers other things to smoke as well—opium, hash, pot. I imagine if I asked for a hit or two of crack he'd have that as well. I thank him and turn it all down.

"Brandy's fine, thanks. I don't like to mix my poisons."

We make small talk while his cigar burns down. He asks me a lot about myself and my background and politely turns away my queries about him. After twenty or so minutes all I know is that he is from Hue, was a general in the South Vietnamese army and left the country after the fall of Saigon. He's now a Thai citizen and owns many businesses.

"It is good for a man to indulge himself; do you not think so, Ray?"

"Sure, builds character I guess."

"I am a man of many, what others might call vices but I prefer to call indulgences. It is my pleasure to share them with my friends and associates."

"That's very kind of you."

"When you arrived you were admiring my tapestry. Perhaps you thought it fanciful. I assure you it is quite realistic in every way. I am very proud of it. I hope it does not sound like bragging, but I am very well endowed for a Vietnamese man. I have a certain, reputation. But please, I want you to feel comfortable, in no way, how do I put this delicately, intimidated."

I'm not. Not by that at least. Is this his idea of guy talk? Are we bonding? Am I supposed to whip mine out now? I don't give a damn how big his dick is. I take a long sip of my brandy.

"Now, Ray, if you have no objection, I should like to offer you whatever else you may desire."

I know I should pipe up with something, a long-percolating fantasy I can tell him about so that he can make it come true, but I'm at a loss for words.

The general raises his hand then turns it to point behind me. I turn around to look.

There's a lineup of a dozen or so women. They must have padded up quietly while we were talking. It could be the cream of the crop of the Miss Universe pageant. They are all races, all shapes, all sizes, all stunning and all nude.

His voice is soft, somewhere near my left ear. "Please, Ray, you may choose whoever and however many you desire. Life can be magnificent if you permit it."

"Um, I, I scarcely know what to say, where to start."

"There is no need for embarrassment, Ray, not about anything. If you prefer, I have handsome men, beautiful boys also available. If you prefer something more esoteric, I can cater to all desires, all whims. Life without indulgence is not life."

I should feel like a kid in a candy store but I don't. My little head wants to shout "whoopee, I'll take 'em all" and jump on in. But my bigger one's talking louder. It's saying that the general is accustomed to owning things and I don't want him owning part of me. And there's that damn nagging voice, the one that's been pestering me the past few months about whether I'm part of this particular problem or part of its solution. The whole thing makes me nervous.

But I can't simply say "no thanks." He's not going to like that. Mike was right, I need to keep him happy.

Thanee is standing third from the left. She looks like an *apsara*, but better because she's not hewn from stone. She smiles at me and shifts a hip slightly in my direction.

I turn to look at Tran. "General, your hospitality overwhelms me. This is a fantasy come true. But I am somewhat old-fashioned, perhaps a little shy. I hope you do not mind if I pick one and ask her to come with me back to my own hotel."

He looks genuinely disappointed, but he can't force me into an orgy, can he?

"Ray, of course I will respect your wishes, but are you certain? What man would not want to have your choice at this moment?"

"I know, General, and I appreciate it. Perhaps I am simply a little tired and I will feel like a fool later on, but if you don't mind I really would prefer to simply take Thanee with me to my hotel."

He shrugs. It looks like a gesture he picked up from the Americans during the war. He waves away the rest of the women and Thanee takes my hand to lead me back to my clothes in the back bedroom. While I change she assures me that it will be fine with her if we stay, if we have sex with other women as well. I do feel like a fool, but I stick to my guns.

She leads me back out to the side of the Jacuzzi and leaves me there while she goes to change into her clothes. The general's in the bubbles, surrounded by all the women I didn't pick.

"Are you certain you will not join us, Ray?"

I apologize and tell him that I will be happy to another time, just not tonight. That seems to be the polite way of saying "no."

He shrugs again and hoists himself up onto the edge of the frothy pool. Before a redhead with lips like two lush slices of melon swoops down on it, I catch a glimpse of his equipment. It is big. Huge even. If anything, the tapestry slightly understates its size. I'm surprised. I always thought that guys who talked about how big their dicks are were lying. He smiles at me and lies back to enjoy himself. I walk around to the other side of the screen where Thanee's waiting, dressed in simple tight blue jeans and a black t-shirt that says, "WWJJD?" There's very small writing under the big letters. I step up close to read it. "What Would Joan Jett Do?"

I don't know. I'm not sure what I'm going to do either.

CHAPTER TWELVE

Stuck in traffic, about twenty minutes away from my hotel, I tell Thanee that she doesn't have to come up to my room. She's welcome to drop me off and have the car take her home.

She looks surprised. She sticks an exaggerated pout on her face. Then she looks thoughtful.

"I know that you find me attractive. I can see how you look at me. Why?"

I'm not sure why. I find her very attractive and it's not like I haven't been with prostitutes before.

"I don't know. There're a lot of reasons. It's complicated."

She puts a hand on my knee. "Ray, please, if you want me to go, I will go, but maybe it will make a problem for me. The general wants me to be with you. He is a man who always gets what he wants. He can be cruel if he does not. Little things, things you might never guess, can make him very angry. Please, may I go with you to your room? I will sleep on the floor if you want."

She knows I don't want. I know I don't want. If she does come to my room we both know what's going to happen. Or what I'll want to happen.

"Okay."

She makes me want to talk. Maybe it's that her English is so good. We settle into my room. I take the chair and a tall glass of vodka and ice. She sits with a Coke on the edge of the bed.

"Where'd you learn your English? It's excellent."

"Thank you, but I am still learning. I go to university, to Chulalongkorn."

"I'm impressed." And I am, that's Thailand's most prestigious university. It's hard to get into. It's here in Bangkok, not far from my hotel. "What are you studying?"

"Business, but I only started a year ago."

"Please don't be offended. Tell me to mind my own business if you want, but why?"

"Why am I a prostitute? What is a nice girl like me doing in a…" Her laugh blurts out like a hiccup and then relaxes. Her whole body eases and she leans back a little on the bed. "American men always ask me that. They don't really want to know. Do you really want to know? I think maybe you do. Why?"

"I was in love with a woman who worked as a prostitute. I'm interested."

"What happened? Do you still love her?"

"Yeah, I do. But it ended badly and I don't know if I'll ever see her again."

"Okay, Ray, come here and sit next to me. I won't bite you, I promise. I will tell you my story, but only if you tell me yours after."

It's my turn to laugh. I get up from the chair and move to the bed. When I sit, she throws her legs over mine. She reaches for my glass and takes a swig of vodka, screwing up her face when it hits her throat.

"I am Khmer, from Cambodia. My family is dead. They were killed by the Khmer Rouge. Other people took me when I was a baby to Thailand, to a refugee camp. I lived there until I was eight years old. One day a rich and powerful man came to the camp, a Vietnamese man. It was General Tran. When he left he took five girls and five boys with him. He took us to his house in Ayutthaya. We lived there. He gave us everything, he sent us to school. They were like my brothers, my sisters.

"He was very gentle, very kind. When I became twelve he came to my room one night and even then he was gentle and kind. When I became eighteen he came to my room for the last time. Afterward he told me that he would send me to university in any subject I want, and then when I graduate I will work for him, in one of his companies. But I must do what he wants me to do, work how he wants me to work.

"It is not bad. My life is so much better than it would have been. I have so many more opportunities. Without the general, without this, I would be nothing. Only a simple, uneducated, poor orphan Khmer girl. I would be living on a farm, a poor farm, and by now I would have three or four children, if they lived, and I would know nothing of the world and have no chance to ever know the world.

"Maybe to you, a Western man who was born with opportunity, with freedom, maybe to you this sounds strange, terrible. But I have a good life. I like my life. It is interesting and filled with hope and even fun. Can you understand that?"

I can. It doesn't mean I have to like it. The older I get, the more I see of the world, the more there is that I don't like, but the less there is that I think I can do about it. I can do little things. Maybe, if I'm lucky, I can contribute my little part to something big. But then I worry about whether or not it's going to backfire. The big things often do.

"I can understand that. I'm sorry you don't have more choices."

"But I don't. So I do not think about them. It would only make me sad to think about what I do not have. I like better to think of what I do have.

"Now what story will you tell me, Ray? You do not have the woman you love; do you think about her often?"

I take a big gulp of my vodka before answering. The burning in my throat brings a bitter smile to my face.

"Yeah, I do, and it makes me sad. I wish I could be like you but I can't. I think too much about things I can't do anything about.

"Her name's Irina, she's Russian. I met her in Indonesia where she was working as a prostitute. We fell in love."

"Were you her customer?"

"The first night, not after that. There was something very strong, very deep between us. It's hard to even say what it was because there was so much of it, it was so complicated."

"What happened?"

"I moved to Hong Kong for a job. She couldn't come with me unless we were married because it's nearly impossible for Russian women to get visas for Hong Kong. But we wanted to be free; we didn't want to be married."

"Why? When you love someone, why do you want to be free? I don't understand this about Western people."

"I'd been married before. I wasn't very good at it. I cheated on my wife all the time. I kept hoping she was cheating on me too, it would've only been fair. I never found out if she was."

"So, you are what the Thai bargirls call, "butterfly.""

"You could say that. And I liked it. I didn't see anything wrong with it."

"Okay, so you are like many men. It is not difficult to understand why a man wants to be free. But what of your Russian woman, Irina?"

"She wasn't all that different from me. She likes having sex with a lot of different people. That's why she became a prostitute. She needed money and thought, why not get paid to do something she liked doing? She makes a lot better living at it than she could at almost anything else she'll ever have a chance to do. She's also cynical about men; she knows us too well.

"We both thought that if we were married, or if we lived together even, sooner or later there'd be problems."

"But you are not together now. What were the problems?"

"That's a long and terrible story. I tried to help some people in Macau, a Russian woman and her lover. They wanted to get her out of her contract with a pimp. One of Irina's best friends, a woman she'd known since they were children, tried to help me. She got killed. Other people got killed, too. I had to kill a couple myself to try and save a woman. I don't know if I did anybody any good, or what was my fault or not. Irina blamed me for her friend's death. She didn't want to see me after that."

"How long has it been?"

"A few months, four."

"Maybe she will change her mind. Maybe you will see her again."

"I don't know. I hope so."

"Is this why you did not want me to come to your room?"

"Part of it, but it's more than that."

"Is it because I am a prostitute? After what happened with your girlfriend and her friend, you feel sorry for prostitutes and do not want to have sex with them?"

"That's part of it, too."

"You do not have to give me money."

"Tran's already paid you to be here. Would you be here if he hadn't?"

"I don't know. Maybe."

"Probably not. You're a young, beautiful, intelligent woman, why would you want to be in a hotel room with a guy in his forties who you just met? Wouldn't you rather be out with friends at a disco? Whatever it is that you college kids do here."

"I don't like discos, they are too loud. I like older men. I feel more secure with them. They are not so stupid as young men. And they are better lovers."

"Thanee, I don't want to insult you, but don't you think you've been messed up by your life? Is this what you really want, or is it what you know? You were raped from the age of twelve by the man who was like a father to you."

She puts her hand over my mouth before I can say anything more and sets her expression into neutral.

"Please, Ray, do not talk to me about psychology. I know who I am, what I am. I know the things that made me this way. My life is better, it is happier when I do not ask questions about these things. I live with who I am, not who I might be in a different life."

Is it that fucking *sanùk*, or is it practical? Would a few years on a shrink's couch make her life better or worse? It's clear that she can't afford analysis, in more ways than one. I feel bad for having asked.

It's been a long day and I'm tired. I hold her hand for a little while, not speaking, not knowing what to say. It takes an effort to not feel sad, or mad. I'm glad she's here, I think. She's smart, interesting, I'm happy for her company. But it's also confusing that she's here. She's sexy as hell, but I feel protective of her, like an older brother or an uncle, and not that kind of uncle.

I get up to take a shower. I tell her to make herself comfortable. Part of me wants her to come in, to slip into the spray with me. I want her hands around me, turning me to her, rubbing our wet, soapy bodies against each other. I don't want to be thinking about all the other reasons why that shouldn't happen. I lock the door to the bathroom behind me.

The hot water pelting on me settles my nerves. It doesn't help to make up my mind about anything, but at least it calms me down. I stay in the shower a long time, letting it beat down on my head.

When I finish and go back into the bedroom the lights are off, the room is dimly lit by the glow from the city outside the window. She's on the floor at the foot of the bed. She's taken the extra blanket and a pillow from the closet. She's on her side, facing away from me. There's no way I'm going to let her sleep on the floor, but I don't want to wake her if she's already asleep. I speak softly.

"Thanee, are you awake?"

She rolls over to look at me. She parts her lips but doesn't say anything. Her eyes rake me up and down and I feel a little faint looking at her.

"You don't need to sleep on the floor. It's a big bed. I won't bite." Her eyes sparkle and her lips broaden into a smile. I laugh, remembering how it wasn't too long ago that she asked me to sit next to her on the bed and said that she didn't bite either.

"What if I want you to bite?"

"We'll see." I slip off the towel I've got wrapped around my waist and get under the covers on the bed.

Thanee rises from the floor, an *apsara* in warm flesh, coursing with blood, hormones that make me dizzy radiating out from her. It's only a few steps but she makes a brief erotic dance out of moving to my side of the bed. I'm on my side, fighting my desire and feeling like an idiot for doing it. She pulls off the covers. She reaches a hand out and caresses my thigh, eases her long, graceful, strong fingers around to the inside of it and gently pulls me over onto my back.

She stands above me, looking down at me. I'm looking back up at her, past her perfect, small, softly rounded breasts and taut nipples, up her long, smooth neck, to the full redness of her lips, into her eyes that seem to crackle with the electricity in the air between us.

She floats down to me, to lie on top of me. Her lips, wet and a little sticky, burrow into the nape of my neck. Her stomach, with a sheen of light sweat, suctions a seal against mine. Her legs slide around me, sinuously entangling themselves with mine. Her crotch, nested with fine, damp, silken hair, settles firmly around mine. My hardening cock presses its way up to rub against her, parting and swelling her moistening lips, sliding along the outside of them.

We lie there like that. It seems like a long time. We aren't moving, we're barely breathing. I'm not even sure if we're awake or not.

Finally, I don't know how I do it. I don't know why. It's not at all what I want to do, not at all what my body's telling me to do. But I roll onto my side, easing her off me onto the bed next to me. I turn onto my stomach. I can't do it. Well, I could, but I won't.

"Go to sleep. Goodnight."

She lightly strokes my side with a fingernail. "Why? I already tell you it is no problem."

"It is for me."

"You think too much about unimportant things."

I'm too tired to discuss it, too tired to give it any further thought. I take her hand, raise it to my mouth and kiss it lightly. I put it back between us and hold onto it. "Have good dreams. Goodnight." I turn my head away from her and it takes me a long time to subside, to settle into welcome sleep.

| | CHAPTER **THIRTEEN** | |

I t'd probably be faster, and surely a lot nicer, to take a boat to Ayutthya. Not that I have much to complain about. The Mercedes is very plush and Thanee turns out to be the associate of General Tran in charge of my tour. This morning, changed out of her t-shirt and jeans into a demure traditional dress, she's all business. It's like last night hadn't happened.

What did happen? Did I make a mistake, or did I do something smart for a change? I'm not really worrying about it and I'm in a good mood. I'd probably be singing in the car if I wasn't listening to her explain what it is we're going to see.

"Ayutthya is the center of the smuggling. It was the second capital of Thailand for close to four hundred years and it has many temples and palaces. Because of that it has a long tradition of stone cutting and sculpture. A lot of the stolen Thai art comes from there, and many of the fakes, both the ones that are honestly sold as replicas and the ones that are sold as real antiques.

"We are going to meet with the family of *Khun* Thongchai. They are the greatest sculptors in the area. It is a tradition with their family."

"Are they legit?"

"Yes and no."

"How can they be both?"

"I will let *Khun* Thongchai explain. You'll see."

"But if it's illegal, why's he willing to talk to me?"

"They are protected, and you have been sent by the general. It is no problem."

I turn away and watch the roadside. It's a long way before we're out of the city and it happens gradually. The buildings grow fewer and smaller, the private houses get bigger. There's more land, glistening with water on its surface and green shoots of rice and the marsh vegetables that are popular. The road is heavy and slow with trucks, ox-carts, people on bicycles, pedestrians. There's a lot more open space in the countryside, but it's as busy as the city.

I turn back to Thanee, reach out and take her hand. "What are you doing later? When we get back."

"Why?"

"I'd like to spend the evening with you."

"Why? I think you do not want me. Last night…"

"I do want you, but I don't know if I can. It's too complicated, too wrapped up in what happened before with Irina and Sasha. It's like you're one of those beautiful stolen *apsaras* and as much as I might want you, you're not mine to have."

"That is stupid. If I am with you, it is because I want also to be with you."

"Because you want to, or because the general wants you to? You're not really free to make that choice, are you?"

"I told you, no psychology. You want to make love with me, okay, we will make love. You want only to buy me dinner, maybe take me to a movie or shopping, up to you. But I will not go with you if you keep asking me stupid questions."

I shut up and look back out the window. We keep holding hands, even though mine's getting clammy.

It takes us about two hours to drive the fifty miles to a large iron gate flanked by two enormous limestone *nagas*. Our driver lowers his window, leans into a small squawk box and coughs out a few words. The gates swing open and we crunch across the gravel into the compound.

Everything's dusted in fine white powder. There are statues everywhere. Some of them look new, some old, a few are complete, many are in ruins. There's a reclining Buddha that's about thirty feet long, half of it looks ancient, the other half like it was made yesterday. *Nagas* slither around the yard, rearing their hooded heads, baring their fangs. Statues of a man, maybe it's Buddha, stand spreading a cape or maybe wings behind them like an antique superhero. There's a crumbling pile of blocks on one side, two gigantic heads of Buddha rising from the middle of it, piece by piece.

There're dogs too, big ones, a roiling pack of maybe a dozen of them. But they're alive, barking and growling and following the car as we roll up to the house. The driver honks the horn. That doesn't disturb the snarling brutes, but it does bring someone out the door and onto the front porch, who yells at them. They immediately all lie down where they are, eyes tuned to the car doors, ears cocked in the direction of their master, but silent.

The driver opens his door and steps out. He isn't immediately set upon and eaten, so I figure it's safe, at least for now. Before he can do it for us I open our door and carefully step out. Thanee steps out with me, sticking close by my side. The dogs make her nervous. I've always liked dogs. I'm not sure about these. They make me nervous, too.

The man on the porch yells "welcome" and beckons us. We pick our way gingerly through the pack, every dog of which moves to sniff at us as we do. By the time we're through them they've no doubt memorized our scent.

The house we're approaching looks like it was bought from the set of "Gone With the Wind." The short, dark man on the front steps, dressed in a colorful batik sarong and matching head scarf with bright yellow flip flops on his feet, looks out of place.

As we get closer Thanee bows her head slightly, slows her pace to a shuffle and places her palms and fingers together in front of her in the greeting that Thais call a *wai*. She climbs the steps toward the man, bowing lower as she goes so as to keep her head below the level of his. I stand back, down a couple of steps, figuring that way I won't have to bow until I know the protocol.

While she and the man paddle salutations back and forth, I look him over. He's short and slight, no more than a few inches over five feet and small boned. His skin is sun darkened and leathery. He has several large, ropy scars across his bared belly and chest. His eyes are narrow slits with bright stars shining out of them. His shoulders are huge and muscular, looking like they belong on a much larger man or a body builder.

And his hands are amazing. They look as if they've been taken from someone else and sewn in place. They're as broad as baseball mitts, with long narrow fingers that seem to move independently, like ten small, writhing snakes. They've been beat up, too. They glisten with drops of dried blood from cuts and scratches. Scars and lines give the map of them as much relief as the twisted and broken knuckles and long, pointed fingernails.

Thanee turns to me and introduces *Khun* Thongchai. I reach out to shake his hand, but he throws me a *wai* instead. I've seen enough people do it that it's no problem to throw one back.

We follow him inside where overhead fans churn the atmosphere at near lift-off speed, forcing ice-cold conditioned air down on us. It was oppressively hot and humid outside in the short distance between the car and here. It's just as oppressively arctic in the sitting room. There's a decorative blanket neatly arranged over the armrest of one of the sofas. I wonder if it would be rude to wrap myself in it. I don't, but I sit very close to Thanee, who scowls at me when I do, but doesn't move away.

Khun Thongchai sits across from us on a beautifully carved limestone stool, a throne. The chill wind doesn't appear to bother him. A very old woman, stooped, her back curved like a longbow tensed to fire an arrow, wrinkled enough for three or four old women who'd been sitting in baths all day, shuffles in with a tray of fresh, icy lemonade that she sets down in front of us.

It's impolite to take a drink before our host. I'm hoping he doesn't have one. I'm hoping he sends for hot coffee, tea or steaming bowls of soup. But he lifts his frosty glass, smiles at us over its brim, takes a long draught and smacks his lips in satisfaction. I take a polite sip and fight off the shivers.

He speaks to Thanee and she scoots a little further from me on the sofa before turning in my direction. "*Khun* Thongchai welcomes you. He says that since you come with an introduction from the General, he will answer any of your questions. He apologizes that he does not speak English and hopes that you will not object to using me as your translator."

I assure him that's fine. I'm sorry I don't speak Thai. Perhaps he could simply describe his business to me, the different types of work he does, how he gets the antiques that he deals in, who his customers are and how he ships his products.

He talks to Thanee for a long time while I concentrate on trying to stay warm. My brain isn't up to the task and I'm worried my teeth are going to start chattering. Finally he stops and Thanee turns back to me.

"His family have been stone carvers for many generations, maybe five hundred years or more. They have always worked here, in this compound. The family did work for many of the temples and palaces in this area. *Khun* Thongchai says that in the past his family has made many of the antiques that are now so valuable, and that their work today is no different.

"The family still carves stone for temples and also for private collectors. In several more generations these sculptures will be the ancient artifacts of tomorrow. Some collectors want new pieces to look old, and they can do that, too. They can make them so that even experts are fooled by them.

"Sometimes they repair old sculptures. They will piece them back together, add the missing pieces and blend all the work together so that it looks like it was never broken. Many of their clients come to them with only a head, perhaps a head of Buddha, but they want the head put onto a body. That is no problem also.

"They have other clients who come to them wanting a copy made of a sculpture. *Khun* Thongchai says that he thinks some of them do that for security reasons; they will exhibit the copy but keep the original in a much safer location. He did not say, but I know that some collectors and smugglers will take the copy to the government's Fine Arts Department to obtain a certificate stating that it is a copy, not an original. That is necessary to ship a piece out of the country. Once they have the certificate, they will substitute the original for the copy. It is a very rare customs official who can tell the difference."

"Where do his customers come from?"

She turns to him and asks. He laughs and hacks out a short word.

"Everywhere."

"How do they find out about him?"

He starts to answer before she can even ask the question. Maybe he does speak some English.

"They are collectors who hear from other collectors. He has customers who are sent to him by the shops in River City. A shop might have a customer who wants something special, and the shop will contact him."

"When he gets real artifacts from Cambodia, how does he get them?"

They talk a while longer this time and I go back to trying not to freeze to death while they do. I've buried my head into my shoulders and am facing down, my eyes squeezed shut, when Thanee taps me on the shoulder.

"They come by truck over the border. Sometimes by boat. Sometimes the government catches a shipment but when that happens it only takes more money to get it back from the border police or the army."

Khun Thongchai suddenly gets up. He drains the rest of his lemonade and motions us out of our seats, speaking to Thanee.

"He wants to know if you would like a tour of his workshops and his storage areas."

I would, of course. He *wais* the both of us, then claps his hands and yells. The old lady comes to pick up our glasses. With her is a boy, maybe twelve years old, slightly pudgy, dressed in baggy jeans and a Metallica t-shirt. He's the youngest son. He mumbles at us in schoolboy English that his name is Tom. He'll take us on our tour. *Khun* Thongchai walks us to the door, then disappears back into the house when we step onto the porch.

The heat hits me like darts, pricking me all over, making my skin tingle and hurt. But it feels good, at least for a moment or two. Then I don't know if it's sweat or condensation but my whole body is suddenly wet under my clothes. I can feel rivulets of liquid cascading all over me, flooding my shoes so that they squish when I walk. No wonder people here wear sandals.

As soon as we step off the porch the pack of hounds has got us surrounded. They're all looking at Tom, waiting for his instructions. I reach down to scratch one of them behind its ears and it growls at me. I withdraw my hand, slowly. Tom smiles when that happens and reaches down to thump a couple of them on their sides. He tells Thanee and me to follow him and we do, the dogs circling silently around us as we move through the dusty yard.

We walk behind the house where there are what look like two large, sheetmetal-sided barns and a lotus pond. The dogs stay outside when we enter one of the barns.

It's a sculptor's studio, lit by floodlights on stands and a skylight running the length of the building. There are nine large pieces in various states of creation. Two of them, the body of a seated Buddha and what looks like it will be a large frieze, are slowly emerging from huge blocks of solid rock. Two middle-aged women are working on each with large chisels and wooden mallets, their silk headscarves wrapped down and around to cover their noses and mouths. Tom gestures at them.

"They are my aunties. My family only can do work here." He leads us past them to a large, solid table covered with smaller sculptures, sorted by type. He takes a place of pride at the top of the table, in front of a small thatch of *linga*, and stone blocks in the process of being carved into penises.

"I am learning to carve. I must start with the simple pieces, then later, when I learn more, maybe I can work with my father on the most beautiful."

He picks up one of the *linga*. It looks more like something you'd see in a sex shop than in an art gallery. It's too realistic, veins bulging along its sides, the head swollen and angry as if filled to bursting. "This is my favorite. But it is only for to practice. It is looking real, so my father say that it is not real, not real like the *linga* from Khmer." He hands it to me and I can see that it is finely carved. The boy's got a good future. I start to hand it to Thanee but he snatches it away, blushing and sputtering something before she can take it.

Tom shows us his father's carving area. There's a leather case of neatly ordered, delicate tools. There are small sanders and buffers and little drills and saws. There's only one piece, an *apsara* that is nearly complete, just the feet remain to be fashioned from the block of stone. To my untrained eye it looks as authentic and beautiful as any I've ever seen.

We walk past other works in progress and out the back of the building. As we approach the second barn a terrible acrid smell fires up our nostrils, causing our eyes to drip tears and a headache to start growing as fast as a grove of new bamboo. There's a box at the entry to the building. Tom opens it and hands us face masks and goggles. I put them on, but I'm not sure I want to go inside.

What's inside is hell, the old-fashioned one with fire and brimstone and vats of bubbling liquids. It's noisy, a loud constant roar like a violent wind and I can't see what's causing that. Thanee and I look at each other. She looks as unhappy about this as I feel.

Tom leans in close to us to yell. "This where make look old. Take bath in acid, burn in fire." He motions us further into the middle of it all. We follow him to stand next to a large, tall, ceramic cauldron with a fog of burning yellow vapor billowing off it. At its side is a statue of a standing Buddha, one of the ones with its arms spread out to its sides, looking a little like Batman. It's about seven feet tall, trussed up in chains that rise above it to a crane and pulley. Its head is duller and more pitted than its body.

Tom yells at us again. "Is Khmer Buddha. Head old, body new. We make body same as head."

He rotates a hand over his head and the Buddha slowly rises above us and moves into the acid mist. I can just make it out when it's centered over the vat and lowered. Then I can't see a thing, but I can hear it as it snaps, crackles, pops. It sounds like a barrage of small arms fire. It would make good sound effects for a war movie.

The fog roils up and boils toward us and Tom waves us away. We move back quick, maybe not quick enough. I'm coughing, my skin and lungs burning. It feels like the bamboo grove is about to burst out through my skull. Thanee's doing the same but she's also stumbling. She looks like she's about to collapse. I throw an arm around her and lead her as quickly as I can outside and far enough away from the building that the air clears.

She lies down on a patch of grass next to the lotus pond. Her chest is heaving; she's gasping for breath. If she was unconscious I'd be attempting artificial respiration, but she isn't. Her eyes are wide open, jetting streams of water. I try fanning her to get the air moving around her.

Tom comes to stand by her side. He looks faintly amused. I ask him if he can get her some water. He looks irritated but goes away and comes back quickly with a bottle that he hands me and I tilt to her lips. She sips from it, then reaches up a hand and pours some onto her eyes. I untuck my shirt and wipe her face with the tails. It's still a few minutes before she can sit up. I sit next to her, giving her something to lean on.

Tom squats next to us and when we look at him he simply points at the pond. We turn to look. It's beautiful. Lotus pods are beginning to erupt into blossom, ducks glide along the surface, a couple of tall, gangly-legged white birds are wading in the shallows. It's soothing to the eyes after the inferno we've been through.

"It's beautiful, Tom, great. What are those white birds?"

"No, look into water, deep, see."

I look again, past the surface. The water's murky and it's hard to see but there is something in there, something round on top. I shade my eyes against the little bit of glare, let them focus down. There's a face down there. A big, smiling face with heavily hooded eyes. It's startling and I shift my gaze away from it to the side and there's another one, this one's frowning.

I stand up and move closer to the edge of the pond, cup hands around my eyes and stare as deeply as I can. More faces look up at me through the murk and the vegetation. More heads are down there, large ones, too large to be human. They've all got different expressions. Everything from amused to upset, contemplative to lustful. There's at least a dozen of them.

Thanee has stood up and is hanging onto my arm for support, also looking into the water. I look at Tom. "What's that?"

"Buddha, many faces Buddha. Khmer, very old."

I've seen the pictures. They look like the heads at Angkor Thom, one of the famous temples in Cambodia, but I guess there're a lot of heads like that. They're big already, but the water magnifies them, broadening their expressions. They're trapped under there, imprisoned, no doubt waiting for a buyer to come and take them away to his house, his museum, some other prison. It seems like an odd place to hide them, if that's what they're doing there.

I've seen enough, seen as much as I can stomach for now. Tom and the dogs take Thanee and me back to the house, leaving us on the porch. We want to say goodbye and thanks to *Khun* Thongchai. We knock on the door and wait.

While we're waiting a truck pulls up in front. It looks like an army truck, but any identifying markings have been removed. Two men from inside, wearing unmarked fatigues and carrying AK-47s, pull aside the green canvas covering the back and jump to the ground. They take up positions at either side of the rear of the truck. A small man with a big pistol in a holster at his side gets out of the passenger side. He's dressed in what look like black pajamas with a red scarf peeking out from the collar.

When she sees him Thanee presses up close against me. She's shaking. I look down at her and she's looking down at the porch floor, but also at the man, furtively through heavily slitted eyes. She's obviously afraid. I lean in to her ear and whisper.

"What is it? Who's he?"

She stutters, something I haven't heard her do before, in a very low voice. "Kkkkhmer Rrrouge."

I pull her to the side as the man strides up the steps to the door. I'm looking straight at him and he doesn't seem to like that. He scowls at me, barks something that isn't Thai at Thanee. It must be Khmer. She presses herself deeper into my side, her eyes down, not looking at him at all.

The man's hand moves to the butt of the gun on his hip. It doesn't look like he's about to pull it, just that he wants us to know he can. He moves close to us to stand in front of the door. I can smell cologne on him, sweet and cloying. It overpowers the sour sweat that's coming off of Thanee.

I don't know what I can do. If I can do anything. If I should do anything. I'm not afraid of him for some reason. Maybe it's adrenalin. Maybe it's stupidity. But still, I'm frozen in place.

The door is opened by *Khun* Thongchai. He greets the man in the black pajamas with a very low *wai*. The man grunts something in response and walks past him into the house.

Khun Thongchai touches Thanee on the shoulder. She looks up at him as he says something fast and low to her in Thai. She looks at me.

"We must go now."

"Please tell *Khun* Thongchai thanks for his time and the tour. If I have any other questions, can I call him?"

"No. We go now. No talking."

I look at our host, impolitely straight into his eyes. Then I toss him a small *wai* and a smile and with my arm still around Thanee I turn us both around and walk us to the waiting Mercedes.

| | CHAPTER **FOURTEEN** | |

As we drive out the front gate I turn to look at Thanee. She's not shaking anymore, not sweating, but she looks tired, exhausted, slumped in the seat like after a very long, hard night without sleep.

"Are you okay?"

"Yes, yes, I will be okay. *Mâi pen rai.* No problem."

"What was he doing there? I didn't think they let Khmer Rouge into Thailand. What's the general got to do with them?"

She looks worried again, on the verge of panic. She looks at the back of the driver's head, then leans in close and speaks softly. "Quiet. Do not ask. Maybe we talk later."

I don't press the issue and we ride in silence to the house where General Tran stashes his wife. Or at least his primary wife. I wouldn't be surprised if he's got a few others.

It's also in a walled compound. Up a long dirt drive through a forest of fruit and rubber trees. The house, built of rich, red teak with a roof that comes to a high peak at each corner, looks as if it's floating in the air, above a lotus pond. The bottom story is solid, unbroken, it's hard to make out even the seams between the planks. The top story blinds me with reflective glass, with only an occasional dark wood beam to hold it all up. I was going to take off my sunglasses but it's a bad idea.

The lotuses in the pond are spectacular. I point them out to Thanee. "They're all in perfect bloom. From the look of the pond at Thongchai's place I didn't think it was full season yet. It's amazing."

Thanee struggles to suppress a smile, then one breaks out on her face anyway. Then she laughs. "You will see."

The Mercedes pulls up by the side of the pond. Other than wading, I can't see how we're supposed to get to the house. The driver gets out with us. He's holding what looks like a garage door opener. He points it at a small box on the side of the house, presses the button, and a tongue of wooden walkway smoothly glides across the water toward us. It stops at the edge, right in front of me, and nestles with a mechanical click into a groove I hadn't noticed before. A door into the house opens at the far end of the walkway. A woman in a crisp black and white French maid's outfit is waiting.

We're halfway across when Thanee stops me and points to a group of huge, white lotus blossoms rising up next to us. "Smell them."

I lean over and take a whiff. They don't smell like anything. They look a little funny, too. I stick out a hand to touch one. It's plastic. It almost feels real. I look up at Thanee and raise my eyebrows. She's shaking with laughter.

"Are they all?"

"Every one. The general wants his flowers to bloom all year long. The general gets what he wants."

The French maid greets us at the door.

One of the most impressive things yet about the general, is that the maid really is French. She's young, pretty, quite a bit haughtier than I'd expect anybody's maid to be and near as I can tell from the torrent of words with which she greets Thanee, speaks fluent Thai. We follow her long legs and short skirt inside and upstairs.

Thanee whispers to me. "Lisette is one of the general and Madame's little jokes. They call her their 'reparations for colonialism.'"

"He's a little young for Dien Bien Phu. So's she."

"We Asians have long memories. And she is very pretty, yes?"

"She also wears very expensive looking panties for a servant. What's the general's wife think of all this?"

"Oh, this is Madame Tran's home. The general is very respectful of that. He has his apartment in the city, where the Madame does not go."

"I guess he'd be in trouble if she did."

"Not at all, Madame and the general are quite civilized. They love each other very much and are respectful of their arrangements."

There's a large, round entry at the top of the stairs with an ornate, gilded bird cage hanging in the middle. A parrot, I think, squawks at me in Thai as I walk past. Whatever it says makes Thanee laugh.

"What'd it say?"

"I always laugh when I hear it talk. It is another of Madame's little jokes. She has trained it so that when a man walks by it says, 'You have two wives.'"

Many men in Thailand, at least the ones who can afford it, do have two, or more, wives. But they prefer to keep it quiet.

Down a hall, Madame Tran is arrayed on an ornate day bed in the atrium. She's dressed in an *ao dai*, one of those traditional Vietnamese dresses with the form-fitting, silky, long-sleeved top that comes down over loose pants. There's a rich, perfumy, floral scent in the air. I know the smell of opium. I'd smoked it myself on a trek in the northwest hill country of Thailand.

Her eyes are closed. She doesn't open them to greet us. Her voice is deep, without much of an accent, and it oozes slowly out of her. "Welcome, Thanee. You have brought the American. It is Raymond, is it not?"

"I'm glad to meet you, Madame Tran. Please call me Ray."

"Indeed, Ray, I am so pleased to have an American come to visit. You are an amusing people. I mean no offense. You are such large people, yet in names you always seem to prefer the diminutive."

A big laugh bursts out of me. Thanee looks startled. I hope it isn't rude. "That's good. It really is. You're right. I haven't thought of it before."

Madame Tran opens her eyes to take inventory. I look her over in return. She's Eurasian, Vietnamese and perhaps Scandinavian of one sort or another. She has bright blue, almond-shaped eyes and a pert nose. She has thin lips, a mouth that could easily look cruel if she wasn't smiling. Satiny, thick black hair flows to below her waist. But she's at least in her mid-forties, possibly in her fifties, so it could be dyed. She's a bit thicker in the body than you'd expect from an upper-class southeast Asian woman, but she's comfortable with it, draped like a fat cat over the pillows. It wouldn't shock me too much if she started purring.

"You are not what I expected, Ray. You are a private investigator, are you not?"

"Being non-descript helps in my business."

"I'm afraid I have an old bad habit of comparing people I meet to movie stars. I am trying, but I cannot yet place you."

"My mother used to say I was more Spencer Tracy than Clark Gable or Bogart. I never knew if I should take it as a compliment or not."

"I defer then to your mother, Ray. And please, do take it as a compliment. Now I am so sorry, I have been a bad hostess. I have had a light lunch prepared. Lisette will take you to a room where you and Thanee can freshen up after your drive and morning's tour. Then she will bring you to the table. I will see you there in a short while."

She allows her eyes to drift shut again, then slowly lifts a delicate hand covered in glittering diamonds in a manner that tells us she's done with us for now. I'm surprised to see that she has closely trimmed nails. They're obviously well manicured, but shorter than I would have thought.

The maid ushers us down the hall and into a small guest suite where towels and robes are laid out on the bed. She shows us a button to push when we want her to return to bring us to the dining room and closes the door behind her.

Why is it that the Tran's want their guests dressed in robes? It's comfortable, but strange. This time I don't let Thanee undress me. I ask about our hostess, trying to keep my mind off Thanee who is being tauntingly slow about changing into her robe.

"Madame Tran's an impressive woman. What is she, part Swedish?"

"Her father was from Vietnam. Her mother from Finland. She went to school in London and Paris."

"She's amazing looking, really striking. I can't even tell if she's attractive or not. She's perfectly made up. But what's with the nails?"

"What do you mean?"

"Her fingernails. I always think of wealthy women as having long, perfectly groomed fingernails. She really seems like the type. It's odd that she doesn't."

"I don't think Lisette would like that."

"Huh?"

Thanee looks at me and rolls her eyes. "It is the problem with the stupid pornography they make for men. So unrealistic."

"What's that got to do with anything?"

"Lisette also has short fingernails. Think about it."

It doesn't take me a lot of thought to get it.

It's a perfectly elegant little French lunch. Pâté, cheese, small pickles, crusty bread and a light salad. Madame Tran lifts her cut crystal wine glass toward the skylight and examines the golden liquid in it. "It is so difficult to obtain truly fine wines here. I hope you do not mind, Ray, this is nothing more than an insolent little Sancerre."

I tilt my glass toward her. "It seems only appropriate, Madame. After all, aren't we Yanks known for our insolence? I'm sure it will be fine."

I take a sip and of course it is more than merely fine. There are obvious advantages to befriending the Trans.

"I have often thought, Madame, that if Hong Kong, where I live, had to have been colonized by any European power, it's a shame it wasn't the French."

"You are not so insolent, Ray. How do you account for that?"

"I'm sure I can be. But I have lived overseas for many years."

"I understand that you are here now on a matter concerning Khmer artwork."

"Yes, my company has a client who is concerned that his company has been unknowingly shipping stolen antiquities."

"And your job, I suppose, is to address the problem?"

"Sort of. I'll look into it, find out what I can, get proof of what's going on, then make a report. It's up to the client what happens after that."

"But surely, Ray, if you uncover illegal activities you must report them to the authorities."

"Not always. It's up to me. Plus, in this instance a lot of the authorities are in on it."

"I'm afraid that is too often the case in our part of the world."

"I think that's the case in a lot of places. It's only the scale that varies."

"You are so diplomatic, Ray. It is no wonder that the general is willing to assist you."

"Madame, do you know much about Khmer art yourself?"

"No, I am afraid that the classics, I find them so, so, how do I put this? Classical, I suppose. I prefer the contemporary, the more youthful arts. I find them more vibrant, more challenging, more supple." She's looking at Lisette, who's standing by the sideboard. The young French maid is smiling back. The whole thing makes me want to squirm, for several reasons.

Lunch is finished off with a rich, black espresso, so thick I could walk on it. Madame Tran lifts a hand in the direction of Lisette, who comes over to take it, helping her up from the table.

"Now, Ray and Thanee. I hope you do not think me a poor hostess, but I always retire for an hour or two after lunch. Please, make yourselves comfortable here in the house. You are welcome to stay for dinner, and for the night if you desire."

I'm intrigued enough by the whole set up that I'm about to say yes, but Thanee cuts me off. "Thank you so much for your invitation, Madame, but we must return to the city. We hope you will not think we are rude if we change back into our clothes and leave."

Madame Tran lifts both her hands and sets a Mona Lisa look on her face. "It is a pity. When you are ready, please come to my chamber. I will ask Lisette to show you out."

The two of them leave the room. Thanee and I find our own way back to the room we had used. "You didn't want to stay? There's something so strange about all this that I'm intrigued."

"No, the general requested that we return by evening."

"I thought you and I were…"

"We are if you wish, it is no problem. But the general wishes for me to be in Bangkok tonight and I must go to see him when we first return. Then I will come back to your hotel."

After we change into our clothes, Thanee leads us to a large, round, open doorway outlined in bright red lacquer at the end of the hall. There's a small forest of sharp, shiny metal spikes at the bottom. About three feet beyond them, into the room, is a translucent Chinese silk screen magnificently embroidered with a lotus blossom that's beginning to open. But it's more than that. The flower looks like it was made by Judy Chicago, the artist who did the dinner party with all the vagina plates. It's thoroughly obscene, and wonderful.

The voice of Madame Tran curls out from around the screen, deep and dreamy, full of smoke and seduction. "Ray, Thanee, please do step around the screen. Perhaps I can convince you to stay."

What with the screen and her voice and the rich, floral poppy smoke that is beginning to coil around us, I'm already half-convinced. Thanee puts a hand on my shoulder, I think to hold me back, but I step around the screen.

The entire room is draped in folds of different shades of red and pink. They are brighter, larger, more billowy, gently moving in a soft breeze near the front, diminishing in size and hue as they close in on a large, round, bright white bed at the far end. I'm familiar enough with female anatomy to know what I'm walking into.

Madame Tran is on the bed, in her same reclining big cat posture. Her face is wreathed in thick smoke that drifts slowly out of her mouth and nose. Lisette, naked, is seated next to her, holding a candle to the pipe. The general's wife is swaddled in a sheer, white robe. It looks like it must have been woven around her by spiders. It accents the naked body underneath it. She's tattooed, completely covered other than her feet, hands and from the neck up. I can't make out the designs but in the spotlight that bathes the bed they are very brightly colored, as if they were new.

"Perhaps, Ray, Thanee, you would care to join Lisette and myself. My chamber is indeed a lovely place in which to wile away an afternoon with the pipe and new friends. It would be lovely to create our own dreams."

Lisette looks impassive and beautiful next to her, attending only to the pipe, stoned, her eyes focused deep into the flame. I can't make out Madame Tran's expression, only the smoke curling around her head and the art on her body.

I've never even bothered to fantasize about something like this because it would seem so unlikely to ever occur. Maybe I'm a boring guy, but I tend to prefer fantasies that fall into the realm of possibility. A few months ago I'd've already been out of my clothes, but now I'm trying to think up a polite way to say no.

Thanee says it for me. "Madame Tran, thank you. But the general has insisted."

"Indeed yes, *quel dommages*. What the general wishes, he must have. Please, Ray, some other time, do come to visit. I have enjoyed your company and do wish to enjoy it further."

Traffic's built up through the day. It's slow going back to my hotel. A few minutes into the drive I give up trying to figure out what our lunch stop was all about and ask. "What the hell was that all about? Did we just stop off to provide amusement for the general's wife, or what?"

Thanee laughs. "Yes, Madame is often lonely. The general sends visitors to her."

"Was I supposed to fuck her and Lisette or what?"

"That was for you to decide."

"What about you?"

"That would have been up to you, also."

Thanee's passivity makes me queasy. "I have enough trouble dealing with myself these days. I wasn't about to decide anything like that for you. It didn't seem like you wanted to stick around anyhow."

"Please do not say anything to the general, but I am bored with Madame and Lisette. Thank you for leaving. Many men would not."

"So you've done this before?"

"It was not only the general who would come to my room when I was young."

"This keeps getting stranger. I guess I'm not in Kansas anymore."

"Kansas?"

"A line from an old movie. It's a farm state in the U.S."

"It would have been very strange if we stayed. You will never know how strange."

I guess I won't, damnit.

| |CHAPTER **FIFTEEN** | |

T hanee's going to drop me at my hotel then go see the general. I ask her to let me off at River City instead. She does. She gives me her mobile phone number and says she'll see me later.

River City's a four-story shopping mall on the bank of the Chao Phaya river. It's Bangkok's center for antique dealers of all sorts; legit, illegit, real, fake, cheap and astronomically expensive. I head up to the fourth floor, where the fanciest shops are. I want to get a sense of how easy it is to buy Cambodian antiques.

It is easy. A Khmer Buddha stares at me from the front window of the first shop at the top of the escalator and to the left. He's spotlit. I have no idea if he's ancient or not. He looks ancient. The small store is called Khunee Phorntip Antiques.

There's not much room to move inside. It's piled high with statuary, and tall glass cases are filled with small artifacts. There's a desk at the back. An electronic eye sets off a buzzer when I walk in, and a woman with short cropped hair and thick glasses rises from behind a tall stack of papers to greet me.

"Hello. Welcome. Is there anything in particular you are looking for?"

She comes out from behind the desk with a big smile, a notepad, pen and magnifying glass. Her glasses now dangle from a chain around her neck.

"I am interested in Khmer art."

"We have very fine pieces. Perhaps you noticed the Buddha head in the window and that is what brought you into our shop."

"Yes. Is it an original?"

"No, it is a very good reproduction though. We have contracted with a renowned family of sculptors."

"*Khun* Thongchai?"

"Yes, you must be a knowledgeable collector."

"I try. Actually, I would very much like to find an *apsara*, an original."

She pauses, and then looks up, slightly wary.

"Pardon me for asking, but how is it that you have come to know *Khun* Thongchai?"

I drop the general's name. If I can't take advantage of the other things he's offering me, at least I can use him for this.

"Ah, today you are lucky. Please do come with me."

I follow her into a back room. She wheels a chair piled high with more papers out of the way of a large safe and bends to the dial. When she turns around she's cradling a bundle of newspaper in her arms. She carries it back to the desk in the front where there's a small clear space.

"I think you will like this piece. We received it only yesterday. It is from Banteay Chmar in the northwest of Cambodia." It takes her a minute to untie and unwrap the package.

Inside is a limestone *apsara* that's been chipped out of a wall. The chunk of stone is about four inches thick and irregularly shaped. The dancing woman herself is maybe a foot high and in perfect shape except for a missing right foot and what looks like it could be a bullet hole at the top corner of her headdress. She's thrusting out her right hip, a hand resting on her left hip, the other inviting me closer. Her head is slightly thrown back, her mouth wide open as if caught in a guffaw. I don't know what's so funny.

If it was a reproduction I'd buy it. Even if I knew for sure it was a fake and the price was ridiculous, I'd buy it. I can't be sure it's a real antique. An expert would need to do chemical testing of the stone to know. But from everything I've heard, what I've found out so far, I suspect it's real.

The woman tells me it's sixty thousand *baht*, about two thousand four hundred U.S. That's real enough. It sounds about right for a genuine piece of its size and type.

I look at the *apsara* for a while. I want to set her free. I want to take her away and bring her back home. I could buy her and donate her back to Cambodia. She'd probably just be stolen again.

I could go to the police and inform on the store. It's illegal in Thailand to be selling these things. But all that would happen is that the police would come, confiscate it, then when I was safely gone they'd sell it back to the store which would raise the price to cover the cost of the corruption.

Finally, I mutter "thanks" and walk out. I go to five other shops over the next hour and find stolen art for sale in all of them. It's depressing.

And it's not just the loss of a country's heritage that gets me down and makes me mad. It's who's involved. I was reminded of that earlier in the day at *Khun* Thongchai's when the Khmer Rouge guy showed up and Thanee shuddered in my arms.

On April 17th, 1975 the communists, the Khmer Rouge, took power in Cambodia, thanks largely to the U.S., which had destabilized the country over the past five or so years. Over the next four years the Khmer Rouge murdered between one and three million

Cambodians, maybe more than a third of the whole population. Then the Vietnamese came and chased them out into the country-side. Then the U.S. and China agreed on something for a change; neither of them liked the Vietnamese, so they supported the Khmer Rouge in the U.N. There's been fighting in Cambodia ever since.

The Khmer Rouge hold on to villages and towns in the west-ern part of the country that borders Thailand, where the Angkor Empire built its finest monuments. They've planted mines around the temples and palaces and farms. The people of Cambodia are still being blown up, killed and maimed simply trying to live their lives. The mayhem is financed by the sale of illegally logged tim-ber, illegally mined gems and looted antiquities. Corrupt Thai generals are major players.

The *apsara* for sale in River City buys landmines for killers. The same guys who killed Thanee's family. The guy we saw at *Khun* Thongchai's compound. Somebody once said "all politics is personal." I think they were talking about a chicken in every pot. But this feels like it's getting personal, too.

Thanee's going to pick me up at my hotel at about nine. I go back to my room and lie down. I want to take a nap, a short holiday from thinking about anything. It's still light outside but I don't have the energy to pull the curtains. I don't even take off my clothes. My body falls asleep quickly. My brain won't leave me alone.

I think it's ancient Cambodia. It looks like it from the drawings I've seen. I'm in a large room with beautifully carved walls. The room's filled with *apsaras*, more than I can count. They're naked and they're dancing, slowly, sensuously. I'm invisible. I wander through them, being careful not to brush against them. But then I notice it doesn't matter. My right arm touches one and passes straight through her body as if through a cloud.

I see someone I recognize. I follow her. It's Irina. I try talking to her. She can't hear me, can't see me. Over her shoulder I see Thanee, but she can't see me either. I feel a cold breath on the back of my neck and turn around. It's Sasha, Irina's friend who I got killed. I think she sees me; she's smiling right at me. She winks, but then she walks backwards away from me, fading slowly into the wall of carvings behind her.

All the other women begin to back toward the walls. They also fade into the chiseled scenes. I'm left alone in the huge room, surrounded by the friezes. I hear laughter, loud, echoing, nasty. It's laughing at me and I feel small. I look up.

There's a gigantic open mouth filled with pointed teeth, a huge forked tongue poking out between them. The mouth is set deep into puffy cheeks, under a wildly flared nose. Blood drips from the teeth; bones and body parts are caught in between them. It's the monster Kala, carved into the ceiling. But is it carved? It looks alive. It looks like the ceiling is closing in on me, the vicious mouth opening wider as it approaches, the laugh coming from deep inside.

The mouth gets closer and closer. I hunker down on the floor; curling up, trying to make myself smaller, to get away. I can see past the teeth and tongue, deep into blackness. There's a small, round red light down there. It flares yellow in three short bursts then softens down to red again. I don't want to go there. I don't want to get any closer to it. But there's nothing I can do. It's coming for me.

I'm about to be devoured when the mouth stops in front of me. The red light shoots yellow another three times, it sizzles. Then a great gust of smoke pours from the mouth, etching its way into my nostrils and up behind my eyes.

"Mr. Sharp. Mr. Sharp." A slap rings against my left cheek and I wake up coughing, disoriented. The red spot is still there, a foot or two in front of my face, heat pushing off it. I focus on it. It's the tip of a cigar. I zoom my vision back to the face behind it.

"General. General Tran. What, what are…"

The cigar flashes yellow again as it retreats to the end of the bed. "You were having a bad dream, Ray. Would you care to share it with me?"

"What, what are you doing here? What time is it? Where's Thanee?"

"I am afraid that I have come in place of Thanee, Ray. She is home, studying."

"What do you want?"

"I have been thinking, Ray. I have been worrying. It is not good when I worry. I regret that I have permitted you to meddle in my business. My business is best left undisturbed."

"Huh? I, I don't think I've been meddling, just asking questions. I'm not investigating you, General."

"In the car, after leaving the compound of *Khun* Thongchai, you inquired of Thanee about my possible business connections with a certain man who you unfortunately saw arrive."

"I don't know what Thanee told you, but I..."

He holds up a hand. "Thanee told me nothing, Ray. For that, she may be punished. You were in one of my cars. I hear everything.

"But that was not all. When you returned to Bangkok, you went to River City."

"Sure, why not? I wanted to see how easy it is to find Cambodian antiques."

"You made inquiries at three of my shops."

"I didn't know they were yours. I went there and poked around. It was a coincidence."

"I do not believe in coincidences, Ray. I learned that quite a long time ago. It is what you might call a 'survival skill.' Perhaps at times I am mistaken, but what is it that you Americans say? You always have something to say. Ah, yes, 'better to be safe than to be sorry.' That's it."

"I don't even know which three shops were yours, General. Even if I did, that wouldn't be part of my report."

"I am sorry, Ray. I am a successful man and it is not because I take chances."

He motions to his right with his cigar and I swivel my head to follow. There's a policeman standing in the corner, a big one by Thai standards. He's holding a gun and I'm not at all pleased to see that it's pointed at me.

"General, won't it cause a stink if you shoot a foreign business-man in a hotel in Bangkok? That's gotta be worse for your busi-ness than anything I've found out."

"That is why you will walk quietly with us to the car out front, and why the lieutenant will take you for a short trip."

"Where're we going?"

"Pattaya. Have you been there before?"

It's the beach. What it's famous for is its foul, heavily polluted bay and a long strip of the sleaziest brothels, sex clubs and bars on the plan-et. It's a popular destination for sex tourists, especially pedophiles.

"Can't say I have. It's never appealed to me."

"No, it is not an appealing place. But it is a very good place for bad things to happen to foreigners."

"General, please, you're making a mistake. You don't have anything to worry about from me."

"Perhaps, Ray, and if so I am very sorry. But if this is not a mistake, then it will save me from a worse mistake."

"People know where I am. I can't just disappear. You're fuck-ing nuts you know, out of control."

He only smiles at me and nods in my direction. The cop hands the general his gun and steps up to me with handcuffs. He clasps them around my wrists loosely in front of me, tight enough to keep me from slipping out of them but not so tight as to leave any marks. He steps back, the general gives him back his gun, and he motions me up and out the door with it.

There's always someone at the front desk. The people who run the hotel know me. They like me. I'm a regular customer. We have to pass the desk on the way out and when we do I'll yell for them to call the cops, the real cops, that I'm being kidnapped. The big cop's behind me, his gun poking the small of my back. But he won't shoot me in the lobby when I'm handcuffed. Would he? That would be too much trouble. Wouldn't it?

But there's no one at the front desk, no one in the lobby. We walk straight out the door to the waiting Mercedes. The orange jump-suited driver opens the back door and shoves me in. The cop walks around and gets in the front passenger side. I struggle to sit up. It's not so easy with my hands cuffed, but I manage. The window's cracked open and the general leans to it from outside.

"Once again, I am sorry, Ray. Perhaps it will please you to know that Thanee likes you. She asked me to let you go. She is young, and a romantic. That is best at her age. There are things about business, important things, that they will not teach her in university. After she graduates I will once again be her teacher and then she will learn to understand these certain necessities."

Is that supposed to make me feel better? It doesn't. I don't say anything. I stare at him and watch as he walks away.

Depending on traffic it can take anywhere from two to six hours to drive to Pattaya. It takes us a little less than three. That's more than enough time to spend worrying about what they're going to do with me. I would have liked it better if they'd have shot me in my sleep. Kala, from my dream, could have simply devoured me and I'd have never woken up to know any better. I'm shaking and trying to think of anything else, to conjure up good memories, something to be happy about. It isn't working.

I think I know what's coming. Foreigners turn up dead with some degree of regularity in Pattaya. They turn up dead in brothels that specialize in children, sometimes with traumatized naked kids by their side, occasionally with dead ones. No one gives a damn. If an investigation happens at all, it's not much of one. No one's going to miss a pedophile. Even the corpse's family is too embarrassed to raise a fuss. It's a great place to kill people.

They've gotta make it look good though. Even corrupt cops can't ignore a crime scene that's too obvious, can they? That means they're going to have to get tricky. There's some hope in that. The more complicated they get, the better chance I've got of escaping. If I can stay calm enough to take advantage of it.

I close my eyes and try breathing slowly in through my nose and out my mouth. Sometimes that works. This time it does, but not enough. When we pull up in front of Daddy's Disco I'm still on edge.

It looks like an overgrown garden shed built of corrugated metal. It's outlined with flashing red and green Christmas tree lights. A small, blue neon sign over the door says "Daddy." There are a few taxis parked out front on the dirt and a bevy of little motorbikes. A terrible, deep thumping is going on inside, muffled by the walls, but still loud enough that I'm surprised the building isn't bulging in and out in time to the bass line.

No one even bothers to look up as I'm walked through the door at gunpoint and up to the bar. I get the sense that the place is crowded, but it's only a guess, it's too dark to see much of anything. At the bar there's a woman in an apron who looks like the mom you wish you had at home baking you chocolate chip cookies. She's swiping out beer mugs with a dirty rag under a lone lightbulb dangling from the ceiling. The cop spits a few rough words at her. She tosses him a few back, hands him a small packet and points to the stairs behind the counter.

We go up three flights. The metal building we came into was only one story so all I can figure is that there's another building attached to it at the back. It's dark in the stairwell, there's one dim bulb at each landing.

At the third floor the cop nudges me along a carpeted hall. It reeks of baby powder and baby oil, stale beer, mildew and incense. He shoves me through a door about halfway down the hall. The room's dim, lit only by a dull, green bulb. There's a large bed covered with stained black sheets and littered with toy stuffed animals—a teddy bear, an elephant, a black panther, a snake, a dog. There's a large bathtub, one of the old kind with clawed feet. It doesn't look like it's been cleaned lately. Next to the bed is a small nightstand with bottles of powder and oil and a glass. The walls are bare, there isn't a window. There's cheap shag carpet underfoot. It's green, or maybe that's from the light.

It's a depressing, ugly room. It's all too vivid at the moment, though. I'm taking in everything about it. It might be the last place I see. The cop shoves me onto the bed and gives the gun to the driver. He picks up the glass from the nightstand, empties the packet the matronly bartender gave him into it, fills it with water from the bathtub tap and stirs it with a finger. He hands it to me.

"Drink."

I take it in my two cuffed hands, put it on the floor and shake my head. If they're going to kill me, they can kill me. It seems unlikely they'd poison me. It's more likely the drink is to knock me out so they can set something up. But I'm not going to help.

The cop laughs and says something to the driver who hands him back the gun then turns and leaves the room.

The cop steps in front of me and roughly shoves the gun into my mouth. I stare at him. Maybe it's harder to shoot someone who's looking at you? That's all I've got. But he doesn't pull the trigger, he takes out the gun and moves it slowly down my body until it's pointing at my crotch. He takes a step back.

"Drink."

I shake my head again. He laughs and pushes the gun up hard into my crotch, then lowers it further to rest against my right knee. I get the message. There're two ways we can do this.

I'm tempted to let him shoot me in the knee. So long as it hurts I'm still alive. Maybe that's better than not hurting and being dead. Maybe not.

I pick up the glass and take a sip. It's a little bitter, but that might be the water. Tap water in Pattaya is pretty bad. I think for a moment that I'll probably get a bad case of the runs. That strikes me as funny and I smile.

The cop taps my knee with the gun barrel and I down the rest.

I don't know what it is or how fast it's supposed to work. My brain is working overtime, trying to come up with a plan. Maybe I can play possum, make it seem like it's taking effect, then I can jump him when he thinks I'm harmless. I've been drugged before. I've taken drugs before. I'm pretty good at fighting them off when I have to.

He's already sure of himself because he puts the gun in his left hand, reaches into a pocket with the right and fishes out the handcuff key. He gives it to me and gestures that I should unlock the cuffs.

"Take off clothes."

I probably could unlock the cuffs with the key but I fumble with it, deliberately, and drop it on the floor. I pick it up and do the same again. I don't feel anything from the drink yet, but I start acting tired and clumsy. The cop mutters something, picks up the key himself, then moves in close to use it.

Timing's everything. He has to juggle the gun to get at the lock. The moment the cuffs open I clasp my hands together into one fist and hit him in the chin harder than I've ever hit anything. He falls back, looking startled, but his hand's still on the gun and he's trying to bring it around at me.

I kick him hard in the face. His head bangs against the floor and his gun hand flails out to the side but he's still conscious. I strike his arm with my right foot, but it's feeble and doesn't buy me much time. I'm starting to feel a little sluggish, like I'm watching myself move. I try to egg myself on to move faster. I jump, or fall, off the bed on top of him, throwing out an arm to grab his hand with the gun, trying to knock the wind out of him with my weight.

My arm's getting weak and I can't hold onto his hand much longer. I remember something an old girlfriend told me she'd learned in a self-defense class. I turn my left palm up at a right angle to the arm, curl the fingers, stiffen it, pull it back a little to pick up some momentum and ram it as hard as I can up against the bottom of his nose.

There's a loud crack and for an instant I think he's got off a shot. I flinch, then hold myself still trying to feel what's going on. What I feel is him going limp underneath me. I look up and into his eyes. They've gone blank, his nose smashed up against the bottom of the sockets. I roll off him, on top of his gun arm to keep it pinned. But it isn't necessary. I'll have to look up that old girlfriend and thank her.

I roll again and reach to take the gun out of his hand. I lie on the floor next to him, holding the gun close. I just want to stay there. I want to go to sleep.

But I have to force myself up, have to keep myself awake. The driver is probably coming back. I've got to get out of here. I get up on my hands and knees and crawl to the bathtub. I stick my head under the faucet and let it run down on me but it only helps a little. I try sticking a finger deep down my throat, to throw up whatever it is I've swallowed. But I can't make myself do it.

I get to my feet and the room's spinning around and I see the bed and all I want to do is lie down and go to sleep. But I don't. I drag myself to the door; each step takes a year or two. It takes everything I've got to pull the door open. I have to grab the knob, turn it, then hold on and let my weight do the work.

Someone's coming down the hall. It sounds like a man and a kid talking. I stumble back into the room, out of sight. With both hands I raise the gun, it's the heaviest thing I've ever lifted, and point it at the door. Or what I think is the door. Three or four people are coming through the door. With one eye shut there's two or three.

It's the driver, I think. He's a large, fuzzy orange shape, holding a smaller, brown shape by what I think is the hand. He stops when he sees the the cop sprawled on the floor. The orange shape moves, turns toward me. The small brown shape is screaming, crying. I think it's that. The sound waves come at me long and deep, slow like everything else.

The orange shape comes at me, it's not far away. I start squeezing my finger. It travels miles on the trigger, requires all my strength. But then there's a sharp, loud boom that vibrates through my hands and up my arms and through my whole body and into the room behind me. My hands jerk up, pain shoots through my wrists. The pain is good. It focuses me, at least for a moment.

The orange shape looks more like the driver now. I can see his face and it looks startled. He doesn't look injured but he isn't moving anymore. He's standing still, about six feet in front of me. I must have missed. I don't know how, but at least I stopped him.

The small brown shape is curled against the wall next to the door. It's a young boy, maybe seven or eight. He's shaking and sobbing, but otherwise I think he's okay. I didn't hit him either. I'm glad for that.

I keep the gun on the driver. I don't think he knows that I probably can't hit him unless he's right up against me. The handcuffs are on the floor. I point at them, then at him. He moves slowly toward them, drapes them around his wrists. I move in a little closer and threaten him with the gun until I'm sure he's tightened and locked the cuffs.

The room starts to turn again, go out of focus. The bed looks inviting; it's where I want to be. I've got to get out of here. I don't know if I can stay awake much longer. I can't leave the driver here but I can't just shoot him either. I'd like to get the kid out of here, too. I would have thought that a shot would attract attention, but no one's come to see what's going on. I don't know how long that's going to last.

I don't know if I've got the strength to do it, but can't you knock a guy out with a tap from a gun butt behind the ear? I motion him to turn around, away from me. He's shaking. He thinks I'm going to shoot him. I probably should.

I turn the gun around in my hand, making sure to keep my finger away from the trigger. I raise it in slow motion then bring it down as hard as I can. I can't tell how hard that is. It feels like I'm moving through thick pudding. I hit him behind his right ear and he crumples to the floor.

Maybe he's faking. I turn the gun back around and poke at him with a foot. He isn't moving. I don't have time to stick around and find out if he's going to jump up after me or not.

I walk up to the kid. I can barely make him out. He's just a shape. This must be how blind people with just a little vision see things. There's a lighter part of him that's pointing up at me. It must be his face. He's probably wondering what I'm going to do to him. He's used to adults doing things to him. What I want to do is get him out of here. I fumble the gun into a pocket and hold out a hand. He reaches up and takes it.

I lead him, or he leads me, out of the room, down the hall and back down the stairs. It's like sleepwalking. I'm enveloped in a bubble surrounded by haze and fog. One foot moves in front of the other, I think.

We reach the bottom of the stairs and the cocoon I'm in starts pulsating with a dull, deep rhythmic boom, like a far away big diesel engine heard from underwater. It gets louder, then recedes as the air around me gets hot and wet. We're outside. I have a faint memory of taxis and I try to speak.

I don't know if I think it, or say it, or if there's any difference. I'm about to fall down but something, someone moves in on my left and holds me up, pushes me forward. I'm lowered onto sticky plastic, my legs pushed in to scrunch against me. There's a slam and a click. I see a light round thing looking at me from in front and above.

"Hotel. Big hotel." Did I say that or think it? Then the light begins to fade. It goes gray, to charcoal gray, to black.

| | CHAPTER **SIXTEEN** | |

"hat'd you do with the gun?"

It's a day later and I still feel groggy. I'm slumped on Warner's visitor's chair. His office is awfully neat, not overrun with crap like mine. He's only got the one two-drawer file cabinet that I can see. I wonder how he does that? Maybe it's an old habit, something he learned in the C.I.A. He burns all his old papers; or chews them up and swallows them.

I crick my neck, slowly, to clear my head.

"Damned if I know, Bill. I came to this morning in a hotel and it wasn't there."

"What kind of gun was it?"

"I'm not an ex-spook like some people I know. I don't have the slightest. It felt lighter than I thought it would, like it was made of plastic. It was really hard to pull the trigger, but that might have been the dope."

"Was it really hard at first, then it felt like it got past a certain point and got easier?"

"Yeah, I guess so. That sounds right."

"Cylinder or magazine?"

"What? Oh. One of those things you jam up into the butt."

"A Glock probably. Sounds like it."

"What the hell does it matter?"

"I like to know what the bad guys are packing. Helps me figure out who they're doing business with. What happened to the kid?"

"I don't know that either. I told you, I conked out in the taxi and the next thing I remember is about six hours later when I woke up in the hotel. The kid wasn't there."

"He probably got scared and ran off."

"I hope so. I hope he ran a long way off and didn't come back."

"How'd you get back again?"

"They wanted the cops to know who I was, so they didn't take my wallet. I took a shuttle to the airport, bought a ticket and here I am. I figured it wasn't a good idea to go back to the Swiss Park for my things."

"Good thinking. Lose anything valuable?"

"Probably not. I can call the hotel and ask them to send what I left. They know me. I might have killed that cop, though. I guess I'm in big trouble."

"I don't know. I'll check into it. It's harder to kill someone that way than you'd think. From what you've told me he might not have been a real cop, or if he was, he was corrupt enough that no one's going to worry too much about him. One of the hazards of his business. I'll let you know."

"It's that easy? It's got me all fucked up. I don't like killing people. Even people who're trying to kill me."

"Good. No one in their right mind does. Are you going to be all right with it?"

"I don't know if I am in my right mind. I wasn't sleeping much even before this, really ugly, scary dreams. Sometimes I start shaking and I don't think it's going to stop."

"Does it?"

"Yeah, I'm not shaking now."

"Good. I know a shrink if you want one. No shame in it."

"It's not a Brit is it?"

"Why?"

"Don't get me wrong, I've got plenty of British friends, but they're different than we are. They think different. What is it that Bernard Shaw said, 'two people separated by a common language,' something like that?"

"I hadn't heard that before. It's good."

"Accurate, too."

"I suppose so. She's Australian. They're more like us."

"Okay, give me her number, maybe I'll give her a call."

"Will do. Meanwhile, where do we stand? Montgomery's called a couple of times, he's antsy to know what's what."

"I've got the big picture, and it's pretty fleshed out on the Thai side. I've got a good idea of what's happening on this side, too, at least from Shenzhen to here. What's missing are some of the specifics in Cambodia and then the links from there to Shenzhen."

"Our Yank client's already taken care of. They got what they needed about Golden Truly. How're we going to make Wellfleet happy? Company like that could be a lot of business down the line."

"They still need the shipping, how the art gets from Cambodia to Shenzhen. If it's really on their boats. They want proof so they can put the screws to their Chinese partner that's running it. If they don't get something solid the Chinese'll deny it. I'll need to go to Cambodia."

"That doesn't sound like such a good idea. Tran's already tried to kill you once. I don't think he'll be happy if you start poking around again."

"Fat lot of good I'm going to be as an investigator if I have to keep out of Thailand and Cambodia. Besides, Tran says he's only involved in the other direction. If I'm poking around his competitors I don't know that he'll care." I'm not so sure I believe that, but I've got to see this thing through.

"In the Agency we might have said you've been compromised."

"This isn't the Agency, Bill, it's private practice. You're just trying to get this business up and running. You can't have me back off now. Besides, this whole thing's got mixed up in my head with all the Russian problems I had a few months ago. I need to see it through, make it work this time."

"Go see that shrink, Ray. Don't use our client to work out your mental problems."

"Let me worry about my hang ups. When they start getting in the way of the company giving the client what it wants, then you can pull me off the case."

What he's thinking plays across his face. I can read it:

'We've got to see this through to the end or we'll lose Wellfleet as a client. I can't afford to hire another operative or leave the office right now. Sharp's got a screw loose, but I knew that when I hired him. He's certainly keen on the whole thing, no matter what it is that's eating him.'

At least that's what I hope he's thinking.

"That Russian business was a mess, Ray. I helped you where I could, but still, it was a mess."

"So, why'd you hire me?"

He shakes his head like he can't believe what he's about to say.

"You stuck to it, you stirred things up. It ended badly but maybe some good was done. I don't know, maybe it was a mistake. Maybe not. Just don't tell me there's a girl this time, too."

It's my turn to shake my head like I can't quite believe what I'm about to tell him. "There's a girl."

"You are fucking nuts. Keep it in your pants."

"No, Bill, it's not like that this time. She's Cambodian. The Khmer Rouge killed her family. Tran took her out of a refugee camp, now he owns her. It's like she's an *apsara* he stole from one of the temples. And the art he's stealing from the temples helps pay the bastards who killed her family and a couple million other people while they were at it. I want to fuck him up. I want to do whatever I can."

"Go see that shrink, Ray. Do something for yourself."

"This is doing something for myself, but that's not your business. All you need to know is that I'm on track to get Wellfleet what it wants."

"This is my company, and it is my business if I think you're about to go off the deep end on the job."

"I won't, Bill. I know what I'm doing. So far I'm doing what you hired me for. I won't be there long anyhow. I'll stay in Phnom Penh, try and make connections to buy stolen art and arrange shipping. That ought to get us what we need."

He puts his chin in a hand and looks at the floor and I don't even want to guess what he's thinking this time.

When he looks up I can see that he's working to keep his face blank, neutral.

"I'm the fucking nutjob for agreeing to this. But we do need to get what Wellfleet's hired us for. It's your funeral. But I don't want you going alone. Take Lei Yue."

"What, for my protection? Is she a kung fu master or something I don't know about?"

"You could use the backup. I don't want you disappearing without anyone around to let me know you're gone. And she might help keep you focused. Plus, it'll be good for her to get seasoning."

"More like basted. You've been trying to convince me how dangerous this is gonna be. She's not ready."

"She can stay put in the hotel, provide logistical support, keep me up to date on what's going on. You're the one who keeps telling me it's gonna be okay."

"If I'm worrying about her it might get in the way."

"Too bad. You're not going without her."

Lei Yue's face lights up when I tell her. "When do we go?"

"I told Bill I don't like the idea. It might be dangerous."

She puts a serious look on her face and her hands on her hips. "Danger is my business."

I crack up laughing. She looks ridiculous. But she smiles when she says, "Don't laugh at me."

It takes a few moments and several gulps of air to catch my breath. "I'm not, I'm not. It's the way you said it, the cliché. You knew what you were doing. I was laughing with you."

"So when are we going?"

"I wasn't kidding about it being dangerous."

"I didn't think you were, but you're overlooking something."

"What?"

"I'm little. People don't take me seriously, they aren't afraid of me. It can be an advantage. You, however, big fella, make people nervous."

"I'm not big. I'm about average."

"Big enough. And White, too. Sometimes your WSP works against you."

"WSP?"

"*Cabrón*, you are *muy estupido* sometimes. White Skin Privilege."

"And I thought it was my charm."

"Don't think too much. It doesn't become you."

I can't help it. I'm already thinking too much about how I'm going to get started in Cambodia. And that, stupidly, leads to thinking about Thanee. She might know something. She's in business school, the general's been training her to work with him, she might know who his competitors are. She's probably got information I can use in Phnom Penh. I can call her.

Or maybe I'm not thinking enough. I don't know where she stands. Why should she risk everything to talk to me?

But then, what's it matter if she tells Tran that I called her? He's gotta know by now that his guys screwed up, that I'm still alive.

And I need to talk to her, to hear her voice. It's probably not fair to her, or myself, or Warner or Wellfleet or anyone else, but she represents something to me. I'm not even sure what. The personal side of why I give a damn about all this in the first place. Something like that.

Whatever, it's an excuse to call her. Maybe it's a dumb one. Maybe it's a good idea. I'll find out sooner or later.

She answers her mobile phone. It sounds like she's in a crowd.

"Thanee."

"Ray? Is that you, Ray? I thought…the general told me…Ray, you are alive. Are you okay?"

"Yeah, it's me. I'm fine. I got away. I'm back in Hong Kong."

"I am happy. But why do you call me? It is dangerous. I should not talk with you."

"I know, I'm sorry. But maybe you can help me. And I wanted to talk to you again. I want to see you again."

"That is impossible, Ray. You must forget me."

"If I ask you something, can you promise to not tell the general?"

She doesn't say anything. I have no idea if silence means yes or no.

I'll take the chance. "Do you know the name of the general's competitor in Cambodia? The other company that sells antiques?"

"It is, I think, Angkor Flower Trading Company. I have heard him talk about it. Why do you ask?"

"My investigation isn't done yet. I'm not looking into the general's company, but I am looking into his competitor, like I told him."

"It is best if you stop, Ray."

"Probably, but I won't."

"Please do not go to Cambodia, Ray."

"I am going. What can I do for you? How can I help you to…"

"Help me to do what, Ray? I do not need any help."

"I don't know, help you get away, away from the general."

"The general is my family, Ray, my only family. I owe him everything. Without him I am nothing."

"That's not true, Thanee. You're smart, you're beautiful, you can make a life for yourself. I can find a way to help."

"This is how I will live this life, Ray. You will never understand. Please do not say more, you only make me sad."

I'm the one who's sad. And she's right, I don't understand. I don't want to, not this. But I shut up.

Thanee's got a catch in her voice that I'm happy to hear when she says goodbye, but it's all I'm left with. She tells me to never contact her again, I will only make trouble for both her and myself.

Lei Yue and I leave the next day, Thai Airways to Phnom Penh. Bill Warner drives us to the airport in Hong Kong. He hands me a slip of paper when we get out of the car.

"Call this guy at the embassy in Phnom Penh. He'll hook you up with a gun."

"I don't want a gun."

"I'll feel better if you have one. With any luck you won't need it."

"I'm a lousy shot anyhow. It won't do me any good."

"There's a public firing range near the airport. Practice. Take Lei Yue. Have some fun. You can even expense it."

I roll my eyes and shake my head at him. Lei Yue's been watching the whole time. She gets a laugh out of it.

We're staying at the Pailin Hotel, on Monivong Boulevard, a long block down Charles de Gaulle Boulevard from Phnom Penh's Central Market. The taxi from the airport isn't air-conditioned. By the time we get there we're like a couple of Chinese dumplings, thoroughly steamed.

We made a reservation for two rooms, but when we walk up to the desk the clerk says they're full. The town's lousy with peacekeepers, aid-workers, consultants and other assorted do-gooders brandishing big expense accounts. He's got the sort of glint in his eye that says a room might clear up if we grease his palm.

One does for an extra twenty bucks U.S. It's on the top floor, and the elevator isn't working. It isn't bad though; there aren't too many buildings over three floors in town. The room's rundown but big and bright with light from large windows on two sides. It looks out over the city toward the river and the Royal Palace.

There's an erratic web of electric and phone wires stretched across the jumble of dirty looking rooftops. On every block there's a gap in the roofline where a building has collapsed, been torn down or was never built. A few pointy towers of *wats*, temples, poke through. They look like they ought to glint in the sun, but they've been rebuilt out of bare concrete—spikes in the rest of the skyline. The spires of the Royal Palace and the Tonle Sap—the river, in the distance—do glisten in the sun.

There's one large bed, but Lei Yue plops down on it and gives me a look that makes it seem a lot smaller. "Don't get any ideas, big boy."

"I'll take the floor." It's tile and there isn't so much as a throw rug.

"Aren't you the gallant *caballero*. It's okay, I don't bite."

"Women keep saying that to me lately."

"The gallant part, or not biting?"

It's hot and humid in the room. No better than the taxi. I crank the window air-conditioning unit to high and it rumbles and shakes into life, rattling the windows and puffing out moderately cool air that smells like molten plastic.

"I'm going to take a shower. Then we can go to the embassy and look up Warner's pal."

"What about me?"

"What about you?"

"I could use a shower, too."

"Fine, you can go first."

"No, you go first. Don't use up all the hot water."

"No problem. The one thing they've got plenty of in this place is hot water."

| |CHAPTER **SEVENTEEN** | |

W arner's pal can't see us. He's "upcountry." But he's left me a bulging manila envelope. I'm shy about these sorts of things. I go into a men's room stall to open it. It's a gun that looks a lot like the one I took from the police lieutenant in Pattaya. There's an unsigned note with it.

"Bill Warner said you have experience with a Glock. I thought you might like the 19; it's got a slightly shorter barrel. I've included two magazines, 15 capacity each. If you only use it for target practice, drop it off back here. If you use it for anything else, get rid of it. The river's fine, but off the middle of the bridge."

I put the gun back in the envelope and go to get Lei Yue. She's watching CNN on a monitor in the embassy lobby.

"Anything new in the world?"

"*Nada.* Nothing we can do anything about."

"At least we can go out to the firing range and shoot guns. Join the crowd."

"I've never shot a gun. That's something you *gringos* are into."

"What about Pancho Villa, Zapata, those guys?"

"I'm Chinese-Mexican, we sold those guys fried rice."

"What about Chairman Mao?"

"I doubt he ever shot a gun either. He ordered other people to do it for him."

"Details, details. If you're going to be a private dick you'll have to learn sometime."

She gives me a dirty look and follows me into a taxi. On the way out to the shooting range near the airport she peeks into the envelope.

"Did you ever shoot somebody?"

"Yeah, a couple of times."

"Did you kill anybody?"

"With a gun? Once." I don't want to get into the Thai cop.

"Why?"

"He was trying to kill me. It was the only way to stop him."

"Are you a good shot?"

"No, I'm terrible. He was very close to me or I would have missed him."

"How'd it make you feel?"

"Horrible, fucked up. I still have nightmares about it."

"Think you could do it again?"

"If I had to, I guess. I don't want to make a habit out of it."

"It'd be a bad habit." She's silent the rest of the way out to the range.

So am I. I'm thinking I'll call Warner's shrink when I get back to Hong Kong.

We can hear the crackle of small arms fire and the occasional larger boom before we get to the range. The driver lets us off in front of a large, unfinished teak building with beer advertisements plastered all over it.

We walk inside and it looks like a saloon out of the Wild West. One of the two Cambodian men who greet us is wearing a big, white Stetson hat. The walls are covered with rifles, rocket launchers, mortars and grenade launchers. A lengthy English menu of gun rental and ammunition prices is set into the middle. A long glass case is filled with pistols, ammunition and what look to be a variety of hand grenades. At the back is a wire cage filled with live chickens. An industrial-scale, glass-doored refrigerator stocked with Angkor pils, Black Panther stout and Tiger lager hums loudly in the opposite corner. I don't know why they need the refrigerator, the place is ferociously air-conditioned. The man in the Stetson is also wearing a down vest and the other guy's in a jeans jacket.

I buy a hundred and fifty rounds of 9mm bullets for the gun I've brought. I don't even know how to load it. The guy in the jacket shows me. It's harder than I thought it would be. There's a very tough spring in the magazine and after the first six bullets it becomes increasingly difficult to push the rest into place. No wonder I've got two magazines; you can't reload one of these things quick. As cold as it is, I'm beginning to sweat a little from above my eyes by the time I've got the gun fully loaded. And my fingers hurt.

Lei Yue has no idea what she wants to shoot. The man in the Stetson suggests an AK-47. It's the world's most popular assault rifle, more than eighty million sold. It's the Big Mac of lethal weaponry; ubiquitous, deadly and dependable. He gives her two clips of thirty rounds each, slams one into place and hands it to her. It looks big in her hands, maybe too big.

She begins to hand it back and he holds up a hand to stop her. He reaches into the pistol case and pulls out a well-worn, red leatherette photo album. It looks like something your grandmother would reminisce over. He leafs through it to about the middle, then turns it around for us to see.

There's two pages of pictures of kids, some of them little kids no bigger than Lei Yue, firing AK-47s. Some of them are in Africa, a few in Asia, a couple look like they must be in Latin America somewhere. One of the kids, dressed in Khmer Rouge black pajamas and red scarf, is a member of a firing squad. You can tell how short he is by comparison with the other four members of the squad. He's in the middle. The man tied to the stake in front of them is slumping to the ground.

This is apparently supposed to reassure Lei Yue that the gun isn't too big for her. She turns to me, holding the rifle tight against her chest, her face going pale. It looks like she's fighting her breakfast back. I take a step away in case she loses the fight and spews in my direction.

"Maybe you don't want to do this. You can wait in here while I practice."

I can practically hear her gritting her teeth. I don't know how her voice gets out past them, her lips don't move. "*Chingate! Vamanos.*"

She walks out fast through the door next to the beer cooler. Stetson Man asks if we want paper targets or chickens. The chickens cost extra but if they're not too shot up he knows a vendor in the Central Market who'll buy them from us at half the price we pay for them.

"What about cows? Got any cows or pigs or sheep or something?"

Understanding sarcasm isn't his strong suit. "So very sorry mister, before we have cow, but too much trouble. You want cow, pig, you pay today, come back tomorrow." I take the paper targets.

He tells me to pick up some beers on my way out. One's included with every fifty rounds of ammo. That's comforting. I'm wondering if maybe body armor is a good idea on the firing range. A bunch of drunk tourists with guns, that's all I need. I hear some of the chickens clucking as I walk away. Maybe it's in relief.

Lei Yue is waiting outside the door. She isn't sure what to do. I spot two open lanes next to each other. No, that's not what they're called. That's bowling. Positions, firing positions, I think that's it. There are about twenty positions in all, separated by thin sheets of plywood with a table top built into them in front. At each position a pair of ear muffs and goggles hang from a small chain anchored to the wood. The ground crunches with metal cartridge shells underfoot. It's slippery.

Lei Yue won't let go of the rifle, so I place the ear protection over her head then turn her to face the target area. I clip the human shaped target to the overhead wires for her and send it back about thirty feet. I've fired rifles before, but none quite like this. I show her how I think she's supposed to hold it, show her how to aim and tell her to squeeze the trigger slowly. Her first shot goes through the belly button. The rifle doesn't have much recoil, so she handles it easily. I pat her on the shoulder and head to my position.

I'm not sure how far back to place my target. Pistols are a close up weapon, not quite hand-to-hand combat like a knife, but not a whole lot better unless you really know what you're doing. I don't know what I'm doing, so I send the target about as far back as I did for Lei Yue. A pistol's not nearly as accurate as a rifle, but I've got more experience than she does.

I hit the target three times out of my first thirty, none of them in the "kill zone." I stand there shooting like I'm supposed to; legs spread and feet planted, both hands on the grip, arms relaxed but strong in front of me. I sight with one eye closed and slowly squeeze the trigger. If the target was shooting back I'd be a dead man. It's a good thing I'm wearing goggles because spent shells fly up and bounce around.

When I finish I step back and look for Lei Yue. She isn't there. Her target is though. It's shredded. It didn't stand a chance. I stand there staring until I hear laughter.

She's still got the AK-47, with two new clips, targets and a pair of goggles. "Maybe I should go out and do the dangerous work and you should stay in the hotel for back up."

"Yeah, yeah. A pistol's a lot harder to handle than one of those."

"I'm a *cábrona* for even thinking this, but this is a lot of fun."

"It's probably not much fun when the target's shooting back."

She wants to try the Glock. I reload the magazines and let her shoot one of them at my target. I've hardly used it anyhow. She plants thirteen of fifteen in the gut. We don't know where the other two went.

"You've got the knack."

"I guess so. I'm not sure that's a good thing."

"Just so long as you don't ever have to use it."

We change targets and I move mine up to about twenty feet. Loading the two magazines takes longer than shooting them, but I'm done in about twenty minutes. By the last thirty shots I'm doing better. I hit the target twenty-three times, I kill it nine.

Lei Yue waits for me to finish because she wants to show me something. Jeans jacket man's shown her how to put the AK on its full-auto setting, turning it into a machine gun. She's got two clips of thirty shots each and figures we can each shoot one. She tells me that the guy warned her to hold the barrel down and that it's not going to be easy. If the metal gets too hot to hold, take your finger off the trigger before letting go.

She puts on the goggles and ear muffs, sends the target back a little further, to about fifty feet and turns sideways, the rifle pointing out across her body to the left. She plants her feet, the left leading foot at a right angle to the right one, like she's about to make a shot on a pool table.

I put on my ear protection as she pulls the trigger and holds it down. I can see her straining to keep the barrel from flying up. The muscles in her forearms are bulging and she's grimacing. It doesn't last more than three or four seconds. When the loud chatter stops and all thirty shots are gone, she stands there. I was watching her, not the target. When I look downrange I see that it's been shredded, only bits of it hanging from the clips.

She puts the still smoking gun down on the table in front of her, turns around and takes off the ear muffs. "Wow."

"Liked that did you?"

"I don't know. I really don't. I don't think I want to shoot guns anymore."

I don't think I want to either. I pick up the AK and bring it back to the guys inside. I touch the barrel and have to yank my hand back fast. It's hot, about as hot as a cast iron skillet in which you've recently fried up some bacon. I lick my fingertips; they hurt and they're turning bright red.

We've got our money back for the unfired clip and are about to leave when a tall blond, tanned guy who looks like he should be on the cover of *Surfer* magazine struts in through the front door. He moves in the center of a tornado of about a dozen small, brown, young, very young, girls in day-glo yellow bikinis with red number tags pinned to them. They've all been rented from the same bar or brothel. We stand back as they roll up to the counter.

"Hey pard, I hear you've got RPGs. I wanna shoot one of them suckers." He's loud and American. I'm embarrassed to be from the same country and I'm fascinated. He wants a rocket propelled grenade launcher. It's a powerful, relatively lightweight, easy-to-use weapon, originally made by the Russians, now copied all over the world, much like the AK.

Jeans Jacket smiles, climbs up on a foot ladder, takes one down from the wall and lovingly presents it to Surfer Dude. Stetson Hat takes the guy's wad of cash, reaches into the glass case for the right kind of grenade and shows him how to load it onto the barrel.

Surfer Dude bounces the weapon in his hands for a moment, then shoulders it like he's going out on guard duty. He sees us watching and winks. "Hey, me and the girls are gonna have us a blast. Come along and watch." He turns like he's on parade, marches to the beer cooler and selects a couple that he hands to one of the girls to carry for him. They walk outside. We follow.

Jeans Jacket leads the twirling storm of girls and the blonde Yank past all the firing range positions, through a field and down a slope to the banks of a large pond. It's a pastoral scene, ducks and geese bobbing on the water, fish pens strung along a plank walk-way, palm trees swaying in the breeze along the shore. There's a small island about a hundred and fifty feet out. It's got a tiny wooden shack on it. Maybe it's where they keep the duck feed.

Surfer dude sets the RPG down on the ground and puts his hands on his hips to survey the scene. He seems to like what he sees. Lei Yue and I have walked up, parting the swirl of girls around him, and are standing nearby. He reaches into a pocket and fishes out a cigarette case and a lighter. He takes a fat joint out of the case, lights up, inhales very deeply and holds it out in my direction, talking without exhaling.

"Want a hit man? It's not that bullshit they sell in the Central Market. This is the real deal." I wave him off politely. He shrugs his shoulders and takes three more long, deep hits before stubbing it out and putting it back into the case.

Then he holds out a hand to one of the girls, who hands him a beer. He pops the top on that and sucks it back like it was another joint. Foam backs up out of his mouth and down his chin. He hands the can back to the girl, then sits down on the grass and picks up the grenade launcher.

Jeans jacket guy helps him settle it on his shoulder. When he looks set, Jeans Jacket yells something to the girls in Cambodian and they quickly clear out of the way behind Surfer Dude. So do we.

Surfer Dude squints through the small sighting tube on top of the launcher, his finger lightly fondling the trigger. I follow where it's pointing. He's locked in on the wood hut on the island. His finger tenses. There's a slight pffft, then a whoosh, then a roar, then a big flash of light and a boom and the sound of shattering wood. The ducks and geese flap wildly, taking to the air, not sure which way to fly. Some of them fly into the smoke where the wood hut used to be.

Surfer Dude cheers, throws the weapon down and rolls around on the grass. The bikini girls pile on top of him giggling and laughing. Jeans Jacket goes over and pulls the RPG out from under the pile. Lei Yue and I walk back toward the firing range with him as yellow bits of cloth begin to be flung aside.

I look at Lei Yue. She looks at me. We don't talk. What's happened to this country? Has the whole place gone nuts? I'm exhausted. I want to go back to the hotel and take a nap.

| |CHAPTER **EIGHTEEN** | |

here isn't much dusk in Phnom Penh. When we get back to the hotel and I look out over the city it's begun to take on a soft golden hue. Fifteen minutes later it's nearly dark.

Lei Yue's gone out to explore. I've crawled under the sheet and thrown my arms up over my ears to try to nap. It's not working. I'm riled up and thinking too much. Maybe if it was dark enough and quiet enough. But the thin, ratty curtains don't keep out the lights of the city. The air-conditioner pumps out as much noise as it does cool air, but it fails to mask the sounds rising from below: radios, TVs, the warm-up thumping of the discos, the sharp sputter from exhaust-spewing, two-stroke-engined motorbikes, the slicing crisp tinkling of bicycle bells, the occasional gunshot or firecracker, a shouting match in an apartment across the street.

How'd this country get so fucked up? How'd I end up having to take target practice in case I have to shoot someone? I've killed two people in my life, maybe a third, probably caused the death of a couple of others. How'd that happen? I'm not a killer. I don't want to be a killer. It's the killers that make places like this. Cambodia's had too many of them: French, Americans, Khmer Rouge, Vietnamese.

I don't want to be one of them. I'm one of the good guys. Is the only way to prove it by fighting the bad guys, by risking my life? It seems like an awful lot to prove something, especially to myself.

I'm here because it's my job, I guess. I'm here because it's the right thing to do, sort of. I'm here because I worry over the puzzle pieces of all this shit and something in me won't let them go until I've worried them into place. As dumb as it sounds, even to myself, I'm here because of Thanee, too. What the hell I think I can do for her, or whether or not she even wants me to do anything for her, I don't have the slightest idea. Why the hell am I here? I guess I don't really know. It just feels right.

Walking helps. It always does. I get up, get dressed and head out to the street.

It's dusty outside. It's the dry season, no matter how humid it is. Dull, crimson grit hangs in the air, suspended in clouds of exhaust. I feel it coating my body as soon as I leave the conditioned air.

There's a hassle of beggars on the sidewalk in front of the hotel doors. In the greenish light from the fluorescent tubes overhead, their faces look slightly red, coated with the dust. There's five of them and only a dozen or so arms and legs between them. They gather around, close but careful not to touch me.

The youngest is a grinning boy of seven or eight who's hobbling around on a crutch. Luckily for him, if you want to call it that, his missing arm is on the opposite side from his missing leg. I wonder how that happened. Maybe it was two landmines.

An old legless and toothless woman balanced on what looks like a skateboard appears to be the matriarch of the bunch. I take twenty bucks U.S. out of my pocket and put it in her blue plastic cup, waving my arm to indicate it's for everybody. She nods her thanks. They all gather around to look at it. It's a lot more money than people usually give them. The young boy nudges my foot with his crutch.

"Thank you, mister. You good luck."

I hope so; for them, for me, for the whole fucking country. I don't think twenty bucks is enough though. I'll never be enough good luck for this place. I smile at him and head down the street in the direction of the Central Market.

It's the tail end of rush hour. Half the people on the street are trundling home in cyclos, the three-wheeled pedicabs that almost everyone who isn't on an expense account gets around in during the day. Crossing the street I'm nearly run down by a family of six piled onto the front bench seat and handlebars of one. The eldest male, probably the father, is perched high on the bike seat, standing on the pedals to get the strength to keep moving. He's got momentum on his side and plenty of weight with him, so he has to plan his stops far ahead. I haven't given him enough time and I barely get out of the way. The whole family laughs as he veers slightly and bangs through a pothole.

I'm watching them, which is why I get knocked down by an enormous pile of empty, ten-gallon plastic containers coming the other way. There must be twenty of them strapped onto a cyclo. It's being ridden by one very angry looking young guy who is glaring at me from behind them, atop his high seat.

I pick myself up and start dusting off. I wave a hand to say "sorry." I'm thinking that maybe a walk wasn't a good idea after all. But then the young guy lets out with a broad smile, a wave of his own, and with a laugh offers me a cigarette he's got set behind an ear. I can't help but laugh also. I wave off the smoke, but help him adjust the containers where they've been smashed out of whack by the impact.

I'm a lot more careful after that. Between the traffic, potholes and crumbling sidewalks, a simple walk requires a lot of attention.

Those people who aren't heading home are coming out for the night. They're emerging from the buildings and setting up folding chairs, tables, small stands to sell things or simply to sit around. Or they're on motos, the nasty, buzzing little scooters that foul the air and assault the eardrums. No one who can help it rides cyclos at night. There's a lot of street crime and they're too slow.

The people move slow, too, even the young ones. Sure, it's a slower moving culture than in Hong Kong or the U.S. And the oppressive heat doesn't encourage speed. But near as I can tell every fourth or fifth Cambodian on the street is also missing a limb or hobbled or damaged in some way or another.

The few older people I see have far-away looks in their eyes. What an American Vietnam-vet once described to me as "the thousand-yard stare." They don't all look physically damaged. But you can tell they've been hurt, and have seen too much that no one should ever have to see.

I can make out the Central Market down the block. It's a huge, yellow, crenelated art deco building, looking like something constructed out of carefully folded cardboard. It's closed for the night. Stragglers shoving along covered pushcarts move away from it, having been there since five or six in the morning. Dim bare bulbs and dangling fluorescent tubes illuminate the few tented stalls still open around the market's edges.

I work my way counterclockwise around the fringe of the market to La Paillote, an old, gone-to-seed French hotel with a sidewalk café facing the market square. I sit down and order a Ricard, an anise flavored pastis that turns from golden brown to milky white when the ice in it melts, or you add water. It's an appropriately colonial drink.

The waiter, thinking I might order dinner as well, brings a menu and a basket of bread. It's nice enough on the terrace, under the overhead fans that rotate barely enough to cool things down slightly and to keep the flying insects away. The breeze can't quite fight off the stench of the market across the street.

I love the smell of Asia's markets in the morning when everything's fresh, dewy, new, distinct. By now though it's simmered in the heat and humidity all day. It's been boiled into a pungent stew of no longer fresh ingredients that in any event don't complement each other. It's as if the yellow building across the road ingested everything earlier, partially digested it, then spewed it up onto the hot asphalt and dirt around closing time.

There are fresh orchids on every table. The people at the other tables are holding them up to their noses, alternating sniffs with sips of whatever they're drinking. I try it, but it seems, I don't know, effete. So I savor my drink, keeping it near my nose for longer than necessary, inhaling its licorice aroma.

A dreary parade limps and shuffles past along the sidewalk, for the most part ignoring me. A man about my age teeters by on makeshift crutches, one leg missing from mid-thigh, the other a crude wooden peg, polished and dyed a toasty brown. He's one of the few who stops. He holds out a tin cup and I fish in my pockets for a coin to give him. I watch his back, listening to the clopping sound he makes when he walks away.

A small cough and a shrill little "mister" get my attention. My eyes edge back to the street in front of me. I'm nervous about what I might see next. Another "mister," that sounds like a whistle, calls my attention down to the pavement.

There's a young woman, gnarled and twisted, pretzled on the ground, one corkscrewed leg thrust out in front of her and one stump pointed nearly straight up. She's wearing the remnants of a khaki military-looking blouse and a green skirt with khaki piping. She's got a faded green sash, covered with brightly colored pins. It looks like the shreds of a uniform, a girl scout uniform.

I can't tell if she's got the broadest smile I've ever seen, or if something terrible happened to her mouth and it's always that way. She's holding out a flat, yellow and red cardboard box with her one finely-shaped, long, elegant hand. I focus on her hand, it's the only part of her that isn't difficult to look at.

I take the box and set it on the table in front of me. It's durian cookies from Malaysia. I've never figured out why anyone would make sweets from the foulest smelling fruit on the planet, but they do. I smile back at her, pull out my wallet and slip a five-dollar bill into her hand. She takes it from me, lashing her fingers lightly and slowly along mine.

I'm curious about how she gets around, how she's going to leave and continue down the street. But I can't bring myself to watch.

I close my eyes to think about what I'm doing here, what I can do here, what's the point of being here. Is five bucks really going to make much of a difference to that girl? Does she give a damn about what's happening to her country's antiquities?

When I raise my eyelids there's another woman, this one holding a snot-nosed kid, standing in front of me on the sidewalk. She's got a hand stretched out. When she sees me looking, she gestures to her child's mouth, then her own.

She's got a rough appeal. Her face is splotched with dirt, her eyes bloodshot, her hair matted, her white t-shirt filthy with oil and grime and sweat. Something deeper, richer and more powerful radiates from her. Her face is solidly proportioned and symmetrical, strong but gentle, with full lips, a pleasing nose, heavy-lidded eyes perfectly set and lit with an internal spark that overwhelms the deep-set exhaustion that's also in there. Her hair is rich, thick, a complex black, obviously long but fastened into a loose bun that perfectly frames her face. She's got an elegant, fluid neck on firm, squared shoulders that even under her shirt give hints of muscle tone. Clean her up, dress her up, and she'd turn a few heads—mine, for one.

She stands at ease, a sense of physical comfort flowing off her. She holds the child with her left arm wrapped loosely around him, his feet balanced on a knotted blue checked scarf around a cocked hip. The kid's about two or three and he's been crying. He's blonde. He must have a foreign father. She's smiling, a warm, inviting, confident smile. It might be too nice a smile for begging. People might not think she looks pathetic enough. I want to do everything I can to help her.

I stand up, pull out a chair and motion for her to sit down. She looks wary and I'm not sure how to reassure her. I hold my hands out flat, palms up, indicating the table, the bread basket, the menu, and I smile.

She smiles back and slowly begins to move around the small iron fence between the café and the sidewalk. The waiter sees her coming and rushes over to head her off. I get up and stop him, gently taking her arm and leading her to the table. The waiter doesn't like it, but he backs off.

We go to my table. She sits, but keeps the kid at her side, perching on the edge of the seat as if ready to spring up and get out of there quick. I pick up the menu and hand it to her, push the bread basket toward her. I point to myself.

"Ray."

She smiles again and it perks me up. I can't stop smiling back.

"Ampora."

That's all we can say to each other. I don't know a word of Khmer and it's plain she doesn't know any English.

She adjusts the kid until he's sitting on her lap. He reaches out for the bread and she looks at me. I hold the basket up within his reach; he takes a piece in two hands and stuffs it into his mouth, looking up at me with wide eyes while he works it.

I open the menu for her, but it's in English and French. There's no way she can read it. I wave for the waiter. He shows up to stand by my side, pointedly not looking at the woman and the kid.

"Would you care for another drink, sir?"

"Sure, but first, please ask the lady what she and her son would like to eat. Explain to her that I will pay for it and they can have anything they want."

"But, sir, I..."

"But nothing. She's with me. We're paying customers. Ask her."

He's not happy about it but he does. It takes a bit of negotiating and she has a lot of questions. Finally he scribbles something down on his pad and walks away. She looks at me and smiles again, holds an open palm out at me then places it over her heart, then her mouth. I do the same.

Once again I point to myself and say my name. Then I point to her son, being careful to do it with a subtle hand gesture rather than the rude Western cocked finger.

She places a protective hand on the child's chest and says something that sounds like "Norodom," the name of the King.

I wish I could ask her what the King's ever done for her, or her child, but I can't, so I smile and repeat the name.

King Norodom Sihanouk is a patron of the arts. He's got a French-educated love of film, theater, music, dance and painting. He's a widely admired and respected aesthete, a philosopher king. But he collaborated with the Khmer Rouge, and it wasn't the only time he sold out his country to hold onto his power or life.

There's something wrong with the whole idea of royalty. I don't even care if the king or queen really is beloved of the people, if they really do perform good or noble acts. The very idea that they've got inherited power offends and disgusts me. A plague on all their royal houses, I say. But I can't say it to Ampora. Even if I could there'd be no point.

Since we can't talk she concentrates on the kid, playing with him, gently teasing him. I get in on the act, making funny faces, showing him I can touch my nose with my tongue. The people on the terrace around us are staring, but I don't care. My only regret is that I can't talk with her, that I can't find out her life story, that I can't find out if there's anything more than a meal that I can do for them.

My second drink arrives on a tray with a large, steaming bowl of beef noodle soup, a plate of glistening green vegetables flecked with slivers of garlic and reeking of slightly sweet, salty fish sauce and a small bowl of rice. Ampora says something to the waiter, who turns to me.

"Sir, she wants to know why you are not eating."

"I'm not hungry. I'll eat later."

He translates and she looks a little confused. I suppose it's hard for her to imagine not being hungry, not eating whenever there's a chance. I smile and lift my drink in a silent toast in her direction before taking a sip. When I put it down she leans over to sniff at it. She comes up with a sour face and a shrug of her shoulders.

She empties the rice into the soup, then scoops a little of everything out and into the small, empty bowl. She pushes it in front of me and gestures for me to eat it. I think it'll make her more comfortable if I do, so I raise the bowl to my lips and lightly scald them with a small sip.

That seems to satisfy her and she bends her head to the steaming bowl in front of her. She makes happy slurping sounds, pausing every third bite or so to blow on what's in the spoon or hanging from the chopsticks before feeding it to her son, who opens his mouth and looks up at her like a baby bird in a nest.

I get her attention and mime holding a glass and drinking from it. She's got a noodle dangling from her lower lip and it quivers when she speaks.

"*Sohm teuk tai.*"

That sounds enough like "tea" that I wave the waiter over and order a pot of it, three glasses of bottled water and another drink for myself. He casts a dirty look at her when she slurps her noodles. I'll bet he does it, too, at home. I decide to stiff him on the tip.

When she finishes I call him back again.

"Please ask her if she would like anything else, ice cream maybe, or something to take away for later."

He does. She does. I order a banana split for her and her son and a double espresso for myself.

When they're done I don't know what else I can do for them. I crack open the box of cookies and hold them up and out to her. She takes a quiet sniff and smiles. She likes durian. I hand her the box.

I take out a small notepad and a pen and write down my name, address, phone number and email in Hong Kong, along with the name of the Pailin hotel here and my room number. I'm sure she can't read any of it. I don't know what good any of it would do her even if she could. It makes me feel better, though, when she looks at it and clutches it in her hand.

After I pay the bill I go back into my wallet and fish out what's left. It's a little over fifty bucks, nowhere near enough to turn her life around, but enough to make the next month or two a lot easier than it would have been otherwise. Or maybe not. I don't know what she'll do with it. Maybe she's a drunk, or a junkie, and I'm projecting what I want her to be.

She's hesitant to take the money at first, wary again. Her eyes go cold, calculating what I might want in return. I insist she take the money. I'm careful not to touch her, not to even brush against her hand when I pass it to her. I don't want anything from her. I don't want her to think I do.

She finally accepts the money and tucks it into the knot of the scarf around her waist. "*Awkun.*"

I'm pretty sure that means "thank you." I smile and spread my hands wide as I get up from the table. We walk out to the sidewalk and it's awkward not being able to say anything. Finally, I point to the paper I've given her that she's still holding in her hand, point to myself, then put my hands together in front of me and bow slightly in a *wai*. Ampora lets out a small laugh, her son lets fly with a chortle that ends in a stream of drool. I laugh back, turn away and walk quickly toward the river.

| |CHAPTER **NINETEEN** | |

don't get far before two small boys with big guns step out of the shadows and stop me. They can't be more than fifteen. They're dressed in the tatters of what used to be army uniforms. They want cigarettes. I'm getting really sick and tired of underage soldiers looking for smokes at gunpoint. Don't they know it's bad for them? I'm also feeling like a jerk for not carrying around a pack or two.

A big grin, a shrug and spread open palms don't get me much. The taller of the two boys, who's still a good four or five inches shorter than me, and I'm not tall, jabs his AK-47 barrel hard into my gut. The other boy takes inventory of my pockets.

He comes up no happier with what he finds than I am with his search. All I've got is my hotel room key and my wallet, now empty of money. I'm not even wearing a watch. The boys confer a little, then both of them point me at the alley they came out of.

I don't want to go in there. I know better than to let them take me in there. But I also know better than to argue. They're smaller than me, weaker, but the guns make that irrelevant. That's the good thing about guns, if you're on the right side of them.

The tall one is sticking close and I could probably fight him before he'd have time to pull the trigger. But the other one is a few feet away, enough to get off a good shot if I try anything. We edge into the alley. I'm looking around and I don't see anyone watching us.

They back me up against a wall. I don't want to die here. I can't die here. It's too stupid to die here, shot by a couple of teenagers. I'll have to rush them. If I have to die I might as well do it fighting back. Maybe they're more nervous than they look and they'll run away.

But they've stepped back. They're out of close range. The tall one has his rifle pointed straight at me, his finger on the trigger. The littler one smiles at me and gestures. I think he wants me to take off my clothes. Maybe they figure they can sell them for something.

I strip down to my boxer shorts and toss everything into a pile in front of them. They motion at me to lie down, my face to the wall. The ground's filthy, viscous with an awful residue, reeking of human shit and piss. I resist doing it for a moment, but the tall one raises his rifle and sights down the barrel at me. I can sense the bore between my eyes. I lie down, wrapping my arms around my head, trying to breathe slowly through my mouth.

An eternity passes. Isn't that what they always say? I don't see my life pass before my eyes; I don't see a bright white light beckoning from the end of a tunnel. It takes a long time, a very long time. I hear them above and behind me in distorted, slow waves of sound; their voices deepened and lengthened, the loud scuffle and shrill chirp of rats in the alley. Water's dripping somewhere. Each drop sounds like a torrent.

At last I hear giggles. I'm kicked a few times in the side. Not hard enough to break anything, but there are going to be bruises. Then I hear more giggles, then footsteps—shuffling at first, then running away.

I wait—feeling relieved, humiliated, exhausted, pissed off. I lie there, the sounds becoming less distinct, the smells more so. I've got to get out of here. I raise myself up in stages. To my hands and knees, to my knees, to a foot and a knee. Finally I stand, holding myself up against the alley wall.

There's a person silhouetted in the light from the street at the mouth of the alley. I don't have anything left that anyone could possibly want and I don't give a shit anyhow. I clench my fists and walk toward them, ready to attack first if I have to, ready to make the first move, to be the aggressor, not the victim, for a change.

It's Ampora, still holding her son. What's she doing here? Did she follow me? Why? I got the impression she spends a lot of time wandering around town. Maybe that's it. Maybe this is a coincidence. I'd like to believe it is. She looks concerned. She gestures at me and holds out her hands, raising her eyebrows, miming the question.

I hold up two fingers, cock two fingers and raise a thumb to look like a gun. She comes close to me, looks me in the face, reaches out a hand and squeezes my shoulder, kneads it. Her flesh is soft but the muscles beneath it are strong. She steps back, turns her hand palm toward the ground and curls her fingers under several times in the polite, southeast Asian gesture for "come here" or "follow me."

I'm not sure why I do. She's a friendly face, her presence is comforting. I can't bring myself to think she means to do me any harm. We walk several blocks down the middle of the street, motos and the occasional car swerving around us. It's safer to be so exposed, but it's embarrassing in my underwear.

We walk in the direction of the river. I can see the Cambodiana Hotel up the street to the right in front of us. It's the biggest, fanciest hotel in town. It sprawls along the riverbank, lit up, inviting. But that's not where she's leading me. We turn left, away from it down the riverfront boulevard, then down a small dirt path until we come to a row of scrap wood shanties built on stilts out over the bank. I can smell the fecund, vegetable odor of the water underneath. I can feel a light breeze off it brushing my face, filtered by the reeds at water's edge.

Ampora leads me to the fifth shack along the row. There's no door, just a flap of tar paper that she pulls aside to invite me in. It's dark, I can hardly see. I stand in the entry waiting for my eyes to adjust or a light to come on. I hear her moving to a far corner, a faint whispering in a tone that tells me she's talking to her child. I hear a creaking of boards and movement back toward me.

Then a flick, sizzle and shsssh of a match lighting. I can see her, bent over a small glass lantern. There's another sizzle and the lantern flares. She turns the wick down and picks it up. She sets it on an upturned crate in the middle of the floor. It throws deep shadows around the room.

There's another upturned crate in the center of the room. In one corner there's a larger crate filled with bedding, her son in it, facing the wall. In another is a bucket with a thick rope attached to it, next to a hole in the floor. There's a shelf with two bowls, two porcelain tea mugs, a couple of spoons, a few old tins.

To my right, by the entry, is another set of bedding, laid out on the wood planks, no mattress, no pillows. Above it there's a rope strung between the walls, clothes draped across. At the head of the bed, on the wall, are two pictures torn from magazines. One is of King Sihanouk. The other is of an American family. They could be a TV family from the 1950s; a mother and father, a son and daughter, sitting on a big, red sofa in a large, middle-class, brightly colored living room, with a decorated Christmas tree behind them.

Ampora pulls down a large piece of fabric from the rope over the bed. It's a sarong, and she hands it to me. She looks amused at my clumsy attempts to tie it properly. She steps up and does it for me, then gestures for me to sit on the crate in the middle of the room.

She goes to the shelf, takes down the two mugs, sprinkles leaves from one of the tins into them and walks outside. In a minute she's back with two steaming cups of tea.

People say that hot drinks are supposed to cool you down in hot weather. Maybe they help balance your inside temperature with the outside. I don't think it works for me. After two delicate sips I'm sweating profusely. I know that's also supposed to cool you down and it does, technically. But it sure doesn't feel like it.

I smile at her. "*Awkun.*" She said it to me when I gave her the money earlier. She smiles back and *wais*.

She sets her cup down on the floor, then squeezes my shoulder again. She steps to the corner and picks up the rope that's tied to the bucket, lowers the bucket through the hole, shakes the rope around and then pulls it back up filled with river water.

Ampora dips a cloth into the water, wrings it out and hands it to me. I use it to wipe my face and upper body, then hand it back. She turns away from me, squats in front of the bucket and starts to take off her shirt. I turn to face the entry. I wouldn't mind watching. But I still don't want her to think that I want anything from her. My money was a gift, it wasn't meant to buy anything. I'm tired of things being bought and sold, especially people.

I hear water splashing and a low tuneful humming, a song I don't know in a scale I don't recognize. It's peaceful here, simple, it lulls and soothes me. It's a relief to be here, my brain emptier than it's been for a long while.

Sometimes I think I want a simple life, with little enough in it there's not much to worry about. I could stay here, live here. I don't have a lot of money but I have enough that I could make the rest of this life more comfortable for her and her child and for me. No one would try to hurt me. I wouldn't have to hurt anybody. I wouldn't have to worry about the things I have, the things I don't have, the things I want.

Am I nuts? Am I completely fucking nuts? This isn't simple. This isn't easy. This isn't peaceful. Poverty's complicated. It's worse than I can possibly imagine. Every day, every minute, Ampora and her son are beaten down, tormented, thwarted in every possible way. They live miserably, they'll die young. In their lifetimes they won't come close to enjoying the options, choices and freedoms I don't even think about because they're the things I take for granted.

What can I do for them? Nothing. The tea leaves in the cup she handed me are a greater gift than the lousy fifty bucks I gave her. I could dress her up, find her a job, send them money every month, put her kid through college. Great for them, but what about everybody else? What about this whole fucked up country? What would it really accomplish? It would be like trying to make tea with those few dry leaves by throwing them in the river that bleeds past beneath us.

The humming and splashing stop. I hear feet padding toward me. A light touch on the back of my neck, then she's standing in front of me.

She's naked, glistening in the dim light, sheathed in beads of wash water. I want her. And I don't. My cock's stirring in the sarong. I want to want her. I reach out my hands and lightly clasp the smooth curve of her thighs, pulling her closer to me. My nose opens wide and inhales her. She smells of freshly blossomed flowers and dark rich soil and a faint wisp of smoke and a bright slice of citrus.

What is it with me and women lately? It's like I've been surrounded by women I want, women offering themselves to me. Susan and Thanee and Ampora, and there's nothing I can do about it. I'm attracted to the *apsaras*. But I can't have them either. They're made of stone and all I can try to do is resuce them.

I can't do this. I'm not going to. It's not going to help; not her, not me, not her son asleep in the corner. I've got to get the hell out of here, and fast. I'm not strong enough to stick around any longer.

I stand up and she takes my hand, thinking she's leading me to the bed. But I hold my ground and gently pat her hand. She turns and I look into her eyes. I want to lose myself in them. I want to feel the press of her lips, the whisper of her breath, the slick, moist rub of her body against mine. She leans in to kiss me and I hold my fingers to her lips before they can get to mine.

I try to make my eyes look sad, but I'm not sure how. I try to tell her with my face, my hands, my posture, how very much I want her but why I can't do it. Why I have to go. If only we could speak the same language. If only I could explain. Maybe that would make things worse. Maybe she'd think I was being stupid, another Western man with confused, romantic ideals. I've got to get out of here before I convince myself of that.

| | CHAPTER **TWENTY** | |

I t's been a very long day and it's only a little after eight when I get back to the hotel. Lei Yue tells me to hurry up and get ready to go out. She asks where I've been. I tell her while I'm getting ready.

"You did what?"

"You heard me."

"Yeah, but I can't believe it. I know I'm too short for you, and you're not my type either. But what the hell kind of guy are you that you keep turning down naked women?"

"Damned if I know. I was trying to be honorable, do the right thing."

"Great, so give yourself a medal. I don't know, though, if it would be for valor or stupidity. Maybe you're gay, ever think of that?"

"Thanks for all your support."

"Don't mention it. I'm glad you got back to the hotel in time to go to this meeting with me. You looked almost cute in that sarong and no shirt though. Maybe if you did some sit-ups or something."

"Enough already. How'd you set this up?"

"I asked about antiques at the front desk. They sent me to a handicraft place down on Mao Tse Tung Boulevard. All they had was fakes, but I was hinting around at wanting the real thing and a driver overheard me. He said he could hook me up."

"He use those words?"

"You know what I mean."

"It sounds pretty flimsy."

"It gets better. He took me back into town, to a Chinese restaurant near the Air France office up the street, then told me to sit in the farthest back booth and order a pot of *boh-lay cha*."

"That's a strong tea from Yunnan Province isn't it?"

"You're smarter than you look. Anyhow, so the waitress is supposed to tell me they're out of it. Then I'm supposed to say I'll have any red tea they've got, but I want it with milk."

"Somebody's been watching too many spy movies."

"Yeah, I know, but it worked."

"What happened?"

"A guy came out from the back and sat across from me. I think he was Vietnamese-Chinese. He spoke Cantonese in that slow, deliberate way that they do in the Chinese part of Saigon."

"What'd he want?"

"It was more about what I wanted, although he did want to see my passport. He had some dumb trick questions that I think were meant to figure out if I was a cop or not."

"How do you know he's really got the goods?"

"I don't, but he sounded right. He told me he works on commission for Angkor Flower Trading. Isn't that the company that's the general's competition? I'm hungry anyway and we're meeting him at a restaurant. The worst that can happen is dinner."

"Okay, so where're we going?"

"It's a branch of some restaurant in Bangkok. It's the world's largest restaurant, or this one is, I'm not sure which. It's got waiters on roller skates, live bands, a tower of flaming seafood, that sort of thing."

"Jesus, those kinds of places are always awful."

"Don't be such a stick in the mud. It'll be fun, and maybe this guy'll be useful."

The car and driver we hire from the hotel takes us across the bridge to the other side of the river. I can just make out the dark area, between the Cambodiana and the bridge, where Ampora lives. We turn up a road paralleling the other bank and finally pull up in front of what looks like the entrance to a big Hollywood premiere. There's a battery of six buzzing, smoking, searing searchlights combing the skies from either side of a wide, bright red carpet.

A bald giant in a red tuxedo opens the car door for us. We walk down the carpeted path trying not to fry our eyeballs on the lights. A riot of sound is rising to greet us from ahead, but all I can see is the river, the few lights of the city across it and a long, bright red dragon in front of us.

The path ends at a railing at a cliff's edge. The dragon is floating in the air a few feet beyond that. We're about thirty feet away when the dragon turns its head our way and lets out a deafening roar that stops us cold. Lei Yue grabs hold of my hand. I don't think she's frightened, just not sure what to do next. Neither am I. We look at each other, then back at the dragon.

The beast tilts its head up and a long tongue of flame fires out of its mouth and into the sky. While that's happening, a large phone booth rises up out of the ground in front of us. The bald giant's twin sister is in it. She's as tall, as bulky, her head shines as much, only her tuxedo is different, it's black. When it stops rising she pushes open a glass door and holds it for us.

I freeze in place. "Lei Yue, I think this has got to be the weirdest place I've ever been. What've you gotten us into?"

"Snap out of it. I'm hungry."

We step into the booth. It's an elevator on a hydraulic device that lifts it from the bottom. Looking out through the glass I can see the dragon, still in the air above us. It's made of plaster, straddling two Roman-style columns that are held up by a metal framework sunk into the cliff face. The restaurant's below, blanketing the river bank. It's a pattern of bright red and yellow circles the size of a couple of football fields, lit by stadium lights along the edges. There's a pond in the middle and a tall, graceful pagoda seems to float on its surface.

Other than a gate, the back of the elevator is open. The buzzing of hundreds of voices, the clatter of thousands of dishes, the shrill amplified voices of singers accompanied by the ting ting ting and plink plink plink and occasional plonk or bom bom of traditional music pushes in and wraps around us as we descend into it all.

At the bottom we're greeted by the giant and giantess's triplet, another man. He leads us to a podium where Lei Yue tells a woman dressed like a geisha who it is we're meeting. She consults a large ledger, then bends her head to a small microphone pinned above her breast and mutters into it, turning back to smile at us when she finishes.

In about a half minute Scarlet O'Hara glides up to us. She's wearing a big, frilly, pink confection of a dress with immense crinoline hoop skirts. She'd need a lot more flesh on her to pull off the pillowy, bosomy look the top of the dress aspires to. She's dusky, her hair a little nappy, a product of the race-mixing that was quietly common in the antebellum American South, and seems to have been transplanted to southeast Asia.

She flops a loose hand into mine. I give it a light squeeze and she lets out a girlish gasp.

"You here to drive us to our table?"

She gives me a blank look.

"It's a big place. How long's it going to take to get there?"

She smiles and shrugs. "Sorry mister, no English."

I smile and shrug back. She collects two menus that look as if they could be the yellow pages for a fair-sized town and tilts her head to indicate we should follow her.

It's hard to keep up. For a moment I can't quite figure out why she isn't taking any steps, how she's moving so swiftly and smoothly. Then I catch a glimpse of the roller skates at the bottom of her skirt. Others are gliding quickly along the wooden walk-ways as well: waiters and waitresses; bus boys and girls, all beauty queen gorgeous; beribboned and sashed beer and cigarette ladies. A soft rolling rumble and rhythmic clicks underlay all the cacophony from the bands, the hubbub of voices, a loudspeaker calling out what sounds like numbers, the crackle of walkie-talkies.

I'm thinking we might need to stop and rest a while, but before I suggest it we get to our table. It's behind a large screen on a slightly raised part of the deck. There are six people there already. I don't know four of them.

I'm glad to see Thanee. She doesn't look glad to see me. I'm not happy to see General Tran.

I stop a few feet away, grab hold of Lei Yue's shoulder and spin her around. "We've got to get out of here quick. I'll explain later."

I turn around, planning to walk away fast, but Scarlet O'Hara's gone and in her place two more of the big, bulky, bald tuxedoed people are in the way. I'd risk trying to shove past them if the one on the right didn't have a small gun in his indelicate hand.

There's a light tap on my shoulder. It's the general, of course.

"Please, Ray, do you and your colleague join us for dinner as planned. Thanee will be pleased to see you and we can have our discussion after we have eaten."

I nod my head at Lei Yue. "Let her go, General. She's not a problem for you."

"Please, Ray, let us be civilized. Of course I insist that Miss Wen join us. I would be a bad host otherwise."

The two big guys sandwich us between them at the table. The general, across a bright expanse of yellow cloth, cracks open a new bottle and pours stiff shots of brandy into snifters. He puts them onto the Lazy Susan and spins them around to us.

I lift my glass, sniff at it, letting small explosions of aroma go off in my head, then gesture with it at our host. "Lei Yue, meet General Tran and his, I'm not really sure what she is, daughter, concubine, protégé, Thanee."

Thanee's had her face lowered, but she lifts her eyes to look at me from under mussed hair covering her forehead. She looks sorry, resigned, sad; at least I think she does. That's how I hope she's feeling.

I take a slug of the brandy, not a sip like you're supposed to. It shocks me inside, puts my body on alert. One will do that; more will have the opposite effect. I'm tempted to get drunk. It's a bad idea.

"General, you told me you don't believe in coincidence. If this isn't one, how'd you arrange it?"

"What is it, Ray, that your boy scouts say? 'Be prepared.' That is it, isn't it? I attempt always to be prepared, in particular when opportunity arises. What many people would call 'luck' I create for myself. Your diminutive colleague, Miss Wen, came to a shop in which I have an interest. The employees there are instructed to alert my associates when someone inquires about any of my businesses. That can lead to sales opportunities or information that will assist in the protection of my interests. As Miss Wen's queries were regarding an activity that is illegal, my associates, how do you say, checked her out. As I am presently in Cambodia for business, this led to our propitious reacquaintance."

"Propitious for you, maybe. What can I do to reassure you, General? There aren't that many places to look for antiques, Lei Yue went to your store by mistake, as I did in River City. We're not interested in your business. We're only interested in it the other way, from here to China to Hong Kong. That's your competitor isn't it? You should want us messing around with him."

"I am so sorry once again, Ray. As I explained before, I have not survived and prospered this long by allowing for coincidence, or relying upon luck. But please, let us not dwell upon unpleasantries for now. I have taken the liberty of ordering for our table. I think you will be pleased. Our dinner should be quite spectacular."

| |CHAPTER **TWENTY-ONE**| |

'm not hungry anymore. I've always wondered if guys on death row really do eat all that fried chicken and ice cream they order the night before their last walk. I've got to get a better look at this place, see if there's any way out.

"General, I need to go to the men's room. Do you know where it is?"

"Indeed. I will have one of my men escort you."

Before I get up I feel an insistent tapping on my leg. Lei Yue's trying to give me something. I wrap my fingers around hers, and around the Glock. She must've had it in her purse. I'm wearing pants with big pockets. That isn't preparation; it's plain dumb luck. My other pair, with smaller pockets, were stolen by the boys in the alley. I slip the gun in my right pocket and make sure that my hand is dangling in front of it to hide any bulge.

The big guy on my left gets up to go with me. He's got his right hand in his tux jacket pocket. Something hard pokes me through the fabric.

As we walk past the general he stops me with a light hand on my arm and a lowered voice. "Please, Ray, do not attempt anything. Your colleague will remain here at the table and there are many innocent people nearby enjoying their dinner." Thanee looks up at me. I'm still hoping it's "I'm sorry" that I'm reading in her eyes.

The men's room is at the far side of the restaurant, near the kitchen. We make our way for several minutes along the paths through the tables. A couple of times we have to quickly shove to the side to let a skating waiter carrying a large tray pass by. If I wasn't worried about Lei Yue, it could be a chance to get away.

The big guy prods me along the side of a huge corrugated metal shed. Hot smoke and steam pour from its vents and chimneys. The air is tearful with garlic and onions, stinging with chilies, cutting with ammonia leached out of seafood, the mineral-rich stench of chicken blood. There's the clatter of pots and pans and knives and spatulas, the inferno roar of volcanic gas flames under gigantic woks, the sizzle of raw food hitting hot metal, the chefs barking commands, line cooks spitting out their replies.

I look back. Even the closest tables aren't paying any attention to the clamor from the kitchen. It's a wall of noise, another piece of the rumpus. The big guy points the way with his pocket and we continue to the men's room.

It's big, too. It has to be, with the number of customers this place can feed. It's empty at the moment, filled only with the racket and the smells coming from the kitchen. The men's room itself has seating for about a dozen and urinals for twenty more. There are six sinks, with a floor-to-ceiling mirror behind them. It's all sparkling clean, and an overpowering reek of disinfectant knifes into me. I have to breathe through my mouth, but even then I feel it searing the lining of my throat.

My attendant nudges me toward the urinals, but I head toward the stalls. I want privacy for whatever I'm going to do, though I don't know what that is yet. He follows.

The stall at the end is extra large, built for people in wheelchairs. That might give me room to maneuver, if I can figure out what to do. When I try to close the stall door, he thrusts out a palm and holds it open.

I've got to get him to let me close the door. I look at him, shake my head, shrug, undo my belt, zip down my pants, yank them and my boxer shorts down and take a seat. He's still watching me, impassive, doing his job.

I flash him a wry smile and start grunting and groaning, making terrible noises like the guy that everyone's heard in the next stall at some point in their life, and that they don't like to think about. I manage to work up and squeeze out a fart; as loud, long, wet and disgusting as I'd hoped for.

The big guy screws up his nose and backs away from the stall, closing the door behind him. I lean forward and as quietly as possible slide the bolt on the lock. I don't know how long that buys me, how long before he checks back in again, how much more rude noise I might have to make to keep him away.

My pants are bunched up at my feet. I hope he's not looking through the space at the bottom of the door, but I have to take the chance. I worry the gun out and into my hand. I have to work the slide to chamber a bullet. More grunting and groaning and the kitchen clamor mask the sound.

So that's done. Now what? He's got a gun, too, and he's better with his than I am with mine. I'm sure of that. I've got to outsmart him, not outshoot him.

I grunt and groan some more to give myself time to think, but he's not very patient and starts beating on the door. He's tall, but the stalls are high enough that he can't peek over. I'm hoping he'll be dumb enough to stick his head underneath, but he doesn't do that either. He keeps pounding.

The flimsy lock is rattling loose of its screws. That gives me an idea. He'll need to put a shoulder to it if he wants to break through. That'll put him off balance. It should be nearly impossible for him to keep his gun on me and bust in at the same time. He's not going to be expecting anything, why would he worry anyhow? He's a lot bigger than me and doesn't know I've got a gun.

I pull my pants up and hook my belt. Then I close the cover on the toilet seat and squat on it, the gun in both hands close to my body, elbows braced to steady the barrel on the middle of the door, my right index finger already slightly tense on the trigger.

My heart's pounding in my chest. His fists are pounding on the door. The uproar of mingled sounds from outside fill the background. My hands want to clench shut but I can't let it happen. I can't pull the trigger unless I have to. My eyes jiggle. Even though it's the big stall, it seems impossibly small. I'm boxed into this tiny place. It's like being buried alive and it's getting harder to breathe, my breath coming out in small, fast puffs.

There's a sharp cracking of wood. The door's about to give. I squint in case of flying splinters. I brace myself, tightening, readying every part that I can, but trying to keep my hands relaxed and my brain clear.

The big guy busts through the door, shoulder first and down like I hoped he would. Everything slows. It takes a moment for his eyes to focus and he's still moving. I'm hoping he sees the gun and that the sight of it stops him before I have to use it.

It's close. He just about has a hand on me when he gets an "oh, shit!" look on his face and stops. I gesture him back a step with my chin. I stand, slowly, on the toilet seat and hold the gun out, pointed between his eyes. He sees my finger on the trigger and he doesn't try anything. He's not paid enough that I'm worth getting killed for.

I prod him backwards a few steps and step off the toilet to follow. Even I can't miss him at this range and he knows it. I hold out my hand for his gun. He gives it to me, gently. I put it in my pocket.

Slowly I turn us around and back him into the stall. I want a little more room between us. I stand back just far enough that I'm still pretty sure I can shoot him if I have to.

He doesn't speak English so I have to order him around with one handed sign language supplemented by chin wags, obvious sounds and facial expressions. The gun gives him the incentive to understand.

I don't know what to do to keep him here. At least I can slow him down. I gesture for him to pull off his shoes and pants. He does. I kick the shoes into the next stall, take the pants and pull out his belt, then toss them as far as I can into another stall.

I toss the belt back at him, gesturing for him to loop it, put his feet into it and cinch it tight. I'm sure it's not tight enough.

My belt's next. I have him tie his hands with it, pull it as tight as he can get it with his teeth.

Keeping the gun on him I squat down to yank his belt end harder. I try tying it tighter with one hand. It works, sort of, but it's not going to hold for long. I do the same with his hands. I unspool a long swathe of toilet paper, wad it up and force it into his mouth. He's staring venom at me and I know he's going to get loose. I just hope I've given myself enough of a head start before he does.

Maybe I can knock him out, like I did to that guy in Pattaya. I move to his side, ease the gun slowly around with me so that he can't see if I'm still pointing it at him or not. I reverse it in my hand, haul back and slam it down behind his ear.

The big guy wobbles, looks dazed, but it isn't long before he's shaking his head, trying to spit the paper in his mouth out at me. He definitely isn't knocked out. I don't know what to do. If I try again I might kill him or I might only make him madder. I could shoot him in the foot, or the thigh. If I'm careful not to hit an artery it won't kill him, but it'll probably put him into shock. That'll slow him down.

I can't do it though. I back out of the stall and look around the room to see if there's anything else I can use to tie him up better. There isn't. I close the door on him, walk a few feet away and listen for a moment, then put my gun in my other pocket and walk out.

Now what am I supposed to do? The big guy won't stay tied up for long. I've got to get Lei Yue out of here, then get us away. I don't think I can call the cops or raise an alarm. I don't know who's working with the general. For all I know he owns this place.

I can't just walk up to the table either. If they see me coming without the big guy, they're going to know something's wrong. I remember the tall, bald, tuxedoed woman who looked a lot like him. When I walk back around the corner of the kitchen I can see her at the front desk. I make my way to her, around the periphery of the tables, hoping no one notices.

Walking up to her I smile and hold out a hand to shake with a twenty dollar bill palmed in it. She takes it and smiles. "What can do, mister?"

"I'm sorry, this place is so big, I've lost my table. Could you take me to General Tran's table, please?"

She looks in the book on the podium and picks up her walkie-talkie to summon Scarlet O'Hara to escort me. I put up a hand and cover the mouthpiece. "Please, could you take me? I don't want to trouble anyone else." With my other hand I edge another twenty out of a pocket and make sure she sees it. She shrugs and motions for me to follow.

I hurry to stay next to her and slightly in front, the way I'd be if she was the big guy and he was moving me along at gunpoint. We come around the edge of the screen and I can see the table. The other big guy is missing. Maybe they were wondering what was taking so long and sent him to find out. That's a stroke of luck.

Lei Yue sees me first. She looks worried. I smile at her. The general sees her looking at me and turns around to look. I move myself in front of the tuxedoed woman as she turns to leave, hoping to obscure her for a little longer. I reach into my right front pocket and grab hold of my gun, ready to pull it out. The other two men at the table begin to get up. They're small men in suits, the ones Lei Yue and I were supposed to meet. I don't know if they're dangerous or not. I can see their hands, exposed, by their sides.

The general's watching us move toward him. I can't risk it any longer. I rush forward, pulling the gun from my pocket but trying to keep it hidden down by my side. The general sees it and begins to get up, his hand moving to the waistband of his pants.

I get within a few feet and hold my gun up and out, pointing it straight at him. His hand stops. I wave my gun at it and it moves away. I point at the chair with the barrel and he sits down. I move up close, poke him in the side of his ribcage with my gun. He says something in Khmer and the two men sit back down. I'm behind Thanee's chair and she's looking up at me.

"Thanee, get up slow and go sit next to Lei Yue. Keep your hands on the table. General, tell your friends to put their hands on the table. Lei Yue, search everybody for guns."

The general is looking up at me, a crack of a smile on his face. "You are more resourceful than I imagined, Ray. I will need to take caution not to underestimate you in the future."

"Take your gun out slow, General. Put it on the table, on the Lazy Susan."

"You Americans are so quaint, Ray. Why a 'Lazy Susan'? Why not some other name? Who was this famous Susan?"

"This isn't the time for linguistics, General. Your gun." I shove mine harder into his ribs and he does what I asked him to.

"Lei Yue, get the gun. Did those guys have anything?" She shakes her head no. "Good, but keep them covered."

So far so good, but it isn't all that far and it's certainly not all that good either. I've got to figure out what to do next, and fast. The table's at the far side of the restaurant, at the river's edge. The screen is keeping it hidden from the rest of the customers. Lei Yue and Thanee are on the side that faces over the rest of the restaurant. It's a better place to be if the big guys show up. I stand the general up and walk him to the far side of the table, where we remain standing.

Lei Yue's holding the general's gun under the table, covering the two other guys, but she's looking nervous. "Ray, *vamos!* We'd better get out of here."

"Yeah, I know. See if you can spot any boats nearby on the river, motorboats." She looks around but can't see anything. She stands on her chair, holding the gun at her side but still pointed at the two men, and swivels her head quickly toward the water.

"There's a small pier with a few boats, but I'm not sure if they're power boats or not. The path to it isn't far from here."

"Okay, that's where we're going. General, I'll be right behind you. Thanee, you and those two guys walk ahead and keep quiet and you'll be okay. If any of you try anything the General isn't going to be happy."

I give the general a shove, but as we start moving I hear a dozen small *pffftts*. The general looks up and I carefully follow his gaze. I can see the tracers of small rockets; they seem to have shot from the top of the pagoda in the middle of the restaurant. They trace a wobbly path upward, then begin to fall back and then there's an explosion of light and color that sears my sockets, followed by huge booming sounds. It's a fireworks display. It might help divert attention from us.

The general stops and turns. "Ray, dinner is served, and it is a shame that you are in such a hurry to miss it."

He's awfully nonchalant. Maybe the stress is getting to him. I step back a couple of feet thinking he might try and do something crazy like grab for the gun. "Ray, what's that? Look." Lei Yue is pointing up and to the left of us. I move the general around so that he'll still be in front of me when I look that way.

There's a large ball drifting down from the top of the tower. It's engulfed in flames, like a slow moving meteorite. I can hear the creaking of wires running through pulleys and the whipping and snapping of the flames. It's coming right at us. I can make out wires leading to a concrete pedestal next to our table. It's got a concave indentation at the top of it. The ball lands in it, nestling perfectly into the hollow, flames shooting up all around it.

There's a loud, sharp crack and sparklers and pinwheels ignite along the equator of the ball. Then another crack and the top half of the ball snaps back and off, falling, flames slowly extinguishing, into a sandbox underneath the pedestal.

It's a cauldron of steaming, sizzling crustaceans; lobster and crab and shrimp and more. A rich, pungent cloud of ginger and chili and vinegar rolls off it. Now I'm getting hungry. It looks and smells stupidly good. Lei Yue is wide-eyed, then laughing. I want to laugh too, but I want to get the hell out of here even more.

The general smiles at me. "Are you certain you would not rather stay for dinner, Ray? You will not get away, so why not enjoy a feast?"

"Some other time, General." I move in again and poke him hard in the gut with the gun. "Move it."

We edge slowly past our dinner. Luckily the tables along the sides of the wooden platform aren't occupied. The path to the pier is about three tables away. I hear commotion headed our way and risk a quick look. The general's men are hurrying toward us. One of them has a gun. The one from the bathroom is pounding along the planks in his socks, his tuxedo jacket and shirt flopping at the top of his bare legs. He's plenty mad.

I've got the general, it's my only advantage. I put him between me and the big guys and keep backing slowly toward the boats. We're about halfway down the path to the pier when they catch up to us. Lei Yue's a little ahead of us.

"Lei Yue, take Thanee, keep the gun on her. Let the other guys go. Get a boat and have Thanee untie the others. Then both of you get into the boat and wait."

I'm not really sure why I want to take Thanee with us. Is she going to be a hostage, a shield? Maybe I think I'm rescuing her. I don't have time to worry about any of it at the moment. I'm running on adrenalin and instinct.

Lei Yue waves the guys away, down the beach, and moves closer to Thanee. I'm moving slowly, careful to keep the general between me and the two big guys who are keeping pace with us about ten feet away. I can see that only one of them's got a gun, but they move apart, trying to flank me.

I reach into my pocket and pull out the gun I took from the guy in the men's room. It's a revolver. I work back the hammer so that it's easier to pull the trigger if I have to. I prod the general's side, letting the two big guys see that I've now got two guns. I point the Glock in their direction, motioning them to move closer together.

"General, tell your guy to drop his gun. Tell them to leave and you won't be hurt."

"I am once again so sorry, Ray. I will not do what you ask. It is, as you say, 'your move.'"

We reach the pier. It's no more than a flimsy, wood-slat walkway a few inches above the level of the river. I can see several boats drifting out onto the water. Lei Yue and Thanee are bobbing at the end of the pier in a small, flat-bottom skiff with a cake beater engine in back.

The big guys are still coming, keeping their distance. The general and I are approaching the boat. I'm trying to concentrate on what I'm doing, trying not to listen to Tran jabber.

"I have many friends in Cambodia, Ray. Many friends in both high and low places. Perhaps you will float away in your boat, but it will not get you far. Stop now, give me your guns and perhaps I will let your little friend go."

Maybe it's selfish of me. I'm not tempted. We get to the boat. Lei Yue's managed to get it started, it's softly puttering. She's squatting at the back of it, one hand on the tiller and the other holding a gun pointed at Thanee who's up front. I step into it, careful not to lose my aim when it rocks underneath me. I move to the middle while pulling the small boat parallel to the pier so I can keep the gun on Tran who's standing on the edge of the planks.

I'm not sure what to do now. One of the big guys has a gun. As soon as we pull away from the pier he can start shooting. I don't want to take the general with us; it's too small a boat for four people. It's dark. Pistols aren't very accurate. I'll have to rely on that.

"Sit down, General. Dangle your legs into the water, put your hands behind your head." He does.

"If you shoot me, Ray, it will not help you."

"I wish I could, General, but I'm not that kind of guy."

"What you are, Ray, only you do not seem to have resigned yourself to it yet, is a dead guy."

"You know, General, your paranoia has got the best of you. I really wasn't trying to do anything about your business before this. Now you've made it personal. I'm going to fuck you up."

"It is unlikely. I will see you soon, Ray. Bon voyage."

I tell Lei Yue to rev up the motor and get ready to take off as soon as I untie us, then to zig-zag across the river and downstream fast.

When the little engine sounds like it's about to blow a gasket I throw off the rope and push us away from the pier.

| |CHAPTER **TWENTY-TWO**| |

A red spot, about the circumference of a lipstick, erupts at the top right of Lei Yue's chest. It's already begun to spread out from the edges before the report registers in my brain. She looks startled, confused, her hands come off the tiller and slap her chest. She starts to say something, I can't hear it, it comes out in bubbles. She crumples where she's sitting, not forward, not back, she dissolves into herself.

We're no more than fifty feet out, moving as fast as we can. It's not fast enough. The middle of the river, the current, we've got to get to it, but it's too far away. Without a hand to guide it, the rudder turns and starts steering us around, back toward shore. Thanee's screaming, laid out on the bottom of the boat, her hands up over her head. I hear another shot. It misses.

I stay low, slither to the back of the boat and pull Lei Yue all the way down, spread her out as much as I can in the middle of the boat. I reach a hand up and grab the tiller and yank hard, pulling the boat back in what I hope is the direction of the far bank. It turns, quick, hitting a log that almost rolls us over.

More shots come, rapidly. Two hit the side of the boat, cracking the wood and making Thanee scream louder. It's hard to hear over the whining of the little engine. I bend down to Lei Yue. It's ragged and weak, but she's breathing.

The shots aren't as loud anymore and not as frequent. I can feel the boat being tugged downstream by the current. We're near the middle of the river. I don't know if it's safe but I sit up for a moment, look back. The lights of the restaurant are fading behind us, moving away around a bend. There are no more shots. I hold the tiller to take us on a diagonal to the other bank, back to the city.

Thanee's stopped screaming. She's whimpering, shaking, curled into a tight ball at the front of the boat. I push out a foot and give her a gentle tap on the shoulder. She looks up, sniffling, a terrified kid behind her eyes.

"Thanee, please, I know this is scary but you've got to calm down. You need to help Lei Yue. See how bad her wound is. I'll take off my shirt, use it to put pressure on it, try to stop the bleeding. Okay? I've got to get us across the river, to the city."

I fumble around, trying to keep the tiller where I want it while taking off my shirt. I toss it to Thanee who is gently lifting Lei Yue, putting her head in her lap, turning her carefully to look at her from both sides.

"What do I do? She's bleeding from both sides."

Shit, I wish I knew what to do. "Put pressure on both I guess. You might have to use your shirt, too."

She doesn't say anything, just nods and unbuttons her expensive blue silk blouse. She wads it up and pushes it hard against Lei Yue's back, then turns her so that she can keep it in place against her thigh. She places my shirt up against the exit wound in front and holds it there, stroking Lei Yue's forehead and cheeks with her other hand.

We've got to get to a hospital, but I don't know where one is. I can see the lights of the Cambodiana Hotel. It's probably got a doctor on call, but we're past it. It'll take precious time to fight the small boat back upstream. The row of shacks where Ampora lives is somewhere in the dark along the river bank ahead of us. If I can find it, we might be able to get some help from her. At least it'll get us safely on shore. I move in as close as I can to the bank and throttle back the little motor, maintaining just enough speed and control to keep from being at the mercy of the currents.

There's the occasional dim light and flickering lantern along the shore. It's not that late and there are plenty of lights on in the city, but they only cast a dim glow on the sky, above and beyond the black wall of the river bank. Not too far ahead I can see the bridge. Ampora's house is a few hundred feet upstream from it. It seems like the current has slowed, that it might keep us close to shore, so I shut off the engine. Maybe I can hear something that will help.

The faint tinkle of a pop song filters out of the darkness. There's a soft green glow where it's coming from, a murmur of voices as well. I can make out a couple of low yellow haloes that might surround candles. Above the line of the river bank I can barely make out dark, rectangular shapes, crude, irregular rooflines in a row. I think that's it. It's gotta be it.

I don't want to start up the engine again, but the rudder isn't very effective without it. The water's edge isn't far but I'm having a hard time getting there. I can't let us drift past the houses on the shore, but we're passing faster than I want. A low overhanging branch is ahead of us. I hope it's strong enough, is attached to something on shore.

I throw my arms up before we get to it. It scrapes but I hold on. The front of the boat veers toward shore. I manage to pull us under the branch and into a small eddy near its base. I can't quite reach the rope at the front of the boat, but Thanee can. She hands it to me and I tie us to the branch.

The water smells like rotting vegetation and diesel. It's deep enough that I swallow some when I jump in. My feet sink into the fine, oily silt of the riverbed. I can make out the black, wood plank floor of a shack hanging over the river. There's a walkway on the other side. I hope it's the walkway that leads to Ampora's house. It's a short, steep climb up. I won't be able to make it carrying Lei Yue. I'll have to get help.

"Thanee, we can't get Lei Yue up from here by ourselves. I'm going to get help. I'll be back soon. Keep applying pressure to her wound."

She whimpers an okay. I scramble up the slope, slipping in the mud, the smaller tree limbs and branches tearing at me.

There's a narrow space between the shacks above me, enough to wiggle through and up onto the walkway. The rough houses all look alike. I'm not sure how I'll remember which one is Ampora's, but I think it was about the fifth in from the upriver entrance to the area. I head that way and when I get to the door that might be hers I knock.

A child starts, making a low whining noise. There's a shuffling and some mumbled words. I see a small, flickering light approaching through the spaces in the sides of the tar paper flap door. Then Ampora is there, holding a candle. She looks at me, a little startled, scared maybe, scowling at me standing there without a shirt, dripping with filthy water.

I look back, wishing I could speak her language. I feel like Lassie in the television series. All I can do is bark, twist my head around, chase my tail and run in the direction I want the rescuers to follow.

My attempts at sign language would be funny if there was anything funny about any of this. I make like I'm paddling a boat, then hold up two fingers and a thumb to say "gun," then mime being shot, then point back down the walkway. I'm trying to figure out what else I can do when she puts out a hand. Her face takes on a look of resignation, as if to say, "Why do I have to keep helping this foreigner?"

Ampora takes a quick look back into her room, at her child, and gestures for me to wait. She walks inside and sets the candle down next to her son's bed, strokes the side of his face and murmurs something. Then she's up and following me down the path back to the boat.

We get to the small space between the houses. I can't explain what I need. Maybe Thanee can.

"Thanee, are you there? Can you hear me?"

"Yes, have you found help?"

"I have a friend with me, she only speaks Khmer. Can you tell her we need people to help bring Lei Yue up from the boat?"

Ampora listens, then puts out her hand to say wait again and hurries back the way we came. In about a minute she returns with a man and a teenage boy. They have a blanket and a rope. She shouts something down to Thanee who shouts back. The boy disappears down the slope with the blanket, unwinding one end of the rope.

Two minutes later the boy appears again—behind Lei Yue, who's tied into the blanket, pulled from above and pushed along from behind. Her body's bent at a strange angle, bent over the rope tied around her middle. She's unconscious, her breath wheezing in and out in little gasps and an occasional low moan.

I untie her, set her on the blanket, show Ampora where her wounds are and mime applying pressure. She looks up at me, puzzled, but she's used to not asking questions, to taking things as they come. She kneels next to Lei Yue and holds the blanket hard against her wound. I throw the rope back down to Thanee. "Do you need some help getting up? I can come back down."

She sounds scared. "What are you going to do?"

Huh? "What do you mean?"

"To me—what are you going to do to me? Maybe I should take the boat and go."

"It's not me you have to worry about. Make up your mind quick though, I've got to get Lei Yue to a doctor. I'm not waiting around."

It's quiet for a tense, nervous few moments. I'm about to pick up Lei Yue and go when I hear rustling in the branches.

"Are you coming up?"

"Yes."

Her head pokes up through the space between the houses, then the rest of her. I take her hand and help her up the rest of the way. She's put her badly wrinkled, now bloody, shirt back on and has mine knotted around her waist.

I hold her hand a moment longer than necessary and squeeze it. "I'm not going to hurt you. I don't blame you for any of this. I can use your help." She looks at me and smiles. I drop her hand and bend to pick up Lei Yue. I carry her as fast as I can to Ampora's shack.

Ampora has gone ahead and when we arrive she is carrying her son out. She stops to talk with Thanee, then walks away.

"She is taking her son to a friend's house, to make more room for us. She says to put Lei Yue in her bed. She knows someone who will go to get a doctor and bring him back. She addressed me as if I'm your wife."

"What'd you say?"

"I told her I was a friend, that you're helping me, and that the other woman is someone you work with."

It's hard to see in the shack by the candlelight. I find the bed and ease Lei Yue down on it. Thanee has found the lantern and matches and soon the hiss, flick and whoosh gives us better light. She brings it over to the bed and holds it up while I get a better look at Lei Yue's wound.

The bleeding has slowed to a slight ooze at the edges. I gently turn her over and look at the entry wound. It's small, round with slightly blackened edges and not much blood. The exit wound is bigger, but not a whole lot bigger. Is that good or bad? It's slightly more ragged and there's more blood. She needs a doctor. I don't want to move her anymore until I know she can take it. I think the bullet missed her heart and any major arteries or she'd be dead already, but I'm sure there's a lot else that could be wrong. I don't know much about first aid but what little I do know tells me to keep her warm and hydrated and to keep the wound clean.

Warm's not a problem. It's hot and humid in here but I wrap the blanket around her anyhow. Hydrated and clean are going to be trouble. She's still unconscious and I can't pour water down her throat. In any case I'd need boiled, then cooled down, water and I don't know where to find any. That's the problem with cleaning the wound, too.

I sit and put Lei Yue's head in my lap. All I can do is wait for the doctor to come. "Thanee, do you think you can find some clean water somewhere? See if you can find some clean cloth, too, and something like alcohol—even booze, if it's clear and potent."

"I will go look. Will you be all right?"

"I hope so. I'll be better if you can find what we need."

She leaves. I hear talking outside. When it stops Ampora comes in. She's got two large bottles of water. They're open bottles and well-used, but I can only hope it's clean. She squats and hands me one, setting the other on the floor within reach.

I smile at her. "*Awkun*." She smiles back.

She gets up and pulls a thin, worn white towel down from the rope above her bed. She sits back down next to me and soaks part of the towel in the water from one of the bottles. She squeezes drops of it out onto Lei Yue's lips, then gently mops her forehead. She pulls open Lei Yue's blouse and lightly daubs at the edges of the wound with the wet towel, brushing away dirt and dried sweat.

She takes the other end of the towel and soaks it, then reaches up and wipes off my face. She points to the bottle, then to my lips. I hadn't realized how thirsty I am and I take a long, deep swig of the water. It tastes faintly of chlorine and that's reassuring.

I'd like to do more for Lei Yue, but I'm not sure how. Her breathing is more regular than it was, but she's still unconscious. I look at her, at the towel and at Ampora, and raise my eyes. Ampora pours water on the towel and squeezes more drops onto Lei Yue's lips. I want another drink myself but I hold back. I don't know why. It isn't going to hurt or help no matter what I do.

Thanee comes back into the room. She's carrying another bottle of water and a bottle with a cork in it, filled with a slightly milky liquid. "This is all I could find, sorry."

I pull the cork from the bottle and take a whiff. It's potent all right, not something I'd want to light a match around. "Ask her what this is."

She waves the bottle at Ampora and asks. Ampora screws up her nose and tells her.

"I think it's like vodka, made from rice. It's fresh, that's why it's white."

Good enough for now. Better than nothing anyway. I reach out for the towel and then douse a dry part with the liquid. The stink of it rises and brings tears to my eyes. I bend over Lei Yue and brush the towel around the edges of her exit wound. When I finish that I hold the wet cloth hard up against the hole in her chest.

Her eyes flick open. She starts sputtering, coughing. I hope that doesn't start her bleeding again. Her lips are moving. I have to bend over further to hear.

"Ow, that stings, what the hell, what's, where…"

Ampora wets a corner of the towel again and holds it up to Lei Yue's lips. She sucks on it, slowly at first, then greedily. Ampora pulls it away and is wetting it again but I stop her.

"Lei Yue, it's me, Ray. You've been hurt. If I hold a water bottle up for you, can you drink?"

Her eyes are wide and fixed on my face. She weakly nods yes. I put a hand behind her head to tilt it slightly up and then hold the bottle to her lips, tilting it barely. She wants more. I can tell she wants a lot, but I'm not sure how much is good for her, how much I can give her without her choking on it. Where's the damn doctor? I pull the bottle away.

"Ray, what, what happened? I don't remember. We were in the boat and…"

"You've been shot. One of the general's guys shot at us and you were hit in the chest."

"Is it bad? Am I going to…?"

"It isn't good. I don't know. You were bleeding but we stopped it. A doctor is coming."

She doesn't hear me. She's out again. Her breathing is a little easier now, steadier. I'm hoping that means something good. I hear laughing from the corner where Ampora's son has his bed. Ampora and Thanee are squatting on the floor talking and looking at me. When they see me looking back they start laughing again. It's good to hear laughter, even at my expense.

| |CHAPTER **TWENTY-THREE** | |

The doctor looks impossibly young. I want to ask for his credentials, a diploma, but he does have an impressive medical kit in a beat up black bag. He's one of the few Cambodian doctors left. The Khmer Rouge killed almost all the others for the crime of being educated. Most of their own leaders had graduated from university in France. So they knew firsthand how dangerous an educated elite could be.

The young doctor's family had managed to get out of the country, to Vietnam, just before the Khmer Rouge took it over and closed the borders. He'd gone to medical school in Moscow.

The doc tries to find a common language for us to speak. He speaks Khmer, Vietnamese, Russian, Thai and some French. I feel like an idiot when he tries all five out on me. My swearing in Russian and few phrases of high school French won't get us anywhere. I don't know why he wants to talk to me directly anyhow. Thanee can translate.

He wakes up Lei Yue, to make sure he can, then puts her back out with a shot of something, morphine probably. In a country that's been at war so frequently and so recently, it's one of the few drugs that isn't in short supply. He uses pure alcohol to better clean the wounds, then puts on a clean dressing.

Lei Yue needs to get to a hospital soon. There's only so much the doctor can do for her. The local hospitals are terrible, worthless. The doctor says we should take her to the clinic at the Cambodiana. It's for guests, but for enough money they'll admit her.

They do, but the hotel doesn't have room for Thanee and me. I can't go back to the Pailin because the general's men know that's where I've been staying. It's getting late, we're tired, and we've got to spend the night somewhere. We're sitting on a sofa in the hall outside the clinic. I'm thinking out loud. Thanee stops me.

"Ampora said we can stay with her if we need to."

"Why didn't you say so before?"

"I did not think you would want to. It is not comfortable. She understands that. She was embarrassed to offer."

"It's a good idea, probably safer than a hotel. But I don't want to put her in any danger."

"I told her everything. She understands, she wants to help."

"Why? All she's done is help me. I've gotta be a pain in her ass."

"She likes you."

"She doesn't know me. I bought her a meal and gave her some money."

"She says you have a good face, a strong heart."

"She's a bad judge of character."

Thanee takes my hand and holds it over her breast. "I think she is right."

"Enough about me. What about you and the general?"

"I owe him much. He is like a father to me. But I am only a possession to him. He did not even stop from shooting at me."

"He was shooting at me."

"Yes, but with a pistol, at that distance, he could have shot me the same as your friend. I am not important to him."

I can't argue with that and I don't want to. It's to my advantage that she believes it. It's probably true anyhow.

"Do you know where the general is, how long he'll be here, what his plans are?"

"He will be here for a week or more. He has special customers, a very big order. He is to meet with them in Siem Reap one week from today."

"Where in Siem Reap?"

"I am not sure."

"Why'd he bring you?"

"He often brings me with him. Sometimes he makes me go for the night with people he is meeting for business. Sometimes I am only his secretary."

"Thank you. I don't know if that's any use, but it might be."

"Do you like me, Ray?"

Yeah, I do, but at the moment I don't care about that. I need to sleep and figure out what to do next. I don't answer the question. "Okay, let's go back to Ampora's, for tonight."

"You like her better than me. She is more beautiful than I am. I am only a whore."

This isn't the time for angst. I want to shout at Thanee, tell her to shut up, grow up, get a life. But it's not her fault. She's young, she's been used her whole life. The man who used her the most, the worst, who she thought loved her like his child, shot at her, made it clear she's expendable. No wonder she's insecure. I want to shut her up. I want to hug her tight and make her feel better.

I stand up, holding onto her hand, and pull her next to me. I give her a hug, lean in to her ear. "Ssshh, I like you a lot. We'll talk tomorrow, after we've slept. You're tired, try to relax."

Ampora greets Thanee as if she's a long lost sister. She greets me with a hand on the shoulder, the other one stroking my face lightly. She offers us tea but we turn it down. Thanee tells her we are very tired, if she doesn't mind, we want to sleep. Ampora says something and they both turn to me, smiling.

"Ampora wants to know how we will sleep. Her bed is small; there is room for two, but not for three. I want to know also."

I look around the room. The kid's bed is way too small. It's amazing that even a kid can fit into it.

"Things are complicated enough already and I'm too tired in any case. You two take the bed, I'll figure out something."

What I figure out is how to toss and turn and scratch on top of the thin sheets, blanket, sarong and a towel I've made a bed of. I can feel the seams in the boards beneath me. I hear Ampora and Thanee whispering across the room. I'm so tired I'm at the mercy of every little crack and creak and sound. My brain is whirling, overly aware of all my joints, where their hard edges rub against the wood planks.

I must have gone to sleep because I only half wake up when the floor starts shaking, the boards start pounding and harsh voices intrude. It's still dark inside, but I can sense Thanee and Ampora sitting up in bed, listening.

"Thanee, what is it?"

"We don't know. People. Quiet."

The tarpaper flap is ripped from the door and two bright flash-light beams skewer my eyes. I can't see anything. A voice, breaking like a young teenager's, calls out, and I hear boots on the walkway coming this direction. I blink my eyes against the light and can make out Thanee and Ampora clinging to each other, terrified, looking trapped.

I start to get up, trying to break through the fuzz in my head to remember where I put the guns, but the flashlight comes closer, then the beam moves to the side before coming back fast and I'm hit hard on the side of the head. It doesn't knock me out but it confuses me. I try to get up again and the muzzle of a rifle appears next to the light, a few inches away. That clears my mind fast.

The room's filling with people. I can't see them but I can hear them, sense them, smell them. Their voices sound young. Thanee and Ampora aren't talking, aren't making any sounds other than their breathing. It's shallow and fast and frightened.

A pair of boots comes closer, a voice from above barks a command. I'm grabbed by at least two, maybe three people. My hands are tied behind my back, my legs are tied together. I try to keep them a little apart so that the binding is loose. It doesn't work. A rag that smells faintly of gasoline is stuffed in my mouth and taped in place; a blindfold's tied over my eyes. I hear Thanee talking, fast, quiet, pleading and then I hear a muffled whimpering.

The voice that gave the order speaks and Ampora answers. It sounds like an interrogation. His voice is gruff, accusatory. Hers is scared, contrite. I hear a slap and something like a fist or a rifle butt on flesh. I strain but I can't loosen the ropes.

The voice barks again and I'm picked up, carried out the door. I'm squirming, writhing, trying to make enough noise and fuss that someone will come out of one of the shacks and at least see what's going on. I hear the cocking of a pistol, feel cold metal against my left temple. I settle down.

We turn left outside the door, so we're heading up and out of the small area of shacks. We don't go far before I can feel that we're turning down, toward the river. It's got to be the general's men, who else would bother kidnapping me? But why didn't they kill me and get it over with? The general should have learned that lesson by now.

There's gravel underfoot, I can hear it crunching. I can hear small river waves slapping up against a boat. The men carrying me splash into the water. Are they going to throw me in? I strain at the ropes; maybe the water will loosen them in time for me to slip out of them before I drown.

They're lowering me, then dropping me onto something bundled and rough. It feels like a coil of rope and it digs into my side. I try squirming into a position that's a little more comfortable. I've just about got it when something heavy drops on me, rolls away, and whimpers. Maybe it's Thanee. Maybe they've tied her up and kidnapped her also. I scrunch up my forehead, working my eye sockets and cheeks, trying to dislodge the blindfold.

I eke out a faint line of sight at the very bottom of my eyes. It's blurry and I have to concentrate to bring it into focus. If I move my head slowly, stop, then work at it, I can see a little. I'm in a motor launch, I think. It's bigger than the one we got away from the restaurant in, but not big enough for any long trips. I'm on a pile of coiled rope. There's another person tied up, about three feet away from me, back to me. It's Thanee and she's squirming, so she's alive.

The engine at the back of the boat pops into action, revs up, motors for a minute and quickly dies down. The boat coasts to a jarring stop, a light thumping continues at intervals. We've pulled along a bigger boat moored in the river.

I'm lifted again, from under the shoulders, hoisted onto the other boat's deck. This one is higher and made of metal. I'm dragged down to the back and shoved up against another pile of rope. It smells of tar and diesel. I tilt my head back, try to make it look like I'm flopping, limber, maybe unconscious. I can just barely see when they pull Thanee on board and drag her over next to me.

I can't talk. I can't even mumble through the rag. I try rolling a little closer to her, making coughing sounds, something to let her know I'm here. My legs bump up against hers and she tenses.

I don't want to scare her and I can't figure out how to let her know it's me. I roll as close to her as I can, my body pressed lightly along the length of her. I try making sounds, any kind of sounds. If she can feel the ropes binding me she'll figure it out. Her body relaxes, a little. Maybe she knows it's me. Hell, who else could it be?

We lie there, in close contact but as far apart as people can be. I hear talk, shouted orders, people moving around. The boat quakes softly, then shudders, then rumbles. Then the rumble becomes a dull, continuous roar and gravity gently pushes on us. I have no way of knowing which way we're headed. Something about the sound, the feel, makes me think it's upstream.

And it's a long way. The sun comes up quickly in the tropics, even quicker it seems with a blindfold on. It's as if someone threw a switch. The temperature rises along with it and before long it's sweltering. There must be a cabin or some structure on the boat in front of us because we aren't getting any breeze or spray or anything to relieve the relentless heat and humidity.

Maybe I can roll into the wind. I can't go to the right, Thanee's in the way. I try to the left but come up against the coil of rope before it does me any good. So I maneuver myself back close to Thanee, but not touching her. It's too hot for contact. I hope she senses me here and that it's comforting. I try to sleep, to disappear inside myself, to detach myself from everything.

Is it sleep? Am I dreaming or delirious? I don't care. There's a waitress, dressed like an *apsara*, our fingers meet around the base of the frosty mug and linger, playing a little with each other, tapping out promises. She bends to my ear and her voice enters me, caressing and soothing my entire body from the inside out. She speaks Khmer, in soft, lilting tones and I understand every word and she's telling me to stay, that she'll be back. She turns and walks away and she glides as if on air, but still, somehow there's an earthy sensuality to it.

It's the best beer I've ever had, near freezing, just bitter enough. The first sip sends small chills down my spine, tingles in my brain, tickles my fingertips. I'm instantly refreshed, revitalized. I lean back in the chair, complete, content, as satisfied as possible.

Music wells up. It's intriguing, mysterious, a blend of all the music I've ever loved: slow Coltrane and Irma Thomas and Etta James and James Brown and Miles and some Rolling Stones and Hendrix and Beethoven's piano sonata number 32 and Celia Cruz and *jaipongnan* from Indonesia and *mor lam sing* from Thailand and *fado* from Portugal and West African guitars and the discordant tinkles and gongs and moaning horns I've heard here in Cambodia. And all of that should be a terrible, ear-splitting cacophony but it isn't. It drifts around me like wisps of smoke. I can see the notes in the air. The sounds mingle and weave together into a new music that embraces me, comforts me, makes me feel safe and warm.

I slowly sip my beer; each taste is like the first. I close my eyes and bathe in the music, savoring the cool, calm spreading within me. I sense someone standing in front of me and open my eyes. It's the waitress, the *apsara*. It's Ampora and she's smiling kindly at me. She's holding her son and he's been crying. His face glistens with tears.

She lifts her blouse and wipes his face. As she wipes it, it transforms, it ages, it grows hard and cruel. The boy in her arms begins to grow, take on muscle tone and bulk. Soon he's too big for her to hold and she sets him down on his feet. Soon he's taller than her and it's General Tran. He stretches and laughs and it's more of a cackle really. He turns to Ampora and slaps her, then points behind her. The saddest look imaginable takes over her face and she turns and shrinks as she walks away.

The general faces me now. He reaches out and grabs the musical notes still swirling around my body. He twirls them in a string over his head and as he spins them they twist into a whip that hisses and crackles in the air. He slowly brings the whip down, snapping it past my face. I hear a whistle, a buzz, then a crack. I sense the bright red blood streaming down off my cheek from below my left eye before I feel the sting of the lash.

The whip curls around his waist like it's alive. He stands in front of me, his hands on his hips, cackling wildly. He's naked and his cock is so hard, so huge, the head so engorged with blood that it looks like a purple sledgehammer. The *nagas* inked onto his legs writhe and slither, their tongues flick out, meeting and entangling in front of my face.

The tongues become one tongue, slender, pointed, strong. It licks at my face, spears into my nose. It wraps around my head and the snake's bodies follow it, curling around me down to my feet, squeezing me, constricting me. I breathe in and the pressure increases. My heart thrums, loud, powerful, each beat expands in my chest, tightening the grip of the snakes. It picks up speed.

All I can hear is the jack-hammering of my heart, the hissing of the snakes and the harsh cackle of the general. His laughter deepens, grows even harsher, echoes around in my head. It's more like a cough now, not from deep in the belly but from the throat, continuous. It evolves into a continuous chatter.

I'm asleep. I must be. It's a dream, only a dream. I can wake myself up, get out of this. There's a small part of my brain I've got control of and I tell it to start screaming, "wake up, wake up, wake up." And finally I do but the throaty coughing doesn't go away. It's still there, in bursts. And there's booms and splashes, too. Sweat is sloughing off me in rushing streams and I'm disoriented, dazed, but I've got to concentrate. What's going on?

The boat's picking up speed, rearing high in front, throwing me hard against the back. It begins zig-zagging and I'm tossed hard against Thanee, then away from her.

I can't get any purchase on the deck. I can bend my knees and waist and I try to keep steady doing that but the boat's twisting and turning, rocking and rolling too much. All I can do is try to keep my elbows, knees and head from banging against the metal underneath me.

The speeding boat makes an abrupt right turn and I'm thrown on top of Thanee. I wriggle to roll off her but as I do we make another sharp turn, this one to the left, and both of us are smashed together against the coiled rope and up onto it.

We don't make any more turns but I can hear banging and crashing, something the boat is running over. There's the sound of tree limbs, branches, scraping fast and crackling along the sides. The chattering has stopped. I don't hear any more booms.

The engine throttles back to a dull burble. In a little while we stop. Voices are shouting in Khmer. I hear a couple of large splashes. Rough hands come and shove me off the ropes, rolling me with Thanee back onto the deck. I'm kicked in the side by a foot in sandals. It's not a boot but I still want to cry out and I can't. I try curling up and am kicked again, in the ass, then the side again. Then the foot steps on my head and tests its resiliency against the deck. It's not quite crushing me, but it's enough to let me know who the boss is. If only I knew what he wanted.

After that, whoever it is leaves me alone. The heat doesn't. It's nearly unbearable. I try rolling onto the ropes again but they've been moved. I can bump up against them but I can't get away from the metal deck. I can't get away from the thirst either. I fantasize about cold water, even warm beer, and it gets worse. We motor for a long time. There's a constant scrape of foliage against the sides of the boat.

Later, much later, the air begins to cool slightly. But that's when the insects come. It's a tossup which is worse, burning up or being bitten to death. I try rolling, wiggling, moving any way I can to keep them off me, but they're too hungry and there's too many of them.

I give up after a while and lie there, a buffet for the bugs. I try to put myself out again, to sleep, to blackout. Even if it means another horrible dream it's worth it. But it doesn't work this time. I lie there immobile, trying to think of anything other than the surface of my skin.

It's dark when the boat stops and ties up. I can hear people on shore and they come aboard. I'm picked up again, carried onto wooden planks, then onto soft dirt, and then heaved with a thump over the tailgate of a truck. Thanee's thrown in, landing on top of me. The bed of the truck is corrugated metal and it's gritty with dirt. It smells like fertilizer.

I figure if we can lie sideways we might be able to brace ourselves with our feet but there's no time. Before I can wiggle around the truck starts up and with a loud grinding of gears begins to move. It's slow going over a deeply rutted and potholed road, but fast enough to keep us bouncing. Burlap sacks filled with what feels like rocks bang against us and the ride goes on too long.

I can't think. My mind's deserted me but it hasn't gone anywhere I can find it. I don't think I want to, anyhow. It's not like one of those out-of-body experiences people talk about. It's all body. I can only feel. And what I feel is pain and discomfort like I didn't think would be possible to live through.

I'm conscious, but not conscious enough to know when the truck stops and I'm pulled out and dropped onto the ground. I know that happens, it must be what's happening but there's no world I know around me. There's no me, only this body, this corpse. Is there a word for a body that's alive but's been abandoned by its mind, its soul?

It's dragged along the ground, sharp rocks breaking through its clothes, ripping the skin on its back, its shoulders, its head. It's hauled onto something soft, something that gives, something stinging with the sharp, acrid stench of ammonia, something that sears the patches of raw flesh. All goes black. It vanishes.

| |CHAPTER **TWENTY-FOUR** | |

revive under a waterfall. My body's so dry that it doesn't seem as though the water is running off me so much as being absorbed. I shake my head to clear it and lose precious drops into the air. Everything's blurry, dim; it takes a while for the world to come into focus, but it does.

I'm stiff and swollen, my skin cracked and raw. I'm not tied up anymore, the rag isn't in my mouth, my eyes are uncovered. I'm in a rough hewn, low shed. There's still that terrible stench of ammonia on top of something slightly sweet. I can see feathers all over the place. I must be in a chicken coop. Water's dripping from between the boards in the ceiling. There's a bucket of it by the door.

I drag myself up and sit next to the bucket, scooping water into my hands and drinking it, splashing it on my face. I doubt I've ever been this thirsty before. The more I wake up, the more I wish I hadn't.

Something tight is around my right ankle. It's a large leather cuff, clamped shut with a padlock, attached to a thick chain. At least the chain's coiled. It looks like I've got a little room to play it out.

The door to the coop has a simple latch. The sun's up but there's a tree nearby that spreads shade on the ground underneath. If the chain'll stretch that far, it's where I'd like to be, away from the stink in here.

I've had enough water for now. I want to drink the whole bucket but that's not a good idea. I'm not strong enough to carry it, so I crawl to the tree, pushing the bucket in front of me.

If I stretch my legs out, pointing directly back at the chicken coop, I can just manage to lean against the trunk of the tree and look around. In the distance are rice paddies. The sun sparks off the water on their surface, silhouetting a few dozen people hunched over at work. I can see the fuzzy black outlines of others, holding rifles, standing on the mud embankments watching over the workers.

There are sounds behind me, behind the tree. A loudspeaker crackles and sputters into life, a shrill voice recites in a monotone. Someone's chopping wood. There's the sound of hammering. A couple of dogs are barking. I stretch as far as I can around the trunk, straining to see what's behind me. All I can make out are the edges of small wood- and grass-mat huts. I guess it's a village, or an encampment of some sort, but I can't see any details.

I'm hungry now. That's got to be a good sign. It would be better if there was anything to eat. I occupy my mind trying to imagine cooking breakfast. I don't know if that helps or makes things worse. I hear footsteps coming from behind the tree. I'm too tired, too hungry, too beat up to do anything other than sit here, waiting to see who it is.

It's a man, maybe in his mid-fifties, with close trimmed white hair and a face that would look kind if it wasn't for a large welt of a scar running from the middle of his forehead down past the back of his left ear. He squints at me with unusually large and round eyes for an Asian. He has the expression of someone who forgot to put on his glasses.

He's holding a battered tin cup of cooked rice, but I've lost my appetite. He's Khmer Rouge, dressed in tire-tread sandals, black cotton pajamas and the distinctive red checked scarf.

He sets the cup on the ground within my reach, then rocks back on his haunches and looks at me. *"Si'l vous plaît, monsieur, manger."*

I know I've got to, so I reach out, pick up the cup and scoop a few small fingers of the cold, sticky rice into my mouth. I've rarely tasted anything so good.

The man watches silently while I eat. When I finish I dip the cup into the water bucket and drink. The water tastes dusty. I try not to look at it. When I'm done I leave the cup floating on top of the water.

"Monsieur, si'l vous plaît, comment vous appelez-vous?"

I look at him. I don't want to be cooperative but I'm afraid not to be.

"Sorry, I don't speak French, not much. Ray Sharp. Do you speak English?"

"I am very pleased to meet you, Mr. Sharp. Yes, I do speak English. I am Kon. I am the commander of this outpost."

I'm surprised. His English is nearly perfect, practically unaccented.

"Commander Kon, I..." He holds up a hand to stop me.

"Please, Mr. Sharp, 'Kon' is sufficient. Though it is perhaps mere semantics, we do not permit ourselves expressions of rank."

"Okay, fine, but where am I? Why am I here? What've you done with my friend?"

"Mr. Sharp, we will talk in due course. At the moment I must attend to my duties. I will have you brought more water and a cloth so that you can wash. I'm afraid that we have little food here, but I will bring you a somewhat more substantial meal later and we will talk then."

Being tied up and bounced around on metal for nearly a whole day hadn't done my body much good. And I don't recover as quickly as I used to. Susan says that the older you get, the more you feel like you've got a hangover, all the time, without even the benefit of the previous night's boozing. I think she might be right.

By mid-afternoon I'm able to hobble in a circle at the radius of my chain. There isn't much to see. Even though I know the sun must be traveling across the sky like usual, the rice paddies are blinding and in silhouette all day. The tree I've been sitting under is big, with a wide expanse of branches, and its shadow sundials around like it's supposed to. It provides enough shade for me to keep in. That's good because when I leave it briefly, trying to test my legs, it's too hot and humid to endure for more than a few minutes.

The new water bucket and cloth doesn't show up until late in the day. An old toothless woman, dragging it and a lifeless leg behind her, brings it. Then she stands gawking at me, picking at her teeth with her one good hand.

I'm well beyond modesty. I take off my clothes, although my pants can't come off the chain, and wash as well as I can. It's a huge relief, but my skin flakes away in places when I scrub it. I don't want to put my filthy, sweat-drenched clothes back on. I point to the old woman's sarong and mime tying one on myself. She nods, goes away and then comes back with a long piece of black cloth that's thin enough to read a newspaper through. It wraps around my waist twice. That's enough.

At first there's just a few insects. As the day cools there's more, until I feel as if my body is disappearing into the swarm of them. I move away from the tree, where the soil is a little damp, and onto the hard baked earth that's been exposed to the sun all day. There's fewer bugs there—still too many, but fewer. I sit hunched up, covering as much of me as I can with the sarong, but that only stops the weakest and biggest.

"We have elephants and tigers in our country, a long history of conquest and being conquered, but I am afraid, Mr. Sharp, that it is always the insects that are most powerful. Long after history has ended, they shall prevail."

I consider ignoring him but I don't think that's going to help. It's better if he thinks of me as a person, not simply a captive. I look up at Kon.

"You don't have any bug spray do you?"

He chuckles as he sits down next to me. "No, Mr. Sharp. If you strengthen your mind and detach your physical sensations from pain and other irritants, you will find insecticides unnecessary. We have attempted to eradicate Buddhism, but some of its precepts are useful to us."

"It's a shame you didn't keep the ones about respecting life, peace, harmony, that sort of thing."

"Ah, like so many Westerners, you harbor delusions about Buddhism, Mr. Sharp."

"How so?"

"Have you not yet seen the bas reliefs at the base of Angkor Wat? They are rooted in our history, and are quite instructive."

I haven't. I've been around a lot of Asia, but until recently it's not been easy for Americans to get into Cambodia.

I'm not sure I want to make polite conversation with Kon, but at least it's a distraction from the bugs. "What do you mean?"

"They are scenes of warfare, Mr. Sharp. Terrible battles fought between Buddhists and Hindus, Buddhists and Buddhists. The history of Buddhism is no more peaceful than that of any other religion, Mr. Sharp. As Marx so aptly noted, 'Religion is the opiate of the masses.' He did not add that when the narcotic affect ceases to work, all religions are perfectly willing to sacrifice the masses. Buddhists are no exception."

"That's what you get when religion and politics mix. There are ways to keep them apart."

"Are there, Mr. Sharp? In theory, perhaps. In practice, I think not. I have always been amused by the Western reverence for

Tibet's Dalai Lama. He is simply a fraud, no more worthy of veneration than any other religious fraud."

"He got the Nobel Peace Prize a few years ago. What was that for?"

"It was merely a feeble political gesture; an ineffective swipe of a declawed paw at China. Once again, the West's poor knowledge of Asian history permits it to maintain illusions.

"Why do you think there was a large, and very active, communist movement in Tibet even before the Chinese sent in their troops?

"The theocracy that ran Tibet from the lamaseries was a brutal, corrupt, avaricious regime. Land and crops were seized at will by the powerful. The poor often starved, while the lamas lived very well indeed. If the people complained or organized they were ruthlessly exterminated. Minorities were violently suppressed. It was far from the peaceful utopia that Westerners seem to enjoy imagining. The peasants of Tibet had been in a state of revolt against the lamas for hundreds of years.

"This beloved Dalai Lama was born into the powerful, ruling elite. The supposed search for the next incarnation never seems to lead to a family from the lower classes. He has fought to regain what he claims is his country's rightful independence. But he has yet to repudiate the despicable regime that spawned him and has said little regarding how he should rule if he were to return to power."

I'd read all that before and tend to believe it. I'm skeptical of any religious leader with a political agenda. But I don't want to give Kon the satisfaction of agreeing with him. I change the subject.

"Where'd you learn your English, Kon?"

"At your University of Southern California, where I took my graduate degrees in business and economics."

I have to pinch myself to make sure I'm awake.

"I thought all you Khmer Rouge guys went to school in Paris, the Sorbonne, existentialism gone horribly horribly wrong, something like that."

He chuckles again, a low, soothing sound. It's disconcerting.

"That is the philosophical branch of *Angka,* Mr. Sharp. I am of what you might call the pragmatic branch of our tree."

"Oh, 'The Poverty of Philosophy' crowd."

"Ah, I see you have read Marx, Mr. Sharp. That is unusual in an American."

"I skimmed it. I was intrigued by the joke."

"The joke, Mr. Sharp?"

"His answer to Prudhomme's 'Philosophy of Poverty.'"

"I think that I am pleased we have captured you, Mr. Sharp. My English has been getting rusty, and it will be good to speak with someone who is educated."

I don't want to ask if he's read Hannah Arendt on "the banality of evil." He'd fit right in.

"Wouldn't it be better to speak with someone who's had a decent meal, who isn't being bitten to death by bugs and isn't chained up?"

He chuckles again. This time I don't like the sound of it.

"I fear, Mr. Sharp, I can do nothing about the insects or the chain, but the evening meal is being prepared and will be brought to us when it is ready."

"Why am I here, Kon? What's happened to Thanee, the woman I was kidnapped with?"

"Yes, well, I suppose we must dispense with those topics first, then we can return to more interesting issues."

"Those are pretty damn interesting to me."

"Yes, you are right. I can understand that. But unfortunately there is little or nothing that either of us can do to change these circumstances. I am under orders to keep you here."

"Orders from who, why?"

"From *Angka*, from the central command. As for why, I have not been told. Perhaps you can enlighten me. I was told that you and the woman would be delivered to us only a few hours before you arrived."

I can guess, but I think I'll keep it to myself for now. Maybe it'll come in handy later. General Tran gets his antiques from the Khmer Rouge. He must have told his contacts he was looking for us. I suppose we're worth some money.

"What's *Angka* mean anyhow?"

"It is rice in the field, Mr. Sharp. It is the foundation of our civilization."

I could make a quip about him and his pals not being very civilized, but I don't think it's a good idea.

"Where's Thanee?"

"She is Khmer, Mr. Sharp. She is in the fields where she can best make a contribution to her country."

I doubt it will do Thanee much good if I argue the point. I'm trying to think what to say next when the old woman who had brought me the water and cloth slumps up. She's got a long wood pole slung over her shoulders with buckets hanging from each end. She sets it down, fetches bowls from one of the buckets and fills them from the other. There's warm rice and a green vegetable that looks like a river fern. Kon gets several chunks of stringy, bony meat. I think it's chicken, but I don't get any.

The old woman looks at Kon's bowl hungrily. I can see her lips moving, the tongue pushing from behind them like she's begun salivating and wants to hide it. I begin to do the same. The scent of the meat's found its way into my nose. If I don't keep swallowing I'm going to end up drooling.

Kon says something to the woman. She reaches back into the bucket, pulls out a small, gray piece of the meat and puts it on top of my rice.

It is chicken. It looks awful, but I think it's the best smelling food I've ever had. I pick it up in my fingers and pop it into my mouth, working the tiny morsels of flesh off it, sucking on it, finally cracking the small bones between my teeth to get at the flecks of marrow. I chew it down to granules of bone, then swallow those.

It's not much, but it's enough to make me ravenous. I know there won't be any more, that I should take my time, make this meal last, but I can't. I ball the rice and greens up in my fingers and eat them fast. They're gone in a minute, or less.

Kon is watching me, spooning his food slowly with his long, thin, elegant middle and forefinger. He sets his bowl down for a moment to finish chewing one of his pieces of chicken.

"Mr. Sharp, where in the United States do you come from?"

"Los Angeles."

"Perhaps you know then of the 'garbage burritos' and tacos near my alma mater. I cannot recall the name of the restaurant."

I wish I had one now. It's a Mexican place near downtown. On Sunday nights they take the leftovers from the week before, throw them together into a huge pot and cook them overnight. The next afternoon they wrap them in extra large tortillas and sell them cheap. It's a lot of food for a little money. Some weeks they're better than others.

"I know the place. I've eaten my share there."

"I have tried to tell my comrades here about the restaurant. They cannot understand it, not anything about it. They cannot imagine that there would be food remaining at the end of a week. What did they cost?"

"Fifty cents."

"Yes, that's right, a half-dollar. To my comrades that is an unimaginably large sum of money to spend on one meal for one person."

"So, this is what everyone eats?"

"No, unfortunately, Mr. Sharp, my comrades rarely receive meat with their meals."

"The privilege of rank, Kon? I thought you didn't have ranks."

He doesn't answer. He picks his bowl back up and silently finishes his dinner. When we're both done the old woman collects our bowls and heads back to the huts.

Kon stretches, then reaches into a pocket in the shirt of his black pajamas and pulls out two cigarettes and a wooden match.

"Would you care for a cigarette, Mr. Sharp? It is perhaps my only vice. I enjoy a smoke after eating."

I shake my head. He puts away one of the smokes, lights his and doesn't talk until he's had three deep, apparently satisfying drags.

"You are an educated man, Mr. Sharp. What are your political beliefs? Are you a Democrat or a Republican?"

For a moment I don't know what to say. What the hell am I doing here, in chains, a prisoner, talking about politics with a man who's probably a mass murderer? I should attack him, strangle him if I can, do the world a favor.

"I don't know, a Democrat I guess. I'm for whatever does the greatest good for the most people."

Am I? I don't know anymore. It seems that every time anybody tries to do a lot of good for a lot of people, something goes wrong. Or their idea of what a lot of good is, is screwed up to begin with. I'm beginning to think that the only real good anyone can do is for one person at a time, maybe a few. But it's a wobbly platform to stand on when talking politics.

"That is very noble, Mr. Sharp, and perhaps, in a rich country such as yours it is possible. Here, in Kampuchea, as we prefer to call our country, we have different priorities."

"Why? What's wrong with the idea of making life better for as many people as possible?"

"Nothing, of course, Mr. Sharp. But before you can develop capitalism, you must have capital. Here, we lack capital."

"Marx would disagree. You have people, you have natural resources."

"Of course, and we invest that capital. We put it to work in the fields. But to do so in a profitable manner we cannot indulge ourselves with inefficiencies such as democratic ideals."

"Sorry if I'm too blunt, but you went to school in America, you know how we are. Didn't you guys waste a lot of that capital in the killing fields?"

"Indeed, but as my French educated comrades would say, 'you cannot cook an omelette without breaking eggs.'"

"I thought you said you were the pragmatic one, not another philosopher."

"Yes, but my pragmatism is in the service of a philosophy, Mr. Sharp. It helps to focus the thinking. In America you believe you have ideals but they are unclear. Your country is perhaps too prosperous; its thinking has grown as fat and lazy as its people. I hope you do not mind my being direct, Mr. Sharp."

I do and I don't. I want to argue with him but my brain is beginning to burn. I'm too tired, worn down, too torn up to hold up my end of the conversation any longer.

"I'm sorry, Kon, I'm tired. I guess I'm not used to being kidnapped, abused, chained up and barely fed. I can't talk anymore tonight. Maybe tomorrow."

He gets up. "Tomorrow then, Mr. Sharp. Is there anything I can do for you before I retire for the night?"

I look up at him trying to keep the incredulity off of my face. "I already told you."

"I am so sorry, Mr. Sharp. We are both prisoners of our circumstances."

That's easy for him to say. He walks away and I don't shout at his back. That's hard for me to do. He's a bastard and he doesn't have to sleep chained up in a chicken coop.

| | CHAPTER **TWENTY-FIVE** | |

The chicken coop is surprisingly comfortable. The ground is soft, padded with feathers, kicked-up dirt and layers of chicken shit. I'm so tired I don't even notice the stench anymore. There aren't so many flying insects at night. I sleep without dreaming for a long time, much longer than usual.

When I wake up there's a clean bucket of water, a bowl of cold rice and a small banana outside the coop door. I don't like bananas. I like this one. There're also three sheets of lined paper and a roughly sharpened pencil.

There's a note at the top of the first sheet. The handwriting is small, precise. "Mr. Sharp, please write, in detail, what it is that you are doing in Kampuchea."

I remember reading that the Khmer Rouge are big on confessions. I don't think honesty is going to be the best policy. If they're making money selling looted antiques to foreigners, they're not going to be happy with me poking my nose into their business.

Then again, I don't know that it matters. I've heard of one foreigner who's survived being taken prisoner by the Khmer Rouge, but only one. Kon's been polite. He even seems interested in what I've got to say. But the fact remains that he's a killer, even if he is one with an MBA from USC. How's that going to look in the alumni magazine? He didn't get where he is without leaving a trail of bodies behind him, without smashing a few infants' skulls against tree trunks. Philosophy my ass. Psychopathy is more like it.

There's gotta be some way out of here. I don't know how long it's going to be before the general's men show up to get me, or if the Khmer Rouge will kill me themselves, but I can't just sit around waiting for it to happen.

The coop's partly made from rusty wire fencing. I break off a couple of inches and try to pick the padlock on the cuff around my ankle.

It doesn't work. The wire crumbles inside the slot. Now I've done it. It probably can't even be opened with the key anymore.

What now? I look around for anything else sharp, anything to scrape at the leather. I try some twigs and they don't get me anywhere. There are pebbles on the ground, but they're rounded. Finally I find a rock that fits snugly into my hand. It's got a slight crack in it. Maybe I can break it against another rock, make an edge. It takes a while but that's what I manage to do.

I've got to sit in a way that no one will see what I'm doing, but at the same time I've got to watch out for anyone coming. I've got to sit in the shade. I'll get heat stroke if I don't. At the moment there's only one spot where I can do all that, but it's not ideal. It's close to the tree trunk but I can't lean against it. I think that might look suspicious. Why wouldn't I be sitting against the trunk? But I don't have a choice.

No one notices. I'm chained up. I have no idea where we are. Why would they need to pay attention to me?

It's thick leather and very slow going. My hands get sweaty and slip a lot. The rock's edges dig into the skin on my hands, slide into and slice the skin on my ankle, drawing blood. I get tired easily and find myself drifting off, not asleep but spacing out. I snap back and realize I've stopped working the leather, or the rock's dropped from my hand and I'm rubbing with my fingers. I try finding ways to keep my attention from wavering. I run songs through my head and scratch in time with the beat. That works for a while but thoughts keep intruding and I lose time.

I hope Thanee's okay, Ampora, Lei Yue. Is it me? Am I the kiss of death for people around me? For the women around me? Can I do what I do without fucking things up for other people? I started all this thinking I might do somebody some good. Now all I want to do is get out alive.

By the time the insects return for their evening meal, I've made some progress. There's a definite cut across the leather. It's not deep, but enough that it has a little play on both sides. I can bend it, deepen it.

When Kon comes for another talk I have to sit on my ankle. I can't put my foot out in front of me or he might see it. The circulation jams up fast and it falls asleep. It's agonizing but I can't stretch it out. I try putting weight on my hands on the ground, more on my butt. I try to do it without his noticing my discomfort.

He asks for my "confession." I tell him I'm still thinking about it and all he does is shrug.

He wants to talk about the "Asian economic miracle," the "tiger economies." He doesn't hear much about it out here in the forest. He loves *Angka,* obeys *Angka,* but he is an educated man and would like to know more about the world.

Kon's skeptical about what I tell him. "All of these governments, these banks, these companies, there is too much corruption, too many deals between friends. It is not realistic, this business.

Too much is based on exaggerated expectations. This 'economic miracle' is only an illusion. It will not last. Capitalism is once again going to prove that it is its own worst enemy."

He's probably right. But no matter how bad any of it is, it can't hold a candle to what he and his pals have done to this country.

"Kon, why do you stay with the Khmer Rouge? You're losing. You can't beat the government again. You're a smart guy, you could probably arrange a settlement, make a good life for yourself."

"Yes, of course, Mr. Sharp. The government is offering an amnesty program if my men and I join them. But I cannot. It is not my nature. For me *Angka* is my life. It is all I need to believe in, to obey. It is, of course, imperfect. But for me it is everything."

"It's like a cult."

"Is there nothing that you accept unquestioningly?"

I hope not. But there isn't time for all of this chit chat. I want him to leave so that I can get back to getting out of here.

Finally he does, apologizing again for our "circumstances." Fuck him. He can be a victim of circumstance if he wants. Not me.

The moon's a slender thread in the densely speckled sky when I finally manage to break through the cuff. There's no sound from the huts. There's got to be a sentry and the dogs are around somewhere. I don't know where Thanee is. If I can, I've got to get her out with me.

Great, so I'm free. Now what?

I need to look around. I've got to watch where I step. I'll have to steal a pair of sandals, if I can find any that aren't too small.

A path from the huts to the fields runs along a raised embankment. If I get on to it I'll have a clear view, but I might also be visible to any guards. At one place it briefly winds through a small stand of palm trees. If I can get there without being seen they'll provide cover.

I take the long way around and don't see anybody. Dogs don't bark, nothing stirs. I keep low and hold the black sarong up to cover as much of my body as it can. There's a lot of damp, rotting dead foliage on the ground. It muffles my footsteps and cushions my feet. I'm not too worried about mines. They wouldn't be planted in the middle of the camp or on paths, would they? But I am nervous about snakes, especially once I get to the palms. Snakes seem to like this sort of countryside. I don't like snakes.

From the trees I can see the camp. There are five small huts with grass roofs and grass mat walls. There's a long, low wooden building under construction, but complete enough that there are probably people sleeping in it. There's a covered central area with a thatched roof held up by one center post, and four in the corners. At one side is a stone-lined pit with a low fire burning. That's where the sentries are, two of them, their rifles on the ground by their sides, none too alert. That doesn't mean there aren't more. One dog is sleeping near them, but I'm sure I've heard at least two.

I watch for a long time. I don't know how soon the sun is going to come up and I've got to move before then. Thanee's probably in the wood building. They'd likely herd the field workers all together, to keep an eye on them. That doesn't do me any good.

I'd like to walk around the outskirt of the entire camp, see it from all sides, see if there is anything more I can figure out. But that's a really bad idea. The Khmer Rouge have a reputation for being mine happy. There're supposed to be two to three million of the hidden explosive devices around the country and there's gotta be some around here.

I'm trapped. The only safe way out is on the road, or along well-marked paths. It's either that or risk getting blown up in the woods. I can't get Thanee out. If I can get away maybe I can get help, come back with the army, something. Maybe I can't. But I've got to try.

The path through the palm grove continues along the embankment through the paddies. It can't be mined, they march the workers along it every day. I don't know where it goes, or how far it goes, but I take it.

They aren't growing a lot of rice. The paddies peter out after only a few hundred yards. The path continues through dense woods. It's hard to follow at times, especially in the dark. I think that's a good thing. There's not much point to mining something this well hidden, either. At least I hope not.

The sky's lightened to about a banker's gray when the path spills into a small clearing with a couple of large sheds in the middle. I stick to the edges, next to the dense brush that rings it. I move around slowly and don't see anybody or hear anything other than some birds waking up. The path continues on the other side of the clearing. It widens and curves through waving reeds.

I need to be out of sight before it gets too light. The sheds aren't a good place to hide, but I want to see what's inside them. A narrow dirt walk leads to them. I stick to it, my feet getting covered in red wet mud.

The doors are padlocked but the construction is slapdash enough that I can peer between the wall boards. One of the sheds is a workshop. It looks like wooden crates are built in it. The other's the warehouse and what's in it doesn't surprise me; heads and whole bodies of Buddha, *nagas* and *apsaras* and everything else I've been seeing in the shops in Thailand, Hong Kong and China.

There's gotta be a large road or a river nearby. They're not just going to pile this stuff up out here in the middle of nowhere. I follow the path through the reeds and around the first bend it ends at a plank dock on a medium-sized river. A small barge, big enough to have a wheelhouse at the front, is tied up at the pier. Its deck is covered with wood crates, tarps thrown loosely over them. A lot of them are open and empty.

Two men are on the boat, on the prow, in front of the wheelhouse, squatting over a small fire and a blackened teapot. If I walk out on the dock they'll see me. I move off the path into the reeds. In a few steps I'm in water up to my knees. I wade out until I'm up against the back of the rusty metal hull. If I jump I can get a handhold on the barge, pull myself up onto it.

But what then? Are they heading out today? Are they waiting to load antiques into the empty crates? I can't stay around here. As soon as Kon and his men discover I'm gone they'll come looking for me.

It's probably stupid but I hoist myself on board and crawl into one of the open crates under a tarp. It's hot, stuffy, terrible. It smells of tar and diesel fumes and limestone dust that gets vacuumed into my nose and makes me want to sneeze. I fight off all my impulses, curl up into the darkest corner of the crate and wait.

| |CHAPTER **TWENTY-SIX**| |

'm lucky. I don't have to wait long. The barge coughs to life, the water at the rear churns and bubbles. It slowly angles out into the current. I don't know where we're going and I don't have a plan, but I figure it's a good idea to stay hidden until we're a long way from the dock. I stretch out as much as I can in the crate. I've been up all night and I'm exhausted.

It's strange that all of a sudden there's an escalator in front of me. I step onto it and it starts moving. It accelerates. It's faster than any escalator I've ever ridden. I hold the handrail tight and bend forward against the push of gravity. I'm surrounded by a whooshing sound. When I look to the side we're passing the light fixtures on the ceiling, but they're a blur from the movement. I pan my head to try and keep the image stable but then I'm up through the hole in the ceiling and the fixtures are receding below me.

I look down and can't see anything holding up the escalator. It's rising up through the air, unsupported. When I look back up I see a huge face. It's Buddha. His nose is askew, like a boxer's. It's been broken a couple of times. He has almond shaped eyes and he's squinting. His fat, long brown lips, pursed into a wry smile, are slowly rippling, a movement that reminds me of the way slugs move through the forest.

The escalator is heading straight for his lips. It's moving so fast I'll be smashed against them. I try stepping back but it doesn't do me any good, the stairs are moving too fast. We're getting closer and my heart is drumming, my stomach churning. I turn around. It takes a terrible effort to fight gravity and stay upright while I do it. I try to run down the moving steps, but at best I'm staying put. I'm too tired to keep it up for long.

Something comes loose around my foot. I look down and my shoe-laces have come untied. They're curling around my ankles and curving under my feet like two thin black snakes. They tangle and I trip.

I spill down the escalator, head over heels, landing flat on my stomach facing up. I can't get up, I'm trapped. Buddha's lips are quivering now, quaking into a big broad smile, then a toothy smile, as I'm carried to him. Then his mouth opens wide and I can see his tongue. It's thick and red and pocked with small craters and it's wrestling with itself in his mouth. It spits out briefly at me and forks into two. The two separate into four, the four into eight that take on hoods and eyes and flicking tongues of their own. And now there's a *naga* there, in Buddha's mouth, waiting to consume me.

Everything slows down, it's like moving through air thickened to the consistency of heavy engine oil. A chorus of voices sinks down to me and I look up. There are five *apsaras*. They're singing, dancing, calling me to them with gesturing hands, inviting bodies. They're familiar. They fill my senses with the scents and sounds and comforting sensations of home, of safety.

My body relaxes, and as it does, it becomes buoyant and rises to where the air is lighter, easier to breathe. I rise past the face of the

Buddha, above his head, into the pillowy white clouds, into the arms of the *apsaras*, nestled against their breasts, luxuriating in their kisses.

I wake up. Stiff and sore, pouring sweat, my head's aching, my lips are parched. My body's puddled into the cracks between the slats of the crate and it's painful to pull the creases in my skin out from them.

The barge's engine is still thrumming, belching exhaust from the small smokestack above the wheelhouse. I risk crawling out of the crate, staying under the tarp but lifting an edge to see where we are.

It must be midday. When I stick my hand out into the sunlight, the shadow is directly beneath it. The river's widened; the banks are a few hundred feet away on either side. I don't see any signs of people on shore or any other boats. If I'm right, we're headed west, or northwest.

I'm desperate for a drink of water. If I can find something to hold it and can get to the side of the barge without being seen, and reach down to the river, I can ladle some up. The river water here can't be all that clean, but there's nothing I can do about that. Dehydration's got to be worse.

With any luck the two men on board will be in the wheelhouse. It's got to be cooler in there than out on deck. I've got to move carefully. I don't want the barge shifting underneath me. If it rocks they might come back to see what caused it.

There's no sign of them when I get a clear view upfront. The back of the barge looks like it's a little lower in the water. I crawl there slowly, trying to stay near the center of the deck. Along the way I don't see anything that will hold water. When I get to the back and stick my face out, I'm hit by spray. It's the best shower I've ever had. I want to lean more of my body into it. I want to thrust my hands down into it, splash it back up on me, bring handfuls to my mouth.

But there's a propeller down there, and I don't know how far down it is. I watch the water churning off the back. It looks like there are two propellers. The water's calmer in the middle. I reach a hand down and skim the surface of it, shooting it back at me. Nothing bites my hand.

It's the worst tasting water I've ever had, but one of the best drinks. It's muddy and leaves fine silt on my skin. I don't want to think about what it's doing to my insides. I just want to keep drinking.

I stop myself before I get to the point where I can't drink any more. It's hard to tear myself away, but I've got to get back under cover. Crawling back to the crate I spot some broken down cardboard boxes. Those have got to be better to park myself on than the bare wood slats. I drag them in with me and make myself a more comfortable nest.

Or is it a cell? I'm still trapped, still not sure where I'm going or what I'm going to do. If I was smart I'd jump off this barge at the first sign of civilization, swim to shore, get to Phnom Penh, get to Hong Kong and forget about everything.

I'm not that smart. I can't bring myself to leave Thanee behind. I can't leave the general alone to his business as usual. If I don't do something to stop him, will I ever be safe again? I haven't even finished the job. I don't have the proof the client wants.

It's about halfway through the afternoon when we turn north out of the river we're in. It's all water to the horizon. It's the Tonle Sap.

It's the largest lake in southeast Asia and I've always wanted to see it, but not like this. In the rainy season it grows to four times as big as in the dry months. The Tonle Sap river runs southeast out of it to meet up with the Mekong at Phnom Penh, except during the rainy season when the river reverses its course and flows northwest. It's what made Cambodia one of the richest agricultural regions in the world, until a lot of the farmland was mined and the farmers had to worry about getting blown up. It's still one of the world's greatest freshwater fishing grounds.

The barge is close enough to the bank that I could swim to land now, but there's no point. All I can see are abandoned fields sprawled over low hills. If people aren't working them, I'm not dumb enough to walk across them. I'm stuck here until we get wherever we're going.

I'm thirsty again, and hungry. I can't do anything about food and I'm trying not to drink too much of the filthy water. I lie in the crate and try to put my brain to work with mental games, lists, dredging up old memories, but I can't control it. My head's spinning out of control, flying off into tangents, breaking up into non-sequiturs. I wish I could sleep, to pass the time, but I can't.

The barge plows slowly along for hours that seem like days that stretch into weeks. It's near twilight when I crawl back to the water for another drink, some more splashes. I hear another boat, then another. I hear a dog barking, children screaming at play, the chugging of a small generator. I chance a move to the side and look where we're headed.

There's a small village floating on the water. Seven or eight houses are built onto rafts. They're surrounded by fenced pens that look like corrals. The small boats I hear are circling just outside, the people in them scooping fish into handheld nets. We're headed for a low jetty that is the only break through the fence. It's a walkway of two-by-fours set on top of truck-tire inner tubes. Naked children are diving off it into the water, screaming and shouting. I crawl back to my crate before they can see me.

The barge starts slowing, gliding in to the jetty. The engine shuts down for a moment then roars briefly in reverse before shutting off again. Then there's a slight bump and the only movement is gently up and down, rocking slightly left and right. I can hear the two men on board talking and then one of them walks past my crate to the back. We must be docking here for the night. The barge rocks toward the jetty and I can hear the men walking away.

I don't come out until it's been dark for a while. Then I keep low, making sure I stick to the darkest areas. There are a few dim lights in the floating houses. I can see the red glow of a cooking fire in a house in the middle of the floating village. Music wafts out from tinny speakers. There's a constant little splish splash coming from the pens surrounding the houses. I can hear the sizzle and pop of food cooking in a wok. The smell of it finds my nose and pummels my gut. My mouth gushes with uncontrollable saliva.

I've got to eat something. I could walk up to one of the houses, knock on the door and ask for help. I don't speak any Khmer but I'm looking like someone who needs help. What else would I be doing here? I don't have any money, or anything to trade, but I'm a white man in the middle of nowhere in Cambodia, filthy and beat up looking. Anyone would get the idea just looking at me.

The people who live here couldn't possibly support the Khmer Rouge, could they? They're probably fishermen and want to be left alone to make their livings and live their lives.

I must be getting desperate because I've almost got myself convinced. Luckily I can still think, at least a little. The guys on the boat work with, or for, the Khmer Rouge. The people in the village are probably afraid of the Khmer Rouge, and for good reason. It's got to be more trouble for these people to help me than not to. They've got enough hardship in their lives without some foreigner bringing even more down on their heads.

Okay, but I've still got to eat something. And I've got to do it fast. What if the two guys have only gone into the village for a little while? They might come back to the barge to sleep. I also don't want to get onto the jetty. Everything in this place is attached to everything else and it's all floating. If I don't want to be caught I can't rock the boat. This is like a frustrating game you'd play as a kid; pick-up sticks, something like that.

My eyes are adjusting to the dark. There's movement in the pens around the houses. They're either fish farms or holding pens for the day's catch. The noises I've been hearing are the fish jumping. It's going to be sashimi for dinner. I don't have a way to cook it.

I've also got to catch dinner with my hands. I can't reach far enough into the closest pen to do it from the barge. But it is close enough that I can slip into it and then toss the fish onto the deck.

The water's cool, refreshing. I wish I had soap, shampoo, a towel, a nice cozy bed to sink into after eating a big meal. I'm relaxing into how good it feels when I'm bumped hard in the side, then in the other side, then the back and around my legs and on my ass. Either the fish are banging into me the same way they bang each other, or they're trying to chase me away, or there isn't enough room for both them and me.

It's a strange and frightening feeling. I'm being beaten by snouts and fins, thrashed by flailing scaly bodies. Nothing's bitten me yet. That's a relief. I try grabbing one by the tail but it wriggles away. I'm treading water like mad to stay afloat and I'm wading through fish. Maybe I'll stun one with my feet and it'll float to the surface.

I try batting one into the air and onto the barge. I succeed in helping it escape as it lands in the water on the other side of the fence. A second one hits the side of the barge, making a thump that sounds loud to me. I look around to make sure no one's coming. They're used to fish noises, or else it wasn't as loud as I'd thought.

Finally, I manage to bat two onto the deck of the barge. It takes all the remaining energy I've got to hoist myself back up. I lie there, next to the flopping fish, catching my breath, but not for long. They're flopping across the deck, working their way to the other side. They could flop back overboard if I don't stop them.

I remember reading that there's a type of fish in the Tonle Sap that has evolved the ability to move around out of water for a few hours. In the dry season parts of the lake dry up fast and the fish wouldn't survive if they couldn't somehow make it over land to find water.

I take a few deep breaths and force myself up onto my hands and knees to chase them. It wouldn't be this much work if I wasn't so tired, but I stop them. I pick them up one at a time and smoosh their heads hard against the metal deck. It makes me squeamish to do it. . A good quick thwack would be quicker and easier, but noisier. I put them into my crate, then try to figure out how I'm going to eat them.

The thought of picking them up and biting into them doesn't do much for me. I'm hungry enough that I will if I have to. Maybe there's a knife in the wheelhouse. No one's in sight so I crawl there. There's no door. There's not much to it; a few simple controls, a chair to sit on at the wheel, a couple of blankets on the floor. It's too dark to see if there's anything else.

Feeling around I find a low shelf behind and under the wheel. There's a flashlight on it. I cup its business end in my hand and turn it on, letting enough light out to make a quick search. There's a couple of big bottles of water propped up in a corner. I can't resist and take a long swig out of the open one. It tastes great. There are three more under the shelf. Maybe they won't remember how many they've got.

There's a large knife on the shelf. It's too big for them not to miss and I don't know if I'll have time to get it back before they return. There are some tools, a folded newspaper and a lot of oily dust. I run a hand back into the darkest corner and come up with a manila envelope. Inside are twelve pages of documents. They look like shipping manifests but they're in Khmer so I can't read them. Two of the pages are on stationary from Wellfleet.

That's a lucky break. If I ever get out of here, maybe I can finish my job. I take one of the pages, fold it and put it in the waist band of my sarong. I'm too nervous and hungry to look around any longer. I put the flashlight back, take a bottle of water and crawl back to my crate.

So what if I have to eat the fish like I'm at a Dark Ages feast? It's tough at first to tear through the skin with my teeth, but once I do it's the best fish I've ever tasted. I have to be careful with the water. It's a two-liter bottle and I want to make it last. After three gulps I'm drunk on it. I feel like singing, dancing, shouting out. But I don't.

| |CHAPTER **TWENTY-SEVEN** | |

The low rumble of the engine wakes me up. It's first light, cool, and I'm more refreshed than I've felt for a long while. I fell asleep after eating. I can't remember any dreams, nothing disturbing anyway. A couple of swigs from the water bottle, a splash into my eyes, and I'm awake, alert even.

Now what do I do? Maybe it was better being groggy, starved and out of it. My mind wandered all over the place on its own. I wish I had a book, a newspaper, even bad television. I try some stretching exercises. They're painful but better than nothing.

I'm pretty sure I know where we're headed and I think there's a good chance we'll get there sometime today. Near as I can tell we're cruising north on the Tonle Sap. That's the direction to Siem Reap, the main town near the Angkor temples. The barge is probably headed there to pick up more antiquities. Then it will take them back to the warehouse I saw, or further downriver to Phnom Penh. From there they can go by truck to the sea harbor at Sihanoukville.

Siem Reap should be a good place for me to get away. From what I've heard, the port on the lake isn't much, but the town itself is popular with tourists. There'll be hotels and telephones and banks and an airport—the things I need.

We tie up at a floating dock around noon, squeezing into place between two long, high-prowed, fantail speedboats. There isn't a pier that I can see.

The banks of the lake and both sides along a small river leading east are lined with tin-roofed shacks built on pilings, hanging out over the water. Every single one sports a satellite television dish on its roof. Some are open-air, with tables and chairs and beer advertisements. I can hear music squawking out of eight or nine places.

A small rowboat, steered and powered by a combination rudder and paddle off the back, bangs up alongside us. The two men get into it and are rowed to shore. They get off at the first restaurant on the right side of the entrance to the river.

How am I going to get to land? The water looks disgusting, choked with garbage and waste. What I can't see is probably even worse.

There are a lot of rowboats wobbling through the water all around. I could easily hail one. But the boat guy's going to want money. I don't think a few gnawed-on fish bones and a near-empty bottle of water is going to get me very far.

I go back into the wheelhouse. Maybe some coins fell on the floor or one of the men left his wallet. No such luck, but there is the flashlight. It's probably worth more than the short trip to land.

I stand at the front of the barge, putting the wheelhouse between me and the restaurant where the two men were let off. As soon as I wave my arms three rowboats turn to race for my business. About halfway, two of them drop out.

The old man who wins the race and pulls up alongside the barge looks like he's at least a hundred, maybe two. I've never seen anyone who looks so frail. He's sitting down, his legs like broken matchsticks in front of him. His knotted arms aren't thick enough to look like rope, more like twine. I think he's looking at me. His eyelids are so wrinkled they look like they're closed.

I get in his boat, sit down on an overturned bucket in the middle of it and point to the closest open-air café. It's on the opposite side of the river from the one that the barge men went to.

The old man sticks out his hand for money. I point again to the shore. He points to his open hand, then points where I want to go. I hand what I've got to him. It's nothing special, a fairly beat up, Chinese made, medium-sized metal flashlight that's going to need new batteries in another fifteen minutes or so of use.

He weighs it in his hands, flicks it on and off a couple of times, sets it down next to him and bends his shoulders to the oar. The little boat sidewinds across the foul water, tossing me from side to side until I get the hang of it and brace my feet against its wales.

We pull up underneath a restaurant built over the water. There are rungs hammered into its pilings. As I climb I can hear the terrible shriek, chop and splatter of a Chinese kung-fu video cranked up loud enough to rattle the speakers on a cheap Korean television set. I have to fight against the noise to clamber over the railing and move to a table that can't be seen from outside.

Within a flash there's a waiter in a torn white linen jacket at my side. In my condition, looking like I do, if I was Cambodian there'd be at least two of them and they'd toss me out. Instead he's all false smiles, carrying a tray with a glass of ice water, a bowl of peanuts and a thick menu. I don't like taking advantage of my skin color, it embarrasses me, but at the moment it's coming in handy.

I motion for him to wait a moment and take a long drink of the water. The freeze of it immediately goes to my head and I get one of those shooting pains in the temples that I used to get as a kid when I'd slurp an Icee too fast on a hot summer day. But that goes away quick and I order an Angkor beer.

I've got to do something other than just sit here and drink beer. I remember Warner's pal, Friend, at the embassy. I can call him. Isn't that what embassies are for?

Employing the universal symbol of holding up a slightly closed hand, the thumb pointing at my ear, pinkie at my mouth, I ask if there's a phone.

The waiter points in the direction of the TV, which is suspended on a platform hanging from wires attached to the ceiling at one end of the bar. There's a bright pink plastic phone sitting on top of a barstool directly underneath it. When I hold the receiver up to my ear I can't even hear the dial tone over the mayhem going on above me. I can't see a volume control on the TV, it must need a remote.

I wave to get the bartender's attention and mime that I can't hear. He nods, reaches under the bar and notches the volume down just a little, but enough. I bend over, hold the phone tight to my one ear and cramp a hand over the other. I can make out the dial tone.

The operator doesn't speak English. I keep repeating "U.S. embassy," hoping she'll understand. "Embassy, America" doesn't work either. She gets frustrated and hangs up on me. I call back and get another operator who doesn't speak English. She doesn't hang up though. She says something, then I hear her shouting away from the phone. A little kid's voice comes on the line and says, "Yes?"

"U.S. embassy, please. I need to talk to the U.S. embassy."

"Okay, one minute."

There's a lot of clicking and clacking sounds. I hope I'm not disconnected.

"Good afternoon, Embassy of the United States of America, how may I direct your call?"

That's a big relief. "Hi, I'd like to speak to Thomas Friend." It's got to be some sort of code name. "Bill Warner told me to call."

I'm passed through three more levels of receptionists and then put on hold. The waiter brings my beer over to me. The first sip is perfect but goes straight to my head. I put it down. I shouldn't drink any more until I've eaten something.

"Friend. Shoot."

"It's Ray Sharp. I work with Bill Warner. You left something for me at the front desk."

"Where are you? I've got people looking for you."

"How'd you know I was missing?"

"A doctor from the Cambodiana called the embassy, said an American had dropped a woman off there then disappeared. He'd been expecting you to come back and make arrangements to get her out of the country for treatment. They found one of your business cards in her pocket. I went to talk with Miss Wen and there was a banged up Cambodian woman there making a fuss, looking for you. It wasn't hard to piece it all together."

"Is she okay?"

"Miss Wen? I don't know. She was in and out of consciousness. She didn't look too good. We got her on a med-evac flight back to Hong Kong. I didn't get much out of her and the Cambodian woman didn't know much either, past her getting beat up and you and the other woman kidnapped. What happened?"

I give him the condensed version. I've got to eat before I can talk much more. He tells me to sit tight. "I'll call a Cambodian army captain I know in Siem Reap, he'll come get you." He asks to talk to whoever looks like they're in charge.

I wave the phone at the bartender. He comes over slowly, like he's afraid of it. I hand him the phone and when he hangs it up he comes out from behind the bar to escort me back to my table. He picks up the menu, smiles at me, points at it, then at himself. I think he's going to order for me.

After that I'm treated like royalty. The waiter brings me a clean towel and a bar of soap, then leads me to the bathroom. It's dirtier than I am but it has running water and a sink. I don't mind the sarong I'm wearing, it's comfortable. But I do wish someone had a clean one for me, and a shirt. Good thing they don't take that "no shirt, no shoes, no service" thing seriously around here.

When I get back to the table the food has begun to arrive. I eat the rice and simple vegetables first, figuring my stomach's got to be a little delicate. But then I can't resist and dig into everything. Forty minutes later I'm bloated and gurgling from all the food I've crammed into myself and my head's a carnival midway with beer. I turn down the offer of cigarettes but accept a thick, rich, sweet, creamy glass of strong iced coffee.

I don't know how restaurants like this survive. It's lunch hour and there are only two other tables with people at them. At one of the tables are four scruffy backpacker traveler types. Something about them looks more European than American. They're sharing one large bowl of soup that they ladle over plates of rice. They're drinking tea. The five men at the other table look like they might be Japanese aid workers. They're eating a lot more and drinking beer. Unless this place does a roaring dinner trade, it's either going to go bust quickly or it's a front for something else.

I'm considering calling for another coffee when the Cambodian captain and three lesser soldiers show up. I gesture to the chairs around my table but they remain standing. The waiter comes scurrying over with a bill and sets it in front of me. I look up at the captain.

He picks up the bill, hands it back to the waiter without any money and snarls at him. The waiter scowls and heads off to talk with the bartender. I look up at the captain. "Do you speak English?"

He shakes his head no and uses a thumb with a long fingernail to point me at the exit. I try miming something about leaving a tip on the table, but either he doesn't get it or he doesn't care. On the way out I shrug my shoulders in the direction of the waiter and throw him a *wai*. He doesn't look happy.

It's another bouncy pickup truck ride, only this time I get to sit up front between the driver and the captain, and I can see where we're going. There's a large hill to our left with ruins on top. The rutted dirt road snakes along at the back of a stream of shacks that line the river to our right. Laundry dries in the dust and heat, kids and chickens scramble out of our way. It seems like everyone we pass looks at us with resigned fear. Mingling with the dust is a strong, sour fishy odor and the air tastes salty. It seems to be rising from hundreds of enormous pots by the side of the road.

I tap the captain on the shoulder, point at the pots and raise my hands in the universal sign for "What's that?"

He smiles, points to his mouth, pats his stomach and says something that sounds like "*prrahk*." Whatever it is, I can't imagine wanting to eat it.

The captain drops me off in front of a hotel that looks like a pink and white, multi-tiered Chinese wedding cake with dark green windows. It towers over the young stalks of rice that bristle from the paddies around it. The roof looks like a lighthouse topped off with a neon sign. It's off for the day, but I can see that it says, "Hotel." I make a *wai* to the back of the truck as it zips away down the newly asphalted road.

I'm near shivering in the lobby's air-conditioning and self-conscious in my filthy sarong, bare feet and chest. A young woman at the counter takes one look at me and rushes away, yelling to the back office.

The Cambodian man who comes back out and around the counter with a fat hand extended is wearing a crisply ironed white linen shirt with a very loud yellow and purple tie and a matte black raw silk sarong.

"Hello, mate. I'm Penh. You're a bleedin' sight for sore eyes, ain't ya?" He pumps my hand hard, it makes my bicep hurt.

I give him a funny look.

"It's the accent, ain't it, mate? I was a driver in the Aussie embassy in '75. My mates snuck me out. Got back last year."

"I'm Ray. I could use a room, some clothes and a phone, but I don't have any money. I can get some wired to me."

"I know all that mate, been expectin' ya. Got a ring from your friend, Friend, at the Yank embassy. He's got you all fixed up. No worries. You've got some credit. I can front you some scratch for clothes and giggles."

Penh calls for his "girl" to show me to my room. "She can show ya a whole lot more than that, too, if you want, mate. Just let her know." He winks and heads back behind the counter to the office.

The "girl" lingers for a couple of beats near the bed after turning on the lights, the air-conditioner and the TV. I shoo her out. She's smiling when she leaves.

It looks like a Holiday Inn room anywhere, except with pink and red painted flowers and a bad, highly-stylized, French colonial, nostalgic painting over the bed. On the snowy TV an American pop band I've never heard of is cavorting through a neighborhood of identical tract houses accompanied by a flock of leggy blondes in very short skirts.

It amazes me that MTV is so popular in places like this. How can people relate? It's alien enough to me. I can't imagine that to the average Cambodian it looks like anything other than science fiction, or a nightmare.

I go to the bathroom and start the tub filling with hot water. I sit down to wait on the edge of the bed and flick through the channels to get to CNN. I find it and there's a couple of talking heads insulting each other about something I can't follow. I turn it off, get up, untie the sarong and get into the tub to let it fill up around me.

The water's hot and soothing and saps me of strength. It's a real effort to scrub myself. Maybe I shouldn't have sent the girl away.

After a while the water's a shade of reddish, brownish gray that I don't want to sit in. I pull the plug, push myself up off the sides of the tub and stand under the shower to rinse. There's some horrible, bubble-gum-smelling shampoo in a small plastic bottle. It feels good to wash my hair.

I lie down on the bed, letting the cold air from the wall unit sweep across me. I turn the TV back on for the noise. I don't care what it is. I don't listen. It helps drown out my worrying about Thanee and Lei Yue. There's nothing I can do for them at the moment anyhow. After a little while I climb under the covers, pulling the blanket tight around me.

| | CHAPTER **TWENTY-EIGHT** | |

For a moment when I wake up, I think I'm tied up again. I don't understand it and it makes me mad, but I resign myself to it. If I keep calm maybe there's something I can do. Then my head clears. I'm simply tangled in the sheets and blanket, wrapped like a mummy in the results of my own tossing and turning.

I kick off the sheets and lie there, luxuriating in simple comforts that I normally take for granted. I flip on the TV and watch enough CNN to reassure myself that the world is still as messed up as ever. Too many powerful people have high stakes in the status quo. If real peace and prosperity and common sense ever break out, all hell will break loose. And I'll be out of a job.

The clock says ten. I think that's an hour earlier than it is in Hong Kong. There's sunlight pricking in through the window slats. I'm not even sure what day it is, but I've got to call Warner.

The phone doesn't have a dial. I pick it up and a woman answers. I give her the number and she tells me to wait a minute. It's less than that before my boss is on the other end.

"Bill."

"Ray? Where the hell are you?"

I've never heard him sound anything other than calm and collected. "Jeez, Bill, I didn't think you cared. I'm fine, in something that looks like a Holiday Inn in Siem Reap."

"What happened?"

"How's Lei Yue? She okay?"

"She'll make it, but it's been rough. She started bleeding again, lost a lot of blood. Was in shock for a while. It'll be a long, slow recovery, but she's going to be okay. She's a tough one. I'm headed to the hospital in a little while. I'm not going to say 'I told you so,' but what the hell happened?"

I tell him the whole story and he's so quiet that I have to interrupt myself a few times to ask if he's still there.

"Yeah, I'm listening, taking notes. What was the name of the Khmer Rouge commander again?"

"Kon."

"You're one very lucky bastard that he didn't shoot you straight off. He's one of the group that's wanted for crimes against humanity. The U.N. would love to get their hands on him."

"Strangely enough, he seemed okay to me, just making bad use of his MBA."

"Where'd you say he went?"

"USC, University of Southern California. We used to eat at the same taco stand."

"And in all my years in government I always thought it was the Harvard grads you had to watch out for."

"Guess not. Anything you can think of I can do for Thanee?"

His groan, and its accompanying expletives are deep and resonant enough to make the receiver vibrate against my ear.

"I like her. I got her into this. I don't think she's any too happy with the general anymore and maybe she'll come in handy."

"She's in the KR camp? Working the fields?"

"Yeah."

"Forget about her. She's gone."

"You said that to me about someone else once."

"And I was right about her, too, wasn't I?"

"It's not good enough."

For who? I can't help but think. For her? I don't know. What can I do? Haven't I already done too much? She was getting along just fine before I showed up and turned everything inside out. Probably the last thing she needs, or wants, is my help for anything.

For myself then? How fucked up is that? What am I? Some sort of wannabe masked avenger out for justice? Whose justice anyhow?

"It has to be. Sorry, Ray. That's just the way it is. Come home. You've got enough to satisfy the client. No need to stick around there when you've got people gunning for you."

"Think I'll hang around for a few days, see the ruins."

"Take a holiday if you want, Ray. Go to the beach; go visit your family back in the States. Eat some tacos and get nostalgic over the good old days with your pal Commander Kon if you want, but don't be stupid. If you stay there, it's off the clock."

He's right, of course. And maybe if I was thinking straight; maybe if I wasn't wallowing in guilt that this whole mess is my fault; maybe if I was convinced I'd done everything I could possibly do to try and fix it; maybe then I'd do the smart thing and get the hell out of here quick.

"Sometimes stupid's what a guy's gotta do, Bill. You didn't hire me because I give up easy. Besides, I've gotta do something to put Tran away. If I don't, I might as well pack up and leave Asia. I'll call you when I'm done."

He's sputtering when I hang up and I'm not sure how anything so idiotically macho sounding found its way out of my mouth. But it did and I like the ring of it.

I pick the phone back up and ask to talk with Penh. He'll send up a pot of coffee, a clean sarong and the biggest t-shirt and pair of sandals he can find. He's got a kid and a moto for me to use if I want to go into town, buy some clothes and arrange to transfer some money. I ask him to call the airport and cancel the flight reservation the embassy'd made for me tomorrow.

When I get out of the shower it's all there, on the dresser. The coffee's strong, bitter. It's perfect. There's an envelope stuffed with soft, wrinkled cash in small denominations and a note saying it'll be added to my hotel bill. The sarong fits, of course they're pretty much one size fits all. I have to rip the t-shirt under the armpits and down the middle of the back to get into it. I'm not a big guy but it makes me feel like the Incredible Hulk bursting out of his clothes. The sandals are hopeless. I'll have to go barefoot until I can find shoes.

The feeble moto suffers and complains under the weight of me and the slight boy driving, but it gets us into town. I keep asking the boy questions, but it's useless, he doesn't speak a word of English beyond "hello" and "dollar." He seems disinterested, kind of grumpy, like there's somewhere else he'd rather be.

There's not much to the town: a whole lot of new, small guesthouses for tourists visiting the temples and a bunch of rock-and-roll blaring eateries serving backpacker fare, like banana pancakes and pizza sprinkled with the local pot instead of oregano. If there's a shopping district for the locals, I don't see it.

There are a couple of banks though. I walk into the biggest one and wait in line behind a group of three Dutch tourists who are expressing their outrage at the two-percent commission to cash traveler's checks. They're yelling in English at the middle-aged woman behind the counter who has a blank expression on her face. I don't think she understands.

Behind her, seated at a table with a large printing calculator and stacks of paper, is a wire-thin boy. He looks about twelve. I'd think it was her son doing his homework if this wasn't Cambodia. But the beleaguered woman at the counter is a front. Customers tend to get nervous about banking transactions conducted with twelve-year-old tellers.

During their four years in power, the Khmer Rouge killed off or chased out almost everyone with an education. Schools didn't even begin to reopen until the early 1980s, about the time the kid at the table was born.

The woman behind the counter finally retreats from the Dutch tourists and bends to whisper in the kid's ear. The boy looks exasperated but gets up and walks over to the counter. The shouting tourists quiet down, not sure what to make of the child facing them.

He explains, in high-pitched, awkward, but serviceable English that the only person with the authority to waive the two-percent fee is the manager, who is not here at the moment. The Dutch huddle and grumble, take back their traveler's checks and march out of the bank.

I step up quickly before he can go back to his table. I'm going to need someone who speaks English. He eyes me nervously, shyly looking me up and down.

"I'm sorry, I need someone who can speak English."

The boy's face falls into the sort of weary attitude that shouldn't have to be there for at least another forty years. "Yes."

"I'm sorry about those people. I hope not all tourists are like that."

He shrugs and ekes out a narrow smile.

"How much money did they want to cash? Two-percent isn't very much."

"Twenty dollar."

Twenty bucks is two or more weeks wages to the average Cambodian. They were making a fuss over forty cents. It wouldn't buy them a chocolate bar back in Amsterdam. I lower my head and shake it sadly. "Assholes."

The boy laughs. "No problem. What want?"

I tell him I need to arrange a wire transfer from my bank in Hong Kong. He directs me around the counter and leads me to the back office. The manager is in after all, seated behind a large roughly finished deep red teak log.

The boy speaks to the manager, who answers in a hoarse, gurgling whisper. He's either got a terrible case of laryngitis or something worse. He looks like he's known a lot worse. His face and neck are plaid with raised scars. A large, permanent, wrinkled welt covers the right side of his head, over his temple. Hair doesn't grow on it.

He stands to greet us, but his posture is cringing, like he's expecting a blow. His eyes are wide and unblinking. The one on the right is fogged over with a blue gray film. The one on the left points in our direction but looks like it's seeing something else, something I don't ever want to see for myself.

I slowly, carefully put out a hand for him to shake. He recoils from it as if from a spitting cobra. I look at the boy. He motions me to bring my ear to his lips.

"Manager Bona, he not like shake hand. He trouble before, Khmer Rouge. He no English. I be translation."

It takes longer than it should to get everything taken care of, but eventually it's worked out. I'll have money in the bank tomorrow and I've got a receipt to show for it.

The boy's name is Rath. Before I leave he insists he'll take the day off tomorrow, and after I pick up my money he'll be my guide to the temples. "No much money mister, you give me how much you like. I good guide, best guide, no problem robber, no problem mine." I agree and he pumps my hand to seal the deal.

Finding clothes that fit is more of a problem. Cambodians tend to be small. In the few local shops the pants, shirts and shoes don't even come close to big enough. There are tailors. I could have something made in a couple of days but I'd rather not wait.

The road to Angkor Wat leads north, out of town. There have got to be souvenir stalls along the way. There are, and they sell large ugly t-shirts in a variety of loud colors decorated with everything from silhouettes of the temples and stylized Buddhas to bootleg brand names and logos from heavy metal bands.

I spend a while hunting from stand to stand for as innocuous a shirt as I can find. Finally I give up and get two light green, cotton t-shirts with angry looking Buddhas on them. His expression matches my mood.

The same stand has a bin of cheap mismatched Chinese rubber flip flops. I dig around and find a pair that will stay on my feet. I can move around better in pants than in a sarong, but I can't find any to fit, not even shorts. I give up and buy a couple of sarongs. The stallkeeper's disappointed that I want plain cotton ones, rather than the more expensive multi-colored polyester.

It's the dumb tourist look, but I fit right in at the crowded café where I stop to eat. It's run by a middle-aged French couple who've retired here from Lyons. If you ask me, it's way too hot and humid for their lunch special of sausages, hot, vinegary potato salad, French fries and a glass of red wine.

A cheese omelet and a small salad go down fine with a cold Angkor beer. They've got an excellent, blistering fresh-made green chili sauce. I don't bother using the shaker filled with dried pot. It's a common seasoning in Cambodia, not strong enough to bring on more than a very mild buzz, but I don't like the way it tastes.

I buy my moto driver lunch but he won't sit with me. He goes into the kitchen and hunkers down in a corner with his bowl of rice and some meat. Afterwards, he gets me back to the motel where I fall into a deep, peaceful, well chilled nap.

When I wake up I want a massage. I'm stiff and my muscles are sore. I pick up the phone and ask for Penh.

"Thanks for the moto driver and the cash advance, everything's taken care of."

"No worries mate. Easy squeezy. What can I do ya for now?"

"What I could use is a massage. Is it possible to get one in the room?"

"You betcha. How ya want it, mate?"

"Huh?"

"What kinda pounding ya want? Ya got your pretty young Sheila who'll turn ya every which way ya fancy. Ya got your medium gal who can rub ya pretty bloody good then take care of whatever's else needs takin' care of. Then ya got your old mamasan who can crack ya into a million bits then put ya back together again, but ya ain't gonna want her anywhere near your equipment if ya know what I mean."

"I just want a really great massage. I can worry about sex later."

"No worries mate, you sit tight, she'll be comin' right at ya."

Ten minutes later I wrap a towel around my waist and answer a solid knock on the door. There's a great-grandmother there. Or maybe a great-great-grandmother, people have kids young here. She's gotta be one of the oldest women I've ever seen, and the spindliest, and one of the shortest. Her arms are so thin they look like they'll snap if she tries to put enough pressure on them to give me a massage.

Her eyes are young though, remarkably so; bright, sparkling, full of energy. She's naked from the waist up and has a towel draped over her shoulders, covering her dark, wrinkled chest. She's carrying a large plastic bottle of oil.

I don't mean to be rude but I don't know what to say. I'm standing there gaping. She emits a noise from high in her throat that might be a laugh, puts a palm out flat on my chest and pushes me back into the room, all the way to the foot of the bed. She reaches down and whips the towel off me, makes a long appraisal of my dick, licks her cracked and wrinkled lips and lets out that sound again. She shoves me hard so I fall onto the bed on my back, then makes a motion with her hand that means turn over.

I do, and I scoot up the mattress so my whole body is on the bed. I hear the plastic bottle opening, then a blurt of oil, then her papery hands rubbing together. She climbs on top of me and sits on my ass. She's light, but her touch isn't. She digs with bony thumbs into the underside of my shoulder blades and for a moment I'm about to shout out in pain. Then I relax into it and it feels good, really good.

She kneads me into submission. I'm nearly asleep when I feel her slither under my right leg. I can't see what she's up to but I feel her sitting up, my leg draped over a shoulder. She settles her torso against it, laying it along my thigh. I'm about to wiggle away when she twists her body, harder and faster than I would have thought possible. I hear a deep crack from around my hip and I wait for the agonizing pain of a break but it doesn't come. The whole area is suddenly relaxed. She does it on the other side as well. Then my arms, my back in several places, my ankles, my neck.

When she gets around to my fingers and toes I hardly notice. I lie there, liquid, every point on my body form-fitted into the bed, like I've been melted down and poured onto it. She flips me over, but it's effortless, I find myself on my back without any sense of how I got there. I'm conscious but beyond thought, way past knowing or caring which way is up or down. She works on my front, down from the top of my head, my neck, my shoulders, my chest, my stomach; pushing all the tension and fear ahead of her hands as she goes, leaving the parts she's pummeled at peace in her wake.

She gets to my groin then moves around my body to my feet and starts pushing up from there, kneading my ankles and calves and knees and thighs and again to my groin. There's nothing particularly sexy about it but my dick is rock hard, as if she's worked all the stress out of every other part of my body and into this one last place.

She massages me there, rubbing and kneading and stroking around my groin, then on my balls, then at the base of my dick. And everything that's been bothering me, all my pain and worry and guilt and indecision, foams and churns and rises up through the shaft and into the head and builds and swells and I feel like I'm going to burst with it and I'm about to scream with the agony of it.

And I do. I lose all sense of everything. It's as if my liquid being has become vapor and dispersed.

| |CHAPTER **TWENTY-NINE** | |

The old woman's gone when I come to my senses. That's good. I'd be embarrassed to look at her. Not because she's a thousand years old, but because, in Asia, it's common to get a handjob at the end of a massage. I ought to be nonchalant.

But I'm not. I wasn't. I don't know what I did. I might have screamed, or sobbed or told her I loved her. Whatever it was, I don't want to know. It's the first sex I've had in a while, if it was sex. I think it was just a massage, a very complete one. And it did what it was supposed to.

I feel great, better than I have in a very long time. I'm full of energy and optimism and resolve. I need a plan, a course of action. It'll help if I've got someone to bounce my thinking off. I call Susan in Hong Kong.

"Ray, where've you been? I've been trying to call. Your office said you're out of town, but that's all I could get out of them."

"I'm in Cambodia, Siem Reap."

"How is it? You'll have to give me recommendations. You still gonna be there next week? That's when my trip is."

"Recommendations? Sure. Don't get shot at by pissed off Vietnamese generals turned gangster. Don't get kidnapped by the Khmer Rouge. Oh yeah, don't drink the water."

"What the...Okay, Ray, what's up? Are you okay?"

"I am now, I think." I give her the medium-length version of the last few days. How many days? I'm not even sure until I tell the story and count them off on my fingers.

"That's bad, Ray. Get the hell out of there. Come back here now, don't be stupid."

"That's what Warner told me."

"Maybe he's got a point."

"Okay, okay, but that's not why I called. Let's pretend for now that you're not in love with me, that you don't care so much about what happens to me. I need someone to talk this out with."

"In love with you? You wish. You're my friend, Ray, but I'd be out of my mind to be in love with you. I'm sure some woman out there is that nuts. It ain't me, babe."

"Don't get your knickers in a twist. I'm joking. But really, hear me out. I've already cancelled my flight out of here anyhow."

"I'm all ears."

"You're a whole lot more than that."

"Enough with the flirting already or I'm hanging up."

"Okay, so here's where it stands. The job I'm being paid to do is done. I've got everything I need. But, the Khmer Rouge has Thanee and that's my fault."

"Not another damsel in distress. Ray, you..."

"Yeah, that, let me finish. They've got Thanee and General Tran's still going about his business, getting away with having tried to kill me and almost killing Lei Yue, and if I don't do something to stop him, there's nothing to keep him from coming after me again."

"And you want to round up the bad guys and rescue the fair maiden. Are you insane?"

"Granted. What do they say in court? I'll stipulate to that. Let's move on to what I'm gonna do about it."

"Okay, so what're you gonna do about it? What can you do about it?"

"The Cambodian army's fighting the Khmer Rouge. I can show them where to find the camp I was taken to. They can attack it. I don't think it's a big camp, it shouldn't be too hard."

"So, if they haven't moved, if the army decides to attack them on your say so, if the attack is successful and if Thanee isn't hurt in the fighting, then that takes care of that. That's four 'ifs' already. What about the general?"

"He's here, or he will be. He's got a big deal going on."

"So what? You're going to bust in guns blazing, and take him out?"

"Something like that. There's gotta be an honest cop around, even here. What he's doing's illegal."

"And you're gonna round up a posse and go get him?"

"It's the right thing to do."

"I suppose that's better than doing it yourself. You're no Clint Eastwood."

"Not since I last checked."

"Be careful, Ray. Maybe I don't love you, but there are some lovable things about you."

"Aw shucks."

"That isn't one of them. Go out and get laid or something, relax, it'll do you some good."

"Don't know if I'm capable. A great-great-granny already milked it all out of me."

"I'm not sure what that means and I'm very sure I don't want the details. Men are disgusting pigs sometimes."

"Only sometimes?"

"Yeah."

"All men?"

"Every one I ever met."

"You ever meet the Pope?"

"No, but I doubt he'd change my mind."

"On that note, I'm gonna get dressed and go out for a drink and some dinner. Thanks for the help."

"What'd I do?"

"Listened. That's enough. It all made more sense when I was telling it to you."

"I'm glad it did to you, 'cause it sure as shit didn't make much sense to me."

I call the desk and ask Penh to meet me for a drink in the hotel bar. It's a small dark room off the lobby, lit by spotlights that bounce off the bright, shiny murals on the walls. The paintings are rendered in lurid colors, *Playboy* magazine versions of temple carvings. *Apsaras* lend themselves to that. It's cheesy, but less of a desecration I suppose than if the subject matter was scenes from the Buddha's life. Penh is halfway through a pint of lager when I sit down across from him.

"How's the rubdown, mate?"

"Perfect, thanks. She really knew what she was doing."

"Damn site oughta with all that experience. Had 'er myself a couple a times, but I usually spring for the younguns."

"You know any honest cops, or soldiers?"

"Don't meet too many of those in my business, mate."

"There's gotta be someone who wants to protect the temples at least."

"I can do ya for that, mate. I know a guy."

"Cop?"

"Army. He's a crook, they all are, but he's an honest crook if you can fancy that. A flag waver."

"In English please."

"He extorts his share of booty from foreigners and business-men like me, but he hates the bloody KR. They killed his whole family. He's got a bee up his arse about this antiques business 'cause it's some of what brings in jack for those bastards."

"That's English?"

"In Oz it is, mate. You want the intro or not?"

"Sure."

"You're gonna need jack, he doesn't do shite for free."

"No worries, mate."

"Stick to the Yank English, willya?"

"No problem."

A phone call later we have a date to meet Captain Ponleak for dinner. Are all the military people in this country captains? Seems like it. I'm buying, of course, with Penh's money, until I can get to the bank in the morning.

Penh drives the moto. It's a marvel that the little thing can move under the two of us, but it gets us there.

This captain's another slight, strong man, military crisp but not flashy or stiff, in a clean uniform with subtle markings that signify his rank. He greets us with a firm hand and an almost impercepti-ble bow. Luckily Penh doesn't have to translate. The captain went to college at Fresno State in California.

"Mr. Sharp, you are no doubt not very familiar with our cui-sine, I have taken the liberty of ordering a selection of our local delicacies. I hope you will be pleased."

"Sounds good to me, Captain."

"Please feel free to call me by my Western name. It is Tom."

"Ray."

A young woman, tightly wrapped in a bright yellow sarong that covers her from neck to ankles, leads us to a cracked Naugehyde banquette at the far end of a dance floor laid with warped wooden planks. The table is set with a large bucket of ice, a bottle of brandy, a bottle of some clear liquid that I don't think is vodka, and large bottles of beer, Coke, Seven-Up, orange Fanta and water. Maybe we're going to drink our meal.

When we sit down the young woman bends by the table, tongs ice, opens bottles and pours each of us glasses of beer, Coke, water, brandy and the clear liquid that smells like paint thinner. She takes away the empty bottles and returns quickly with a large, chipped ceramic bowl filled with shiny, oily fried bugs.

The insects are our salty drinking snacks. The captain picks up the bowl and presents it to me. "I know that in America you do not eat crickets, but here they are a delicacy. I assure you they are quite delicious."

I take one and hold it up for inspection. "Is there any trick to eating them?"

"No, I will demonstrate." The captain takes a fistful and flips them into his mouth one at a time like popcorn at a movie theater. From the sound, he could be eating potato chips, except for the little legs that poke from his mouth and that he delicately pushes back in with a pinkie. He washes them down with the paint thinner.

I try it and it's not so bad. They don't have much flavor, just crunch, salt and a light dusting of chili. Like all salty bar food, it's hard to stop eating them once you get started. I take a small sip of the clear booze —it tastes like paint thinner, too, then I switch to beer.

Dinner finds its way to the table one dish at a time. It's a jumble of meat, fish, fowl and vegetable dishes in no particular order. It's all good, though heavily laden with slightly sweet fish sauce. In the middle of the table is a large bowl of thick gray paste with little specks of red chilies and shallots, surrounded by lightly cooked vegetables. The captain tells me with a smile that it is the national dish, something called *prahoc*. It's the dreaded "*prrahk*" I asked about on the drive to the hotel.

The captain picks up a carrot stick, scoops a glob of the gunk onto it and hands it to me. The smell hits me first—rotten fish. Fish gone so rotten it has a faint vinegar odor to it. It makes my eyes water. I smile and put it in my mouth. It takes all I've got to avoid spitting it out. It's like the most thoroughly overripe, stinkiest French cheese you could possibly imagine. But it's fish. I choke some down with one of each vegetable: the carrot, a cucumber, a green onion, some kind of white radish and half a baby eggplant. It's salty too, so I've got a good excuse for washing it down with a lot of beer.

We don't talk business until the last dishes are cleared and we've stirred brandy into thick gritty mixes of bitter coffee and sweetened condensed milk. The captain takes a long swig, wipes white foam off his upper lip and adds more brandy.

"Ray, what is it that you want the Army of Cambodia to do for you?"

I've never been offered the services of an army before. This ought to be interesting.

"Captain, Tom, crooks are taking your country's treasures. They're working with the Khmer Rouge, who use them to finance their operations."

He holds up a hand to stop me. "Ray, I already know this. What is your concern with this? What is it you would like me to do?"

"There's a man, an ex-general in the South Vietnamese army named Tran. He's one of the biggest dealers in stolen Cambodian antiques. He works with the Khmer Rouge."

"I have heard of this man. What of him?"

"He's here, in Siem Reap, or he will be tomorrow. He's got a big deal about to happen."

"How do you know this? And again, why are you concerned and what do you want me to do?"

I tell him, everything. It takes as long as it takes to slide down two slow glasses of the increasingly delicious brandy, coffee and sweet milk goo. When I'm done I bum a cigarette from him. I don't smoke, but I want one now.

"Ah, I understand, Ray. What you want is revenge and to rescue the woman, is that correct?"

"Revenge, justice, I don't care what you call it. I want Tran out of business. If we can save Thanee, I want that, too."

"You Americans are so romantic. I think it is why you lost your wars in Vietnam, Laos and my country."

"Sure, puppy love, bad tactics and a screwed up worldview. I won't argue any of that with you. I just want to win one small battle, save the girl and get Tran off my back. It'd be a good win for you, too."

"It would indeed. You know, of course, that there is a reward offered for the recovery of our national treasures. If the transaction you speak of is large, the reward may be substantial. You will, of course, want your share of that. How much do you want?"

"Nope, all yours. Consider it your payment."

"Ray, the Army of Cambodia does not accept outside payment for its actions. There is a chain of command."

"Captain, if you and some of your men help me do this, it won't be on orders from your command. It's what you might call, if you were back at Fresno State, 'extra-curricular activities.' I would not be surprised if some of your men moonlight at other jobs. This is no different."

"Indeed, Ray, there may be costs and there will be risk. There is no guarantee of a reward. If we do this, I will permit you to cover our expenses."

I'd hate to start toting up how many laws I'm in the process of breaking. Plenty, here in Cambodia. A few in the U.S., too. Maybe even an international treaty or two while I'm at it.

"How much do you have in mind, Captain?"

"Perhaps it is best if you inform me of your budget, Ray. I can try to accommodate you."

This is ridiculous. How the hell am I supposed to know what it takes to hire soldiers? I'm going to tell him too little, or too much. Worst of all, it's my money. I'm sure Warner isn't going to let me charge it to my expense account. He already told me I'm off the clock. What's it worth to me?

"Will fifteen hundred U.S. be enough? You'll have to take a note; I don't think I can get that kind of cash in time."

It is. We shake on it. I don't have to mention that he'll also be pocketing the reward if we recover any stolen antiquities. The captain will provide four soldiers and himself.

He's also got people he can use as informants around town. He hadn't known about Tran's pending deal, but now that he does, they'll find out what they can about where he's staying, who he's meeting and what he's up to.

When we're done, he invites Penh and me to continue the evening at a local brothel. I'm tempted, out of curiosity if nothing else. But I'm also tired and a little drunk, and I want a clear head over the next few days.

I turn down the offer. Penh lends me his moto to get back to the hotel. He and the captain head off in a beat up old Mercedes.

| | CHAPTER **THIRTY** | |

The next morning, the bank's got my money. I get it in U.S. dollars, the preferred form of cash in Cambodia. I go into the manager's office to count it, divide it up and hide it in as many places as I can think of around my body. A thousand bucks is enough to get killed for a dozen times or more around here.

Penh drove me into town. Rath, the boy who really runs the bank, takes over as my chauffeur, guide, and, showing me the butt of an old pistol stuck into a fold of his sarong, apparently my bodyguard. I try to give him forty bucks, hoping it's enough that he isn't tempted by the rest of it.

"No now, mister. You give money later, after service." I have him drive me to the army post so I can give Captain Ponleak a down payment on his services and find out if his spies have discovered anything.

They have. "General Tran will arrive today and will stay at the Grand Hotel d'Angkor."

I'd passed by it on the way into town. "It's a construction site. How's that possible?"

"The hotel is being renovated. There has been much activity in the past three days to ready a suite of rooms. The restaurant where we dined last night is preparing a catered banquet. A private plane is scheduled to arrive at the local airport at four this afternoon."

"How can we confirm that it's Tran? How're we going to find out what he's up to?"

"My wife's brother owns the restaurant. She has an uncle who is a supervisor of the construction at the hotel. We will have men inside. You will wait in the trees across from the hotel and watch with binoculars to make certain that it is your General Tran."

"What then?"

"We will listen, and watch. It is only if we can catch your general with looted treasure that we will reap the reward. We also wish to capture his associates."

I agree to meet the captain at three-thirty in the woods across from the hotel. It's only ten now, so I ask Rath to take me to Angkor Wat. I've got a few hours. I might as well play tourist.

The boy knows a back route to the temple. He tells me it's the best way to get there and that we can avoid paying the twenty U.S. dollars for a permit to enter the area. I make him drive us to the checkpoint anyhow and I pay the fee. Cambodian citizens get in free, foreigners don't. Nothing wrong with that.

After collecting my pass, Rath turns us around and drives back the way we came for about a mile, to a small dirt road leading into the scrub forest. We bounce slowly along for another mile or so. We stop in front of a roll of barbed wire that blocks the entrance to a narrow footpath. There's a bright red sign with a skull and crossbones, some Cambodian writing and the words, 'Danger!! Mines!!' in English.

The two exclamation marks make me especially nervous. That's what they're supposed to do. Rath doesn't get it though. He hops off the moto and gingerly picks up one side of the razor sharp wire to move it aside.

"Rath, what the hell are you doing?"

"No to worry, mister, no mine on path, only mine on side."

That's not reassuring. The path is rutted, pitted, bumpy; no wider than three or four of the moto's tires placed next to each other.

I sit tight. The kid's got to know what he's doing, doesn't he? Even if he wants to kill me he probably doesn't want to kill himself. He gets back on the moto and turns around to look at me.

"No make foot go dirt, okay?"

He doesn't have to worry. I'd stand on the seat if I could.

In less than a minute my thighs are burning with the effort to keep my feet in the air. My fingers are gripped so tight on the seat underneath me that I don't know if they'll ever unfold. We bump and weave in small fits and starts. Rath guns the engine to get over little hills and nearly slows it to a stall to coast through rough flats. At one point we begin to skid on a small patch of sand and I come close to jumping off, hoping to land in the path and not on a mine.

I don't, though, and we get through. But is a special approach to the temple worth all this? I doubt it. It's the longest ten minutes of my life.

We stop at the base of a forested hill. The path winds steeply up, through low bushes and tall trees. Rath parks the bike and starts up on foot. I follow, making sure to keep to the path. There are other footprints, and when I can, I step in those. There's rustling in the brush. If it's animals I hope they know how to avoid mines. I'd hate to be blown up by a careless rodent or a fat snake.

At the top of the hill the path opens into a small, cleared meadow with a wooden lean-to on one side. In the middle is a large pile of carved rocks, some archways, a small tower, pedestals where statues once rested. The perimeter is surrounded with barbed wire, festooned with the red skull-and-crossbones signs. I guess the meadow's safe. Rath points to the ruins, "Phnom Bokheang, very very old, more old Angkor Wat. No time see now."

We approach the lean-to and Rath calls out something in Cambodian. A soldier, or a teenager playing soldier, pops his head and his AK-47 out and watches us approach.

I hear three short, low booms, like thunder far away, then a burst of crackle, like lightning. I look up and scan the sky. There's only a couple of fluffy white clouds. I put out a hand to stop Rath.

"What's that?"

"Army, Khmer Rouge make fighting."

"Where? What are we doing here?"

"No worry. No close. No problem."

I'd read in the papers that there are still battles, at least sporadic ones, going on between here and Anlong Veang, north of here, near the Thai border. But that's a long way away, isn't it? It doesn't surprise me that I can hear artillery from a distance. Small arms fire, which I think accounts for the crackling, is something else again.

We stop at the lean-to. The soldier bums a cigarette off Rath, who doesn't smoke but carries a pack to make friends. I keep forgetting to do the same thing. It's a good idea; cigarettes for adults, and cheap ballpoint pens for kids. Those are universal currency, like chocolate, gum and nylon stockings in Europe after the Second World War.

The two boys chat while the soldier finishes off a cigarette so that Rath can give him another. I wander over to the wire to see what I can. I don't see any mines, or anything that looks like a mine. I hear a faint stirring in a bush near where I'm standing and look in time to see the tail end of a thick black and yellow banded snake slither away. I walk back to the lean-to, watching carefully where I step.

The soldier boy puts the second cigarette behind his ear and waves us to the other side of the meadow with his gun. The path continues there. It's broader, better kept up. It leads back into the woods, hemmed in by the barbed wire and the red warning signs.

We turn a corner and a stone spire rises on our left. It's shaped like a rocket ship with eight or nine stages. Ornately carved, it's maybe fifty or sixty feet high. It used to be taller, but it's worn down, battered by the nine hundred years of weather and warfare since it was built. It's a football field away, thrusting up through the tangle of brush on the other side of the wire. I can make out empty niches and a few smooth areas where it looks like it's been shaved.

Even looted and pocked by bullets it's magnificent. Somehow, through everything, it's endured. I'm in the woods, surrounded by snakes and landmines, being led by a kid who should be in school but runs a bank, in a country where a large portion of the population is missing limbs, and where at least a couple of people are looking to kill me, yet seeing this tower gives me a strange sense of hope and calm.

We move along the path. As it begins to turn down the hill my eyes are skewered by hot pokers of bright diamond light. They close reflexively. I turn my face down and open them, looking at the dirt until they recover. I lift them slowly, carefully, approaching what's in front of me obliquely, trying to sneak my vision up on it.

There are towers, five of them, spaceship-shaped like the one we passed, only much larger. They're slightly above the glare, rising from within it. They look like space shuttles all launching at once. There should be a terrible roar; they should be lifting off, picking up speed, spewing flame beneath them. But they hover, motionless on the light, swollen with energy like in the very moment that a spark hits a cloud of gas and the explosion is there, it's been created, but it hasn't exploded yet.

That sounds stupid, I know. Like something a skinny guy with a loin cloth and a gold Rolls Royce might say. But it seems right, and stupid or not doesn't matter. It's my first sight of Angkor Wat.

I stop, staggering at the view, my eyes and brain bathing in it.

"Mr. Ray, Mr. Ray, I tell you is beautiful, yes? You like, Mr. Ray, you like?"

Of course I like. I wish to hell the kid would shut up and leave me in peace. Wouldn't that be nice? Wouldn't it be great if everyone would leave me here in peace and quiet?

"It's beautiful, Rath. Thank you. I want to stay here and look at it for a little, okay?"

"Okay, Mr. Ray, I quiet now. You say when go."

The glare is off a large rectangular pond at the front of the temple, it's bisected by a causeway that leads to the main entrance. Squinting, I can make out two specks of yellow, monks I think, in a boat lazily skimming the water among the reeds. Knots of tourists and worshippers make their way across the causeway in a jagged, colorful procession. Thin trails of smoke from coils of incense wind into the air.

The sputter of motos bubbles slowly up through the thick air. A dog barks. A trickle of song eases from a boombox on a scaffold of bamboo covering a small tower. The battle in the distance has settled. I can't hear them lobbing artillery shells at each other anymore.

But then a long, fast burst of automatic weapons fire needles into my ears like the warning of a rattlesnake.

"Come on, Rath, let's go."

The rocky path down to Angkor Wat is steep, the carved broad steps stitched all along with barbed wire and red warning signs. As we descend, the towers of the temple rise before us, higher and higher until we're standing at the beginning of the causeway, in front of a seven-headed *naga* rearing up, either in greeting or to guard against us.

A swarm of raggedy, shouting young boys crowds up against us, wanting "Bic, candy, dollah, me best guide, meester." Rath shoos them away. As we walk toward the temple entrance they follow, but quietly and at a respectful distance.

At the temple gate there's a young woman sitting under an umbrella, with a large red cooler full of ice, beer, soft drinks and water. I buy a bottle of water for myself and a Coke for Rath who grunts disapprovingly when I overpay. The woman is gorgeous, with a smile that makes me feel good about life.

Are most of the women in this country beautiful? Or only the ones who go out in public? Or is it just me? Has something snapped in my brain and that's just the way I'm seeing things? This beautiful woman's missing a leg.

I buy six more Cokes, for the boys who've been following us. I hand them out, making a gesture that I hope means they should share them. The two biggest grab them all and run away. Rath looks disgusted.

"You see, Mr. Ray, they fighting now. No good buy Coke temple boys, only making problem."

He's right. I've got a lot to learn.

He doesn't know much about the temple though. As we stroll slowly through the grounds, climbing steep steps to see the intricate carvings at different levels, Rath merely points out the obvious. "Is beautiful woman, Mr. Ray. Is bad monster, Mr. Ray. Is big snake, Mr. Ray."

After a while I give him five bucks and tell him to meet me back at the woman with the cooler in about an hour. He scurries off happily.

I wander aimlessly. I know there's a right way to do it, an order to follow so that it all makes sense, but I don't have the time or the inclination. There's too much. It's too big, too detailed, too complex. The whole thing, including its moats, is nearly a square mile.

One battle scene, intricately carved out of the limestone, is as tall as a basketball player and a hundred and fifty feet long. Thousands, tens of thousands of warriors and gods and elephants and monkeys and demons are interwoven in a fight unlike anything Hollywood could dream up. Gods, a dozen or more in carts being pulled by different animals, race into battle from the left. Other gods, debased-looking evil ones, rush to fight them from the right.

My eyes go bleary and I begin to get a headache trying to take it all in. I have to concentrate on small pieces. A soldier grimaces as he's run through with a spear, a monkey chutters wildly swinging from a low-hanging branch, above it all a god, fondling the breast of an *apsara*, looks impassively down on the scene, apparently only mildly interested in the outcome.

Along another long gallery a tug of war is going on. One set of gods yanks on one end of a huge *naga*, another group pulls against them. The thrashing of the giant snake churns the sea between the gods. Fish and serpents and strange creatures are caught up in the storm it creates.

I climb steep, shallow ancient steps to the shady, colonnaded recesses of the higher galleries, where *apsaras* frozen in mid-languid motion, await the victors of the battles below. I'm honored to be among them, soothed and calmed by their presence above the fray.

I take a seat on a ledge in the shade, resting my back against the cool limestone, cupping a hand over my eyes to cut the glare from beyond the overhang. What the hell have I got myself into? I ought to be up here, surrounded by these luscious women, enjoying life, rather than down there doing battle with demons. I get tired thinking about it.

I take several deep breaths, in through the nose, out through the mouth. I run my eyes along the curves of an *apsara* to my right. I let my eyes go blurry and it brings her to life. Her hands move in slow, broad circles as if to fold me into her arms, to bring me to her and pillow my head on her breasts, to offer herself to me. And I want her, want to be with her. And I want Thanee to be safe. And I want Irina back. And I want things to be right, good. And that's worth fighting for.

My eyes water, my knees crack and my legs tremble as I slowly push myself up and out into the harsh sunlight. I lumber down the well worn stone steps, passing a Japanese tour group panting their way up, to find Rath and the beautiful woman with one leg. It's time to head back, to meet Captain Ponleak, to finish what I've started with General Tran.

| |CHAPTER **THIRTY-ONE**| |

There's not much for me to do once I've confirmed that it is Tran who's come to town. Ponleak's guys will find out what they can. All I can do is wait. I do that at the hotel.

I consider another massage but I'm too keyed up. Penh offers to send the "room girl" to me but I don't want that either. I take a cold beer and some peanuts back to my room and turn on CNN for company. The phone wakes me up a couple of hours later.

"Your General Tran will meet with his contact, probably Khmer Rouge, tomorrow morning at the Bayon."

"Ponleak?"

"Yes, of course. We must be in position before the General and the other men arrive. I will come to pick you up at three this morning. Can you shoot a gun?"

"Not very well. Will I have to?"

"It will probably not be necessary. These smugglers do not like to fight with the army. They prefer to use corruption. But it is good to be prepared."

"I'm better with a rifle than a pistol."

"Then I will bring you one of each."

I ought to go back to sleep so I'm fully rested when it comes time for the trouble to start. I can't. I borrow a five-day-old *International Herald Tribune* from the front desk and sit down with the stale news and a plate of greasy fried noodles in the hotel's coffee shop.

According to the newspaper, it's business as usual. Nothing ever changes. A couple of big banks have collapsed, a huge conglomerate is teetering on the edge, stock- and property-market valuations are at ludicrous levels. The son of a Hong Kong zillionaire threw a party recently, at which he filled his yacht's swimming pool with expensive champagne.

If Commander Kon, the erudite Khmer Rouge killer was here, he'd smirk and say, "I told you so." Stalin supposedly once commented, "one death is a tragedy, a million is a statistic." Do you have to be cynical to be powerful? I guess it helps.

In a few hours I'll be heading out with a couple of guns and my own small, private army. It makes me nervous, makes me feel weak. I can't finish my noodles, not even when I cut the grease with strong lashings of a searing hot chili sauce. I finish my beer, consider another, but go out for a walk instead.

The cicadas are making their racket, motos sputter in the distance, a Chinese diesel truck creaks past, wheezing, coughing and grinding its gears. I walk from the hotel, across the road and out along the embankment on one side of a large fish farm. I can hear fish jumping out of the water, splishing back into it. The moon's coming up at the far end and sets its rays down on the dappled surface of the pond. A low white light bathes everything. It must twinkle down from all those stars.

A small shed made from bamboo poles is in my path. A faint red glow swells and ebbs inside. I make some noise as I approach. I don't want to startle anyone. The glow rises. As I get closer I can see it's the tip of a big cigarette in the mouth of a small man. He takes clearer shape when I'm a few feet away.

He might be my age, but if he is, he's lived a lot harder than I have. He's not wrinkled, but he's lined and scarred, his flesh shined and smoothed by burns. He's got all his limbs, but looks like something else is missing, something significant inside. He watches me walk up out of the side of his eyes. It's rude to look directly at a stranger, or maybe it's forbidden, something he's had well beaten into him.

I stop in front of him and smile, wave my hands around to take in the scenery, point to myself and make a walking motion with my fingers. I point to myself again. "Ray." I stick out a loose hand, turned slightly down.

The man smiles slightly, takes my hand and holds it for a moment, then slides his along it as he takes it away. He holds his hand over his heart. "Chann." He turns and points to the moon. It's beautiful, half-round and bright and comforting.

Chann squats and pats the ground. I squat, too, but only for a moment before I have to sit. He smiles again, a little larger. He reaches behind him and brings out a battered plastic container and a cup. He pours tea and offers it to me. I can smell it. It's rich with minerals and dust and a faint sour odor. It's made from a local herb and farm water, probably fish farm water.

He's a poor man. It makes him richer to share what little he has with a stranger. I nod my thanks and drink deeply. I hand him back the cup, he takes a smaller sip and then puts the cup down between us.

He brings out a carefully folded packet of newspaper and unfolds it on the dirt. It's tobacco with marijuana mixed in. It's moist, cut very fine, the strands clumping together. He nudges the paper toward me, another offering. He holds out a small stack of torn pieces of newsprint. I've heard that Cambodian pot isn't very strong, just strong enough to keep you from freaking out. There's a lot that can freak you out in this place.

I roll a clumsy cigarette, wetting it with my lips until it holds together. Chann takes a large, deep drag on his own cigarette, the red flare at its end bursting into a small yellow flame, and hands it to me. I use it to light mine.

I inhale deeply and cough. He looks concerned. I wave a hand and smile, let out a small laugh. I inhale again, shallower, letting the smoke linger in my mouth to cool, letting it ghost down my throat into my lungs. Chann's smiling broadly now. We don't speak the same language, but it's okay. We don't need to talk. We simply share a good moment, in a hard place, at a hard time. For now at least, that's enough.

I lie down with my head outside the shed, looking up at the night sky. Chann gets up and moves down the embankment. I can hear him wading in the water, working, tending to the fish.

All the small sounds swell and fill the air. No dreams disturb me. No sleep comes. No thoughts, no worries, no sensations. I'm simply here, another small part of the world. I don't need or want or feel anything else.

It's a little before two when I get back to the hotel. I'm relaxed, ready to go, ready to do what needs to be done. I take a long, hot shower and am waiting in the lobby when Captain Ponleak shows up.

He takes me out to the parking area to give me a quick tour of the guns he's brought. His four men watch, amused. The pistol's a revolver. It looks like a Wild West six-shooter. Ponleak's brought me a holster and belt. I strap it on. Should I practice my quick draw? Firing it isn't the problem. Hitting what I want is.

I might be able to hit something with the AK-47 he hands me if I take it off automatic and aim one shot at a time. If I have the time. If I don't, and I simply hold down the trigger, it'll get off all thirty of its shots in three seconds. That didn't seem like much fun at the shooting range.

He walks me across the street and shows me how to fire it in short bursts. A quick flick of my index finger and three or four bullets flash out. If I keep a hand pressed on top of the barrel I can hold it down enough that the shots go in the general vicinity of where I want them.

We load into a pickup truck, the captain and me in the front seat, the four soldiers in back. The moon's sunk low, but it's bright enough that we don't need lights to drive.

| | CHAPTER **THIRTY-TWO** | |

The town's quiet as we softly rattle through to the north. We're past it and into the woods without seeing anybody. The highway to the temples is empty. As we approach the guard posts, the captain flicks the lights and the gates lift without slowing us down. We skirt around the left side of Angkor Wat. It's lit with a soft glow and looks like it's floating on top of the ground fog.

We pass down a road, flanked by two enormous *nagas*. We roll through an archway with a giant face of the demon Rahu looking down on us. I see only the faint silhouettes of trees and piles of rubble. It's as if the monster really had swallowed the moon.

We come to a stop in front of the biggest dark pile I've seen yet. It's a shapeless lump, a different shade of black from what surrounds it. Ponleak nudges me.

"We will get off here. My men will hide the truck and come back to meet us. We will take positions in the temple."

"This the Bayon? Doesn't look like much."

"No, not now. Later, when the sun rises, then you will see. But then you must be paying attention to other things, to your general and his associates."

"Don't worry, I know I'm not here to play tourist."

"No, you are not. But a good soldier is always aware of what surrounds him. So when you are able, you will see all that you can. You will see it as a tourist, but also for strategy."

I've read Sun Tzu, but I don't recall anything about tourism in *The Art of War*. Maybe I had a different translation.

We get out of the truck. I try carrying the AK-47 in one hand, barrel down, but it's awkward. I don't want to put my finger over the trigger until I have to, so I fiddle with it. Finally I give up and hold it with two hands, one on the wooden handle behind the trigger, the other on the wood grip in front. The gun's pointed to the left. Ponleak notices and moves around to my right.

"Stay close, Mr. Sharp. Be careful where you step. We will walk very slowly. I have only a small light and I will use it only inside the temple."

I'm not sure what he means by "inside the temple." It still looks like a jumbled heap of rocks. The moon's gone and any useful light with it. I wish I didn't have to use both hands to carry this damn gun. I'd hold on to the captain if it wouldn't be embarrassing.

We edge forward along a stone pathway. It's worn smooth, and my toes, sticking out of the flip flops, brush against an occasional weed or small pebble. As we approach the Bayon it looks bigger and takes on a basic shape of walls and terraces. I can't make out any details.

Up a couple of steps, through an arch and we're on a broad walkway. The walls rise no more than five feet on either side. We get to a staircase. The steps are rough and unevenly worn but well spaced for walking up blind.

At the top we stop and wait. I look back. There isn't much to see. Low walls, a much higher wall of trees in the distance. Straight ahead there's a crooked, bent shape. It might be a giant, frozen in place and withered with time. Or it might be a gnarled tree, petrified where it stands, polished and shaped by the winds and rains. Above are the stars, not quite as many as before, some obscured by clouds.

After a few minutes I hear footsteps, the slight clanking of metal, the pad of well-oiled boots on stone. It's the captain's men and they come up to us. Ponleak speaks to them in a low tone and they disperse in four directions.

I feel Ponleak's hand on my shoulder. "Come, we will go to a central point, a higher courtyard." He turns me the way he wants me to go and I walk slowly, trying to keep in touch with him for guidance.

We curve around to the right and up more steps, then along a narrow corridor through a series of arches, to another flight of stairs and up those. Ponleak stops us at an open space, a courtyard maybe. There's still nothing to see other than dark, looming, ill-defined shapes. There's a large stone, or a bench, and I sit on it. Ponleak stands nearby.

"Any idea when they're showing up?"

"Sunrise, maybe little later. Do not talk, please."

I try to adjust my eyes, edging them slowly from dark form to dark form. They do, a little, but I still can't make out details.

A loud parade of worry is marching through my head. How do soldiers do it? The anticipation makes me sick to my stomach. Once the fighting starts you don't have time to think. Thinking's the real enemy, the one you can't protect yourself from. One of these days an inventor's going to come up with the thought-proof helmet and make himself a fortune. I'll be first in line to buy one.

My head's down, eyes unfocussed. Something whooshes past me, zooming left to right at tremendous speed. I bring my head up and try to follow it. I can't see anything. Then there's another from right to left. Then behind me, above me, more sounds circling. Before long I'm swathed in sibilant sound, sharp squeaks cutting through, allowing my ears to fix on something. But what? It's ee-rie, frightening. What the hell is it?

Ponleak taps me on the shoulder, leans into my ear. "Bats, they go home. Sun is coming."

I look up and the sky is lightening, a faint glow over the treeline to the east. The contours of the dark things around me are sharpening, faint features beginning to emerge.

A slow dim yellow beam lumbers through the trees, it's as if I can watch it moving toward us. I turn to follow it behind me and there's a face, big, three or four feet from chin to the top of the forehead, slit-eyed with a sardonic expression. I can't tell if it's a man or a woman. It's split into blocks, dark complexioned and mottled gray. It looks as if it's about to say something I don't want to hear.

I turn my head away but then someone turns up the lights, like slowly moving a dimmer switch. Another face appears, this one to my right and laughing. Laughing at me, I guess.

More light and more faces. This one looks like it's about to cry. There's a crazed one, its eyes bulging. There's a sad one, a smart one, an impatient one, a contented one. I'm surrounded by faces. They're all different and yet they all look the way I sometimes feel. The confused one, the worried one and the dumb one look the way I feel now.

That reminds me. I've got to pick up my heads from Tommy back in Hong Kong. If I ever get back to Hong Kong. That's how this all started. I don't think I'll ever look at my heads the same way again.

These heads are Buddha, but not quite. They're Lokesvara, the incarnation of Buddha before he achieved enlightenment. And they're modelled after Jayavarman the Seventh, the king who built the place. He's been here, in all his changing guises, for eight hundred years.

His faces were all carved the same, but weather and war and time has pushed and prodded and hacked them into their varied states. Like anybody, he wasn't born with all these moods, life made him that way.

If Lokesvara's moody like everyone else, like me, what makes him so special? Why's he worth worshipping, or emulating or being inspired by?

I'm not getting anywhere trying to figure it out when I hear a truck grind and squeal to a halt in front of the temple. I can see Ponleak now. He's got a finger to his lips, cautioning me to be quiet. It's not necessary.

He crooks the finger, telling me to follow him. I move slowly, steadily, the AK-47 held tight to my side with the barrel down, my finger near the trigger. We creep around the side, up a couple of steps to a parapet. The faces watch our backs, more watch us approach. Each has a different expression, a new look, more than I've got myself.

Maybe that's it. Buddha or Lokesavara or the king who built the place isn't much different from me or anyone else, only more so. He's got more moods. He knows more. He's been around longer, so he's moodier. I always thought he was supposed to be ethereal, other-worldly, but I was wrong. He's earthier, more human than I'll ever be.

I ease my eyes over the stone wall and look at the road. This isn't the time for philosophy.

There are two trucks and a jeep. Ponleak hands me his binoculars, showing me how to shield the glass so it doesn't reflect back at what I'm looking at. I hold the up to my eyes. I feel like a guy at the door to his old high school gym, trying to decide if he wants to go into the reunion or not.

Tran's holding a big bright orange Adidas gym bag. He's got his bald giants from the restaurant on either side, only they're in casual clothes this morning. They're holding guns. The guns aren't pointing at the other guys, but they're not pointing away either.

The other guys are Khmer Rouge, small, dressed in black, and deadly. There are six of them including Kon, who's the only one without an AK-47. Thanee is standing behind them, swaying in place, her hands tied behind her back.

I don't know why they've chosen to meet here. Maybe it's Tran's flare for drama.

Tran unzips the gym bag and holds it out for Kon to look inside. It's got to be cash. It doesn't look heavy enough to be gold or anything like that. Kon motions for the general to put it on the ground. He squats next to it and starts counting. Tran looks impatient. He says something to one of his men who laughs.

Kon looks up and he isn't pleased. He says something to one of his men, who turns and knocks Thanee to the ground with the butt of his rifle. He stands over her, pointing it at her. I start, rising and pulling up my rifle, but Ponleak pulls me down.

"Not yet."

Tran holds up his hands, says something again and looks contrite. Kon looks at him and nods. He barks at the soldier, who yanks Thanee back to her feet and shoves her forward, toward General Tran.

The general slaps her. She stands straight and takes it. He pushes her behind him roughly. One of his men unties her hands and moves her behind him. She stands still, rubbing her wrists and cracking her fingers. I hand the binoculars back to Ponleak.

It's getting bright. We move into the shadow cast by a head that looks like it has indigestion. The captain leans in close.

"We go soon. Your general has paid. I am certain the Khmer Rouge have brought antiques in the trucks. I want to see the business completed."

It's beginning to get hot and I'm getting squirmy. I'm tired. I've been on my feet for too long. I slump down, my back against the parapet wall. My head crumples forward on my neck a couple of times. It's hard to keep upright, my eyes open. This is nuts. Am I developing narcolepsy or something? I've never been one of those guys who stress makes sleepy. I've heard of that. It always sounded stupid to me.

But before I can give it much thought or succumb to it, I startle alert to the sound of shouts, a loud crack, then another, then a short burst of chatter, screams and clicks and thuds. What the hell's happened? Who started shooting? Why?

I'm sprawled on the stones, my AK-47 partly under me. Ponleak's above me, flattened hard against the face with the upset stomach, his rifle raised, coughing out single shots, then short groups. I skitter to my feet behind him and peer out.

Two of the Khmer Rouge are sprawled on the ground, not moving. Everyone else has taken cover. I can't see anything to shoot at but I guess some of the captain's men can. I hear bullets pinging and clanging and clattering through the slab metal sides of the trucks.

Ponleak lets off a burst. I have no idea what he's aiming at, but his fire's returned. Hot, sharp limestone chips flit around me. I jump back, putting the ancient profile between me and whoever's shooting.

The captain squats down below the top of the parapet wall to change magazines. He turns and smiles, then waves and points along the walkway to the other side, where a face that's laughing like it was late to get the joke makes another pool of shade.

It's safe enough behind the thick stone wall as I scramble to the other side. It's standing up that's got me worried. I get to the deepest part of the shadow, but it's not as dark as I'd like. I watch Ponleak calmly move up and down, in and out of exposure, firing short bursts and never returning to quite the same place.

I have a hard time making my fingers do what I want them too. I move my trigger hand away from the grip to work the safety lever. It makes a sound that draws the captain's attention. He grins and points out toward the road.

I stand up, taking cover behind a prominent nose. I take a deep breath, then slowly let it out. When my lungs are about empty I roll around the nose, keeping flush against it, point the gun in the direction I think it ought to go and squeeze the trigger.

The AK erupts in a coughing fit. I can't hear anything else over the sound. I don't really look where I'm shooting; it's a haze of light blue smoke and blur. It's a longer burst than I want, maybe a dozen bullets. I roll back and down, move a couple of feet to my right. I've drawn some fire. I can hear the stone chipping nearby, the whizz and crack of bullets.

Looking at the face above me, I shake my head and laugh with him. Here we are trying to save Cambodian antiquities by getting into a gun battle in the middle of the greatest of them. Is this what that army guy meant during the Vietnam War when he said, "We had to destroy the village in order to save it"? I always wondered what he meant.

I pop up and fire another burst, a shorter one this time, maybe four or five rounds. I think I might've hit the jeep. I hope Thanee's somewhere safe.

A bullet nicks a sliver from my protector's nose. It splats into my forehead, sticking above my right eye. It stings bad, but nothing more than that. I hunker down and tweeze it out between two fingers. I have to blink away a short gush of blood, press the back of my hand hard against it to staunch the flow.

I'm about to come up again shooting when I hear shouting and a truck horn honking. Ponleak's edging out behind his gun to look. His smile says he likes what he sees. I get up to see what's going on.

Tran's two guys are dead, or doing a very good job of faking it, sprawled in the jeep. They must have got in hoping to get the hell out of here.

The three remaining Khmer Rouge soldiers have come out from cover. They've got their hands over their heads. One of them carries a piece of white cloth, a t-shirt, and they're slowly walking toward the temple. I can't see Kon, Tran or Thanee.

The Khmer Rouge step onto the raised walkway. I hear a voice off to their right, shouting at them. They get to their knees, hands clasped behind their heads. I see the captain's men moving in slowly from the side, keeping the surrendering soldiers covered.

There's more shouting as one of the Cambodian soldiers moves closer to them, maybe ten feet away. The Khmer Rouge shake their heads, saying "no" or they don't know, or something. I walk over to Ponleak. I take his binoculars and look at the surrendering soldiers. They're teenagers, one of them no older than thirteen. They're terrified, quaking.

The one on the right suddenly looks startled, like someone's snuck up behind him and thumped him on the back. Then they all do, their heads pivoting around to look behind them. The rattle of the AK comes to me in slow motion, through the dense morning air.

The boys fall forward, blood gushing in front of them as if it might somehow cushion their fall. The captain's man is hit and falls to his knees, his gun pointing toward the sky, his finger tightening on the trigger, unleashing a final burst that lasts an interminable three seconds.

Ponleak fires at the muzzle flashes coming from under one of the trucks. His men do, too. Dust and rocks are chewed up from the ground underneath. Bullets bang hard against the truck's undercarriage.

There's a flash of quick movement in my peripheral vision. I turn to watch Tran come out from behind the jeep. He's got Thanee in front of him as a shield, with a gun to her head. They keep low and move fast to cover behind the rubble of a low wall.

It must be Kon under the truck. I doubt he could have survived the fusillade. It's stopped now and the shouting's started up again. Ponleak's men are warily coming out from behind their cover, rifles ready. The four men on the walkway aren't moving, not even moaning.

I don't think anyone's noticed Tran and Thanee. I want to point them out to the captain, but he's already gone to join his men. I move down and around to the left, quiet as I can, and quick. Maybe I can get behind Tran.

The last head I can hide behind looks troubled. His brow is creased, his lips pursed. I'm glad someone cares. I pat him on the cheek for good luck. There's a well about twenty feet away. The built up sides of an aqueduct lead away from it, the way I want to go. I don't know what General Tran can see from where he is, but I bend over and run to the cover.

No one shoots me. That's a relief. I stay down and move along the waterway. Reeds grow in it, sticking up above the wall, helping me keep out of sight. It runs about a hundred and fifty feet before it comes to another well, this one with a five-headed *naga* rising from it.

I peer around the big snake. I'm behind Tran. He's sitting on the sloping bank of a pond, Thanee's in front of him. He's still holding a gun loosely on her, but he's playing with her hair with his other hand, stroking her face, whispering to her. He knows there's nowhere for him to go. Maybe he's playing to use Thanee as a hostage.

I move onto the ground between us, the AK out in front of me, ready to fire. I've gone a few steps, maybe there's still fifty feet between us, when Thanee looks up and sees me. She tenses, causing Tran to look up. He smiles, lifts his gun and pushes it up hard against Thanee's right ear.

"Do not approach any closer, Mr. Sharp. You will not be happy if I kill our friend Thanee."

I don't stop until I'm about ten feet away.

"If you kill her, General, there's nothing to keep me from killing you."

"It is possible that I have underestimated you, Mr. Sharp. But I do not think you are a killer."

"You wanna find out?"

"We are then, at an impasse, Mr. Sharp. A…what was it that your soldiers would speak about in Hue? Yes, I recall, a Mexican standoff."

That makes me smile. It's a shame Lei Yue isn't here to hear that. She'd like it.

"Not really."

"And why not? Enlighten me, Mr. Sharp."

"With all these religious figures around, you ask me for enlightenment? The thing is, Tran, you're not getting out of here. If you kill Thanee or me, all that will do is bring Captain Ponleak and his men running. They'll kill you or capture you, either way. You've got better prospects if you're alive."

"Ah, yes, Mr. Sharp, American pragmatism."

"I prefer to think of it as common sense."

"My death would be a pity, Mr. Sharp, and a waste. This is Cambodia. It is no matter if your soldiers jail me. They will be well paid and I will be home in Bangkok within a week."

He's right. If I could bring myself to shoot him it would save a lot of trouble. I can't, though. I'm not like him.

Tran takes his finger off the trigger of his pistol and tosses it away. Thanee twists to get away from him. He holds her briefly, then lets her go. She moves quickly to put me between him and herself.

"It appears that you have inherited my protégé, Mr. Sharp. Take good care of her, but do not turn your back. I have raised her, made her what she is."

"What's that?"

"A whore. She is only a whore. She will always be a whore. You will find her company very expensive."

She's already behind me and I'm not too worried. I can hear her crying, softly. I reach back and pull her up next to me. I tell the general to stand up. I'm about to walk him back to the trucks when Ponleak comes up to us.

"You have captured your General Tran, Mr. Sharp. I have recovered much stolen treasure. It is a good day for the both of us."

I roll my eyes. Tran snaps out a short laugh, more of a snort.

"Is it not a good day, Mr. Sharp?"

"I don't know, Captain, is it? Men are dead, boys. We saved some statues. But what's the point? It's just a small amount of what's stolen and how soon's it going to be before the general's back in business? And even if it isn't him, it's gonna be somebody else."

The captain nods at me. He looks sad, as if he's about to cry, as he slowly eases the pistol out of the holster at his side. He turns away from me, toward Tran, holding the gun along his thigh.

He steps up to the general and I'm not sure what he's going to do. I guess he's taking custody of the prisoner. Tran smiles at him.

"Captain." He frowns when Ponleak doesn't respond.

I hear a squeal of brakes, a clank of a bad transmission. I turn toward the road. I can make out the top of a tourist bus, the first one of the morning. It's screeched to a halt in front of the temple. I hear the hydraulic door hiss open to let out hordes of camera wielding sightseers. I don't know if they can see us from there or not.

When I look back, Ponleak has his gun to the general's temple. It reminds me of that famous photo from Saigon in 1968. Before I can say anything he pulls the trigger. The sound is muffled, deep, brief. Tran's head explodes out the other side in a geyser of red and gray, flecked with pieces of white bone and black hair. Thanee and the general crumple to the ground simultaneously. The young woman with a ratcheting sob that rises into a wail. General Tran in a loose, empty-bag posture, nothing left to animate his falling body.

The captain holsters his gun and walks to me. Lines furrow his brow and his face sags as if he's gained a dozen years in the last few moments. He nods his head down to indicate Thanee, who is still on the ground sobbing, her body shuddering. "Calm her down. Bring her to the trucks."

"Captain, I, what about…" I nod in the direction of Tran's body.

"Leave him. The war here, it is not over, Mr. Sharp. Perhaps it will never be over."

| |CHAPTER **THIRTY-THREE**| |

The bodies are in the other truck. Ponleak's men heaved them in the back with three large Buddha heads that look strangely like the see-no-evil, hear-no-evil and speak-no-evil chimps. It's limping along behind us on two mismatched spares.

The captain's up front in the jeep, one of his men riding shotgun. Thanee's getting a ride in the army truck that brought me out here. The truck I'm in is bringing up the rear.

I'm in the back with a couple dozen *apsaras*, swaying and bouncing along the road back to town. If I squint I can imagine they're dancing around me, dancing for me, celebrating their rescue.

I look over at Commander Kon. He's slumped against the low, hard metal sidewall of the truck. I'm supposed to be guarding him, but he isn't going anywhere. His legs are all shot up. Every bounce, every jar makes him grimace.

"They'll probably give you something for your pain when we get to town, Commander."

"I am quite certain that there is nothing to help my particular pain, Mr. Sharp."

"Why'd you shoot your own men, Kon? I doubt they taught that at USC."

He laughs, more of a cackle really, punctuated with a harsh gasp when we hit a pothole. "No, it is more the curriculum of my comrades who attended the Sorbonne."

"You think it's funny? They were kids. You're a monster."

"In my country, Mr. Sharp, we either laugh or we are dead. Even if we are talking and walking and breathing, if we are not laughing we are dead inside."

"What would you know about it? Every shred of humanity's dead inside you. You and your comrades, you aren't fucking human. Like I said, you're a monster."

"There is nothing so monstrous as man, Mr. Sharp. I am only a man, a simple man who does some of the things that men do, and who does not do others. There is me. There is Captain Ponleak and also your General Tran. The government of Cambodia will not be pleased that a tourist group arrived at such an unfortuitous moment.

"Then there is yourself, Mr. Sharp. You think you have saved these dancing maidens. They are but carved stone. They will disappear into a dark government warehouse and will be forgotten, perhaps even before we are. You think you have saved the girl, Thanee. For what? We are a continuum."

"I hope to fuck not, Kon. We might be the same species, but that's as far as it goes."

"Species is everything, Mr. Sharp. It is all there is. It is destiny."

"Now you believe in destiny? Or is it Darwin? You've got too much education, Kon. Fat lot of good it's done you. You'd have been better off working in the fields, another one of your tired, illiterate peasants. We'd have all been better off."

"You see, Mr. Sharp, we do understand each other."

I shut up. I've had enough. I let my mind wander, my vision drift. The *apsaras* dance around me, happy, free, beautiful. The bumps on the road are only that. I can barely feel them.

| | AUTHOR'S **NOTES** | |

This story is based on the facts of the illegal trade in Cambodian antiquities. The event that triggers the investigation in the book happened to me when I lived in Hong Kong in the mid-1990s. I took a sculpture to an art supply and framing shop in Central Hong Kong, to have a stand made for it. When I returned to pick it up, the owner of the shop took me down the block to his small warehouse filled with looted Cambodian treasures. I called the Hong Kong police, but at the time it was not illegal to sell these particular antiquities in the Territory. It is now, but it is my understanding that the laws are not strictly enforced.

In December 2003 I was in Bangkok. I went to a shop in River City (which is a real place) and discreetly asked if they had any *apsaras* for sale. After asking me a number of questions, the shop-keeper took me into a back room, where she unlocked a safe and took out a small, very beautiful *apsara* that had been chipped from a frieze in Cambodia. She was asking about US$1,500 for it.

A friend of mine in Bangkok, who works for a corporate investigation firm, confirmed that the trade still goes on, largely unmolested. Raids at River City are not uncommon, but it is seldom long before the confiscated pieces find their way back into the shops.

The Khmer Rouge no longer control the trade in Cambodian antiquities. Other than a few rogue bandit groups, the Khmer Rouge has ceased to exist. As of 2007, trials of the surviving leadership, for crimes against humanity, seem to at last be about to get underway.

The conversations between Ray and Commander Kon were inspired by a fascinating book—*The Gate*, by Francois Bizot. The author was one of the very few Westerners to ever survive capture by the Khmer Rouge. In the book he describes a remarkable relationship that he developed with Duch, a Khmer Rouge commander, who is likely to feature prominently as one of the defendants in any upcoming trial. Much of the Khmer Rouge leadership did indeed attend the Sorbonne in Paris. None, to my knowledge, had a degree from U.S.C.

Unfortunately, the Phnom Penh restaurant from which Ray escapes with Lei Yue and Thanee does not exist as such. It is, however, based on the real world's largest restaurant. *Mang Gorn Luang* (The Royal Dragon) is in Bangkok and does feature, among other attractions, roller-skating waiters and a flaming platter of seafood that descends to tables from a central tower. It seats 5,000 people. The spectacle is, sadly, a lot more impressive than the food.

Any similarity to real people or companies is, of course, strictly coincidental. Although, that said, the Thongchai Family of sculptors (not their real name) is indeed all too real. There is an excellent, and depressing, book that includes a chapter about the activities of the family on whom they are based: Nagashima, Masayuki,

The Lost Heritage: The Reality oj
Asia. Post Books, Bangkok, 200'
    Cambodia is still a country wi'
poorest countries in the world, an
ought to be for impoverished fam.
and other forms of slavery. There .
American Assistance for Cambod
(AAFC). It was founded in 1993 by
Krisher. It operates interlinked progra.
eas of education, health, rural developmn.., _
its many programs is one that provides incentives to poor rural families to keep their daughters in school, rather than selling them into
brothels. I have made contributions to this program from the money
I have been paid for this book and will continue to do so from future earnings. If this story makes you wonder what you can do to
help Cambodia, AAFC's website—www.cambodiaschools.com—is
a good place to start.

‖ ACKNOWLEDGMENTS ‖

Bill Krauss, for a great first read and several smart suggestions that really got the story moving.

Janet Reid, my agent, for keeping the faith in the face of the numerous bumps tossed into our path by the vagaries of the publishing biz.

My publisher Benjamin LeRoy, who I first met at a party at Bleak House's headquarters. He was standing at the grill flipping burgers at the time and I knew right then that he'd be great to work with. He is.

My editor Alison Janssen, who is also a delight to work with. Smart, too. Thanks for the girl scout, Alison.

Paul Bromberg, an old pal who helped with information about the work of corporate investigations firms.

Jackie Green, my publicist on my first two books, from whom I learned a great deal about the wonderful and terrifying world of publishing.

My father and step-mother—Martin and Connie Stone; great friends and fellow writers—Meredith and Win Blevins; ex-colleagues—Amit Chowdhury and Ip Mei Wah; and a host of others, just because.